The Original
Old Rails' Tales

Anecdotes, Stories, & Memoirs

On The Road & In The Yard

(new abridged family edition)

The _Only_ Book Of On-The-Job True Stories Told By Four
Generations Of Engineers, Firemen, Conductors, Brakemen,
Switchmen, Dispatchers, Yardmasters & Superintendents on:
Santa Fe, Western Pacific, Southern Pacific & AMTRAK

© 1991-2005 Alan Kernoff

© Copyright 2005 Alan Kernoff
All rights reserved. No part of this publication may be reproduced, stored in a retrieval system, or transmitted, in any form or by any means, electronic, mechanical, photocopying, recording, or otherwise, without the written prior permission of the author.

Note for Librarians: a cataloguing record for this book that includes Dewey Decimal Classification and US Library of Congress numbers is available from the Library and Archives of Canada. The complete cataloguing record can be obtained from their online database at:
www.collectionscanada.ca/amicus/index-e.html
ISBN 1-4120-5113-4

TRAFFORD

Offices in Canada, USA, Ireland, UK and Spain
This book was published *on-demand* in cooperation with Trafford Publishing. On-demand publishing is a unique process and service of making a book available for retail sale to the public taking advantage of on-demand manufacturing and Internet marketing. On-demand publishing includes promotions, retail sales, manufacturing, order fulfilment, accounting and collecting royalties on behalf of the author.

Book sales for North America and international:
Trafford Publishing, 6E–2333 Government St.,
Victoria, BC v8t 4p4 CANADA
phone 250 383 6864 (toll-free 1 888 232 4444)
fax 250 383 6804; email to orders@trafford.com

Book sales in Europe:
Trafford Publishing (uk) Ltd., Enterprise House, Wistaston Road Business Centre,
Wistaston Road, Crewe, Cheshire cw2 7rp UNITED KINGDOM
phone 01270 251 396 (local rate 0845 230 9601)
facsimile 01270 254 983; orders.uk@trafford.com

Order online at:
www.trafford.com/robots/05-0008.html

10 9 8 7 6 5 4 3 2 1

fig. 1 – a would-be brakeman

© 1991-2005 Alan Kernoff

All Rights Reserved

Foreword by Studs Terkel

What is Oral History, Oral Journalism & Oral Tradition?

— it's about little things that tell a lot ... about ordinary people, in their own words

[AA] Studs, when you were a kid, did you like trains?
[Studs Terkel] Of Course. I loved trains. The sound of a train whistle is like nothing in the world. I just loved the sounds of trains. Thomas Wolfe, in *A Time On The River*, has almost half a book about a trip on a train from Nashville to Boston.

My memory is coming to Chicago, when I was a kid, eight years old. And the trains that I saw excited me. And the trip by myself on the train, later, when I was about ten. That was one of the most exciting periods of my life. That was day-coach. And they stopped at Buffalo and different places; the vendors came on. The guys coming on board to sell the paper from Buffalo, from Syracuse, or Pittsburg, or from whatever city we went through, was very exciting. I bought a wonderful cheese sandwich, and a little 10¢ bottle of milk.

That was a train memory.

Well your name's a household word. And I always thought of you as being a writer.
No; I was in radio primarily. In fact it was radio interviewing in a way that led to the books. You see, it's oral, it's talking out loud, basically. It's called *Oral History*. It's kind of oral journalism, I'm not a historian, really. Historians are basically by-and-large scholars. I'm not a scholar; that's not been my major emphasis.

I'm interested in history, as remembered by people who lived then ... what was it like to live at a certain time? What was it like for an ordinary person to live during the Great Depression of the 30's, see? What was it like to live during World War II? You see, these are two of my books.

I interviewed non-celebrated people, ordinary people.

I would ask, "What's the first thing you do when you wake up in the morning?" Questions like that. It had to be little things. Little things that tell a lot of things.

"What's your job? What's it like to do your job?"

You see, telling a story, is what it's all about.

What has been most important to you in your career?

No one thing. I didn't plan to do what I'm doing. I came out of the depression; my dream was to have a civil service job, a steady, civil service job. And see a ball game during the summer time. Go to the bleachers. See an occasional good movie. And subscribe to the Nation magazine. Basically, that was it.

What has been your career?

I went to law school. I was in the Writer's Project under the New Deal, and I learned to write. And I was a gangster on radio soap opera. Then I became a disc jockey playing jazz music primarily, and folk music. Then I got on television, very early television, that was *TV Chicago Style: Stud's Place*, along with *Garroway at Large*, and *Kukla, Fran and Ollie*, were the three programs called *TV Chicago Style*.

And then I got on this FM station, WFMT, I've been here thirty-eight years. I'm seventy-eight years old, seventy-nine in May.

Does Oral History and Oral Tradition such as these stories of daily life by four generations of rails belong in American history and literature?

It's terribly important. Remember, there was oral history long before there was written history, before the printing press. Most people in the world were illiterate, they couldn't read.

But most people would tell stories, from one generation to another, they'd tell the history of a family or a clan, or a people.

What good are these kind of stories?

I think it's to make us richer people inside.

fig. 2 — West Oakland, 1948; washing-out boiler impurities in the roundhouse.

What is it like to live at this bewildering, crazy time, where our knowledge comes from a ten-second-byte on t.v. ... and that's our philosophy of life — from ten seconds, y'see.

What is it like to live at a time when there's no past. We have no past. Our past has been eliminated. We have to face up to the fact, that there's a history, that we can be wrong as well as right.

These stories about how ordinary people live ... it's important, because the traditional history books don't have that. Traditional history books through the years have been about makers and shakers — the big ones; officials, presidents, kings, industrialists, great artists.

But for the ordinary people, what was it like?

Griever's Forward

by Roy Onstott, Santa Fe Engineer, & United Transportation Union Griever

When the railroads first started, as you well know, state and federal government officials, the president, and everyone else, were elected by the railroads, which were really the big land barons. The big land barons held an iron fist over everything.

They killed ranchers to get their land. They didn't care about killing off their employees. The average life-expectancy was one year or less, for a brakeman, or an engineer, back at the turn of the century. The railroads have historically ruled by fear. They've never changed. You can talk to a hundred people out there, and ninety-nine of them will tell you the railroad's all right. But you become a mouse, and you get into a locker, or into the shanty, and people are so tired, so angry, and so stressed out, that they're almost ready to kill somebody. Even our bosses are called trainmaster. It's that master-slave relationship. That's the way railroads have always worked; and rails are very tight-lipped because of that fear. Fear of things that go bump in the night — and the railroads do go bump in the night quite a bit.

Even if you didn't put in the persons' names who told you the stories in this book, or anything that could be traced back to them, they might say something to a friend, and the word gets back. The railroads always seem to find out, and once they do, that person will be fired — not for that, but the railroad will invent something; they'll make something up, and that person will be fired. That is the way all railroads work. Anybody who speaks out against the railroad is soon fired. They'll make up charges. They hide in bushes, literally, they hide in toilet stalls, to listen to us — that's not an exaggeration; this is done all the time. So people are in fear; they are afraid to talk. Afraid to be candid, even if they don't use their own name; 'cause the word does get out. That's why I'm sayin', the railroads rule by fear. You're afraid to talk to anybody; 'cause you will lose your job.

Prolog — A 60-Yr Old Grandson's View of His Family of Rails

Hampton L. Brady, Jr. recalls his Grandfather Henry Stapp, Master Mechanic on the Western Pacific

My grandfather was a master mechanic, *the master mechanic,* on the Western Pacific. He lived in Elko, Nevada. He moved from Texas to Elko Nevada in about 1913. Between 1913 and 1942, he was master mechanic. A master mechanic is the top mechanical authority of everything that works on the railroad from a water faucet to a locomotive — everything mechanical is under his purview. He was not a steam locomotive engineer; he was a mechanical engineer. So he supervised everything of a mechanical nature on that section of the Western Pacific railroad. He studied as a mechanical engineer in his schooling. And he was in that capacity on railroads all his life.

My great grandfather, was a railroad engineer. My great grandfather was born in Fort Smith, Arkansas, back around 1875.

My grandfather had a badly crippled foot, due to the fact that he and his brother were swimming in a railroad water tank. They knew they'd catch heck ... and they heard the train coming — that their father was driving — so they climbed out of the water tank, ran through the woods, and my grandfather stepped on a hawthorn off of a Haw tree, and it infected and then crippled his foot for his lifetime. Now, his brother, that was swimming with him, became a steam locomotive engineer; and at the time that he retired — or was forced to retire — he was the oldest operating locomotive engineer in the United States. He was running a switch engine back and forth in the Stockton freight yards at the age of eighty-one.

He was good. He really knew his stuff. His nickname was *Sea Biscuit,* due to the fashion in which he drove an engine up and down the Feather River Canyon — he was noted throughout the railroad as a speed-burner; and somebody nicknamed him Sea Biscuit after the famous race horse. But I think he was working at that advanced age, largely due to the fact that his son was the boss there at Stockton. Finally he had some kind of a minor mishap with the engine, and his son came out and said, "Dad, get down out of that cab!" And there was almost a fist fight on account of it.

My uncle, was a conductor. He had been a brakeman for years, and worked up into being a freight conductor. He was involved in a mishap on the railroad — he was riding in the cab of a freight train on the Feather River Canyon, and he and the entire crew got carbon monoxide gassing from a leak in the engine. Many years later he died from it. The whole crew got whoozy and passing out – then died. So they figured out what it was.

My cousin worked briefly as a brakeman through family connections on summer vacations in college. So I've had about four generations of railroad people in my family.

I never had the interest to work for the railroad. If I had wanted to, I certainly had the family connections. The old men, my grandfather and his brother, would get together ... they had a pretty racy career for a while. For a while they were railroading together down on the Mexican Central Railroad during the time of Pancho Villa. At one point the Mexicans had a two-headed train, with a boiler on both sides of the cab; and the fireman had to feed both of them.

As a kid I used to kid my great uncle, Henry, Henry Stapp.

"Uncle Harry, did you ever get anybody with your locomotive?" I said.

"Yeah. I got six of 'em!" he said.

At one time he was going across the Keddy Tressel. Near Keddy, in the Feather River Canyon, there's this tressel must be one-hundred-fifty feet off the water; it's a great big high thing — he was going along on this scheduled run, and I guess there was a handcar with, as he generally termed them, five 'ragheads.' They had a lot of Hindu section hands — and some of 'em were comin' from the other direction in this handcar, right in the middle of the tressel ... I guess a handcar versus a locomotive generally comes out second-money.

And he said he'd got somebody in an ox cart in Mexico, who was in the wrong place at the wrong time. But he was a funny old duck. Tough as a pine knot.

Uncle Harry lived in Keddy. He had a house right there in Keddy. So he would run between Ogden and Portola. He died quite a while ago; my grandfather died in 1945, and I think Uncle Harry died about ten or twelve years later. My uncle was quite well along; he was in his eighties, very spry, right up to the end.

I reaped the benefits of having a grandfather in the railroad. I rode trains almost constantly when I was a kid. I rode on the train with my grandmother and grandfather who had passes, so I never paid a nickel — the train didn't make much money off of me, but I sure got a lot of ridin' done.

I was born in 1933, and was about twelve or thirteen years old when I really start riding trains around a lot. My parents lived in San Francisco, and my grandfather and grandmother lived in Oroville, so I'd take the ferry boat across the bay and get off at Oakland, and got on the Western Pacific and went on up to Oroville. At that time, it was the better part of a day's railroad trip to get there. I used to enjoy it. The thing that was really enjoyable about the trains at that time, was the dining car. They used to put out wonderful food.

The men weren't home a lot. They'd be gone for three or four days, and then back for eight hours or whatever. I guess the women got used to it. Of course my grandmother had five kids in six years ... my grandfather *was* home. Due to the fact his job wasn't like the train crew's job. His was more of a desk-type job. He was a supervisor. He supervised rebuilding of locomotives; the repair of any mechanical problems they would have had, say if a shipment of brake shoes was wearing out too fast or something — that was his bag of tricks. I got tours up in the cab through many of the engines, but I never rode out on the road in them. I got taken through the roundhouse, which was interesting.

I was a little kid at the time, nine or ten, and everything is so massive around railroad machinery. I guess that was the fascination for kids before the great mechanical age of airplanes ... trains were the biggest things around. You wanted to be a locomotive engineer. The roundhouse was interesting to me because of all these ten thousand jobs going on of welding and all the sparks flying; it was very interesting.

But as I say, for some reason, I didn't ever consider it a vocation for myself. I spent twenty years in the news business instead.

The thing that surprises a lot of people is how many railroads there were in the United States; literally thousands of them. Some of them were just a couple of miles long, a couple miles of track, and those are classified as a railroad. A lot of industries put in their own railroad.

The railroads weren't regulated until 1906. And the railroads ran the country. One of the biggest railroad barons was Jay Gould; one of the most crookedest sons-of-a-gun to ever grace the United States stock market. And the Crockers, and Stanfords and others, they exploited with their dictatorial powers the working man, really. They called the shots, and in many ways triggered depressions, booms and busts to meet their own ends.

The biggest land give-aways in the United States was to the railroads. When they built the Trans-Continental Railroad, they gave away every other section of land — a section of land is 640 acres — every other section of land along the track, hop-scotching back and forth across the railroad track in a checkerboard fashion on either side of the railroad tracks — all the way across the United States. It was the biggest land giveaway in history. And it was given to the railroad barons, Leland Stanford, the Crockers, et al.

Railroads were the only method of transportation other than horses and wagons or ships. The railroads came along, and monopolized the transportation of goods and people and services. Look at the fight that the railway unions had with the railroads. The strikes and so on. There was a lot of labor strife in the railroads.

The old-time slang for a railroad worker is a 'Ghandi-dancer'. There were lot of east Indian section hands on the railroads out here. The East-Indians were doing track work, pick and shovel work. Now they had lots of Chinese building the railroads, but never working on them. The Chinese never worked on the railroad as employees of the railroad; they were construction workers. They recruited the Chinese men from China, but they didn't bring in Chinese women; only men. The men were recruited mainly from Canton. They offered 'em money. Let's see. They started bringing in Black slaves into the U.S. before the constitution was framed around 1720 or so and stopped around the 1820-30's. Then at a later point they start bringing in Chinese and Hindus.

fig. 3 – *SD-9*, an early diesel

Table of Contents

Family Edition Of Old Rails' Tales

Foreword by Studs Terkel	iii
Griever's Forward by Roy Onstott	vi
Prolog — A Grandson's View of His Family of Rails	vii
Glossary of Rail & Railroad Slang & Terms	327
Caption Narratives	337

John Hogan (born 1928)

01. Sanitary Jake	1
02. Runaway Boxcar	5
03. I Saw Ninety-Ton Cars Flipping Over Like Toys	7
04. You Don't Get Too Many Chances Like That	9
05. The Time I Stuck My Foot On The Drawbar	11
06. The Grim Reaper	12
07. Old Timers	12
08. Funeral Train	13
09. Old Timers' Stories	14
10. Duke — Dog Of The Texas & New Orleans Railroad	15
11. The Kid In The Wheelchair	16
12. Old Ben	18
13. Pappy Way	20
14. It Brought A Tear To Pappy's Eye	21
15. A Workingman's	22
16. Woman Hoghead	24
17. Woman Switchman	25
18. Eve	26
19. Hoboes	27
20. The Hobo Capital Of The World	28
21. Stanahan	28
22. One Night	30
23. Little Red & The Fuze-ies	30
24. Little Red	31
25. Really Heavy Cars	34
26. Famous Curves Throughout the U.S.A.	33

27. There's the Keddy Y.	33
28. In The Desert	34
29. Roasted Coal	34
30. The Friendship Train	36
31. My Personal Pullman Car	38
32. A Humpyard	43
33. The Drop	43
34. Attila the Hun	44
35. Pete	46
36. The Card Houses In Tracy	48
37. Deadhead	51
38. Deadheading	51
39. Stallin' Around	53
40. Dell	53
41. Harold Clark	54
42. Beginner's Luck	55
43. The Silver Lady & The California Zephyr	55
44. The Time I Did Turn My Back	57
45. Not A Pretty Sight	60
46. Hitting Pedestrians	60
47. We Hit This Car One Time	61
48. Not All Fun and Games — Sometimes It's Not Very Pretty	62
49. We Hit A Car One Time	63
50. Hitting A Truck Full Of Potatoes	65
51. My Old Lantern	65
52. Another Dent In That Old Lantern	66
53. The Story About The Private Car	67
54. Nobody Said Nothin'	70
55. Running Through The Fog In Fresno	72
56. I Got Knocked Off The Top Of A Car Once	73
57. Baptist Special	74
58. Insurance Special	76
59. Celebrities	76
60. Coachyard Johnny	77
61. Off The Record	77
62. The Daylight Special & The Coast Starline	78
63. The Time The Fireman Let The Tank Heater Overflow	80
64. The Daylight Special	80
65. Mr. Lui	82
66. Here Comes Mr. Lui	85

Dick Murdock (born 1917)

67. There Was A Camaraderie Amongst The Men	89
68. I Was Hooked At An Early Age	90
69. Riding My First Train	90
70. The Suntan Special	90
71. Ray Barber	91
72. It's A Rough Darn Life	92
73. Iron Mike Harold & Youngblood the Indian	93
74. A Steam Engine Had An Almost Human Response	95
75. A Human Response	95
76. Striking It Rich On My Last Student Trip	97
77. Jay Moss — Port Costa Winter of '42-'43	97
78. Willie Marshal	98
79. Dorothy	98
80. Dutchy Luhr	99
81. A Ride Dorothy Never Forgot	100
82. The Gaudy Oilcloth	100
83. My Best Moments On The Railroad	101
84. My Big Thrill Was Getting Called For Number 19	101
85. Sandin' The Engine Out	102
86. You Had To Be Careful In July	104
87. You Could See The Sparks Coming Out Of The Flue	104
88. Diesels Were Worse Than Steam Engines Starting Fires	105
89. The Worst Experience I Ever Had	105
90. An Accident	108
91. Another Accident	109
92. The Shasta Daylight	110
93. Forgiven Taxes	112
94. Water Fights	112
95. Two Great Big Guys & A Firehose	114
96. It Wasn't Funny At The Time	115
97. Old Bill Knapke	117
98. Hey, Billy	118
99. Bill Knapke Told So Many Stories	120
100. Knapke Did Tell Me This One	120
101. Building The Dam Up At Boulder Dam	120
102. Tucson	121
103. The King of the Rails	122

104. While The Angel Watched	124
105. One of the Prettiest Curves	129
106. The Curve at Lake Shasta in the Moonlight	130
107. More About The Old Days	130
108. Max Howard	132
109. 1948	133
110. Black Widows in the March of '51	134
111. Shop Talk	136
112. The Burnt Journal	138
113. Deadheadin' in the Caboose – Drifting Through Escolat	139
114. Archy Livingston	140
115. Dunsmuir — In Tunnels Full Of Smoke	141
116. At The Old Rails Club in Oakland	143

Grant Sherwood Allen (born 1897)

117. The Work Record of Grant Sherwood Allen	145
118. 1918 or 1919	146
119. The Story No Boomer Can Match	148
120. Las Vegas	150
121. How A Cut-Off Dispatcher Ended Up Supervising	151
122. Workin' Again	152
123. Out Of A Job, Again	152
124. Workin' Again	154
125. I Get A Break	154
126. My Time In The Timekeeper's Office	155
127. That's Show Business	155
128. Shovelin' Out The Shovel Runners	156
129. What Goes Around Comes Around	156
130. The Icing On The Cake	156
131. 'Saint Peter Don't You Call Me 'Cause I Can't Go'	156
132. A Big Change For Me	157
133. Johnny & Paul Do It Their Way	157
134. The Old Number 8 From Mt. Tamalpais & Muir Woods	158
135. 4% Grades	160
136. 'Here I Go Again,' I Thought.	161
137. The Key To Successful Operation Was The Men	162
138. The Lousy Dispatcher	163
139. The Wolf	163

140.	Train Sheet Of A Single Day's Work	163
141.	Cut Off Again	166
142.	Startin' Seniority Someplace	167
143.	Superintendent Of The Indian Valley Railroad	167
144.	Assistant Trainmaster At Tobin	169
145.	Mile Post 253 In The Feather River Canyon	169
146.	Superintendent of Transportation For Western Pacific	172
147.	Those Eleven Years Were The Happiest Years Of My Life	174
148.	The Private Business Car	175

Bill Millard (born 1912)

149.	I Belonged To Engineers' Union 45 Years	179
150.	My Grandfather, My Father, & I Were Steam Engineers	179
151.	Pride in Belonging To The Engineers	180
152.	The Deep Freeze	180
153.	1871	180
154.	My Grandfather's Boots	182
155.	1904-1917	183
156.	Bright Spots	184
157.	Sanding Them Out	185
158.	A Story About A 4100	187
159.	I Wanted To Tell You About These Engines	187
160.	The Sand-House	189
161.	There Was Nothin' At Kirk	190
162.	The Big Issue Was Always Lumber Up There	191
163.	Spuds From Tulley Lake on The Spud Digger	191
164.	One Morning Out At Madeline	193
165.	*'Pop! Pop! Pop! Pop! Pop!'*	194
166.	Charlie McLaughlin	194
167.	What The Hossler Did	194
168.	We'd Put Picket Fences Into The Firebox	195
169.	*Here She Comes!*	197
170.	The Happiest Time I Had On The Railroad	198
171.	The Feast	199
172.	One Of The Biggest Thrills I Ever Had	201
173.	*Plop, Plop, Fizz, Fizz*	202
174.	I've Hit A Beet Truck	202
175.	We Hit A Spinach Truck	203

176. Marvin Hargess	203
177. Frank Tirral — Full-Blooded Italian	205
178. Razor-Neck Flynn	206
179. Barney Price	207
180. Frank Shoemakker	208
181. Real Characters	209
182. Johnny Cooper	210
183. The Curve at Keg Pit	211
184. When Snow Melts & Freezes On A Train On a Siding	212
185. Red Cinder Ballast	214
186. More Curves	214
187. The Bridge To Leaf	215
188. I Was Out Of Air	216
189. Dick Was Out Of Air	216
190. *Pops* When Feelin' The Seat Box	217
191. You Hadn't Given It Quite Enough	218
192. You've Got To Be On The Ball	219
193. How Is A Woman Going To Handle A 110 lb Knuckle?	219
194. Joe Cooper	221
195. The Broken Knuckle	221
196. Joe Cooper Got A Drawbar Once	221
197. Mr. Brae	222
198. 410 In The Fog To Tracy Waitin' For The Owl, Old 53	222
199. A Brakeman Can't Signal Any Better Than He Can Talk	224
200. That's The Time I Stopped	224
201. Another Time I Was Shovin' Another Track	225
202. The San Jose Pool	226
203. You Owed Your Life To The Company Store	226

Jack Smith (born 1947)

204. Cartoon in Fresno	232
205. On The Mainline	233
206. Curves	234
207. Running In The Fog	234
208. You Count To 8, Or 9	235
209. Cab Signals	236
210. Rain's No Big Thing	236
211. Divided Responsibility	236

212. The First Person I Hit – Or The Train Hit	237
213. What Happened One Time	239
214. That Part I Don't Like Too Well	240
215. The Part I Do Like	240
216. You Wear A Beeper	241
217. The Tops of The Sierras	243
218. A Typical Day The Way The Railroad is Going	244
219. A Rail Turns Over	246
220. Fog and Sleep	247
221. Some People Get Sleepy	248
222. In Your Blood	249
223. That Sixteen-Hour Day	250
224. There Was A Lot Of Sleeping Back In The Caboose	252

John Brown (born 1951)

225. We've Hit A Lot Of Automobiles	255
226. Get Down	256
227. My First Railroad Job	256
228. The World's Largest Whiskey & Water Salty Dog	257
229. AMTRAK	259
230. You Get To Eat, Too?	259
231. Violence On The Reno Fun Train	259
232. Business As Usual	260
233. A Major Mistake By A Yardmaster	261
234. Protecting The Traffic	262
235. A Quick Way Home	262
236. Wow! Man. Look At The Sparks	263
237. Accidents	264
238. Have You Ever Been Hit By A Train?	265
239. The Witch Of Davis	266
240. The Lady With The Bag Full Of Ticket Stubs	266
241. Suicide On The Tracks	267
242. Love Story	268
243. An American Indian Who Couldn't Stop Crying	269
244. Are We Almost There?	271
245. Life On The Job	271
246. Tough Street Guy On An Eleventh Hour Run	272
247. There's Only Two Of You	273

248. Old Folks	274
249. Cops & Saturday Night At The Opera	274

Patricia Lollis (born 1953)

250. 'Nothing Is Yours Until You Pass It On To Another.'	277
251. Those Old Guys Were My Favorites	279
252. Being With The Old Timers Was Wonderful	280
253. My Favorite Person	280
254. 'Liebschen — Meaning 'Dear One'	281
255. Herman's Gooseberry Pie and Papa Duck	282
256. Papa Duck	283
257. The 'Alerter'	284

Wendy Weisman (born 1949)

258. One Guy Shoved Me Into Some Cars That Were Moving	289
259. A Fire In The Dark & The Cold	290
260. One Thing That Happened One Night	291
261. 'Walk Like A Man If You Can'	293
262. Pink Cadillac	293
263. I Hit A Car	294
264. 'The Baby-Doll Train'	295
265. Van The Man	296
266. No Matter What The Weather Is	298
267. Good I Don't Get Colds Easily	298
268. One Of The Most Interesting Things	299
269. 'Flip-Flop'	300
270. 'Not-So-Bad'	301
271. 'Tap-Dancin' Don'	301
272. 'Giggles'	301
273. 'Chicken House'	301
274. 'Leaky Roof'	301
275. 'Shaky' Shayhan	302
276. 'Knuckles'	302
277. 'Be-No'	302
278. No Secrets on the Railroad	302
279. Those Old Steam Engineers	303

fig. 4 – a steam engineer's throttle, forward-reverse, & gages

280. Favorite Curves   304
281. Wheel-Slip   305

Linda Niemann (born 1946)

282. An Interview   306

List of Illustrations

(caption narratives begin on page 337)

fig. 1 – a would-be brakeman	ii
fig. 2 – West Oakland, 1948; washing-out boiler impurities	v
fig. 3 – *SD-9*, an early diesel	xi
fig. 4 – A steam engineer's throttle, forward-reverse, & gages	xx
fig. 5 – Tuolomne, CA, 1952; *'Climax Engine'*	4
fig. 6 – Mountain View, CA, 1951: collision with gravel truck	10
fig. 7 – Sierra Railroad Overland Ltd; open observation car	17
fig. 8 – *switch engine* in Berkeley, CA, 1957	23
fig. 9 – roundhouse *switch engine* in west Oakland	29
fig. 10 – erecting hall, Sacramento, engines under repair, 1946	35
fig. 11 – washing-out boiler; getting scale out; Oakland CA, '43	37
fig. 12 – *Western Pacific*	39
fig. 13 – *'Back-Up' Mallet;* running model John made	50
fig. 14 – *4-6-2, 'milk bottle' boiler'*	50
fig. 15 – running models John built, *GS-4* on the turntable	56
fig. 16 – part of John's train board	58
fig. 17 – a *'rear-ender'* near Pasa Robles in 1942	64
fig. 18 – *California Zephyr (Silver Lady)* Oakland, 1968	71
fig. 19 – job of a *Redcap* is to load luggage on carts & train	75
fig. 20 – Oakland	79
fig. 21 – *Blinky* (bottom) was always blinking his eyes.	83
fig. 22 – *Overland Ltd; F-7* arriving Berkeley from Chicago	86
fig. 23 – Great Salt Lake, north end at Monument Point	87
fig. 24 – 12-mile tangent – 4 miles from Sacramento	88
fig. 25 – *Engine 24, 2-8-0, Sierra Railroad*, Tuolomne, CA	96
fig. 26 – *Sierra Railroad*, west of Jamestown, CA	106
fig. 27 – *The Race Track Special,* at Bay Meadows	113
fig. 28 – *4-4-0 American-Type engine,* c. 1875	119
fig. 29 – *4-6-0 Ten Wheeler,* c. 1885	119
fig. 30 – *4-8-2 Mountain-Type,* 1934	125
fig. 31 – *El Gobernador, 4-10-0,* 1860-1903	125
fig. 32 – *4-6-6-4,* used in Nevada flatlands	131
fig. 33 – *2-8-8-2,* as big as they get	131
fig. 34 – a dispatcher's centralized traffic control board	147
fig. 35 – dispatcher for Feather River Canyon just after WWII	153
fig. 36 – 1919, Grant Allen on 'one of those track motorcars'	159

fig. 37 – Margarite, 1918; Grant's wife, Ogden, Utah 165
fig. 38 – Grant Allen's home one winter when layed-off 171
fig. 39 – *Ten Wheeler No. 77, Western Pacific,* Sacramento '41 173
fig. 40 – Southern Pacific coachyard, San Francisco, 1959 177
fig. 41 – Sierra Nevada Mts., *Huntington* at Alta, Placer City 178
fig. 42 – playing pinochle in the switchman's shanty 181
fig. 43 – *4-8-4 Northfork & Western* 213
fig. 44 – *Ten -Wheeler, SP* Ogden Division shop; Ogden Utah 227
fig. 45 – Niles Canyon, the *California Zephyr,* 1967 228
fig. 46 – railroad excursion trip to Tracy CA, 1960 231
fig. 47 – *F-7 diesel* in the shop, Roseville CA 242
fig. 48 – caboose 253
fig. 49 – a train wreck on the *Western Pacific* 254
fig. 50 – an excursion train from Oakland to Oroville in 1955 275
fig. 51 – engineers: Patricia Lollis & Herman, Christmas 276
fig. 52 – Sierra Nevada's, *Nevada* at Colfax near Placer City 305
fig. 53 – Patricia's qualifying run on *Amtrak* 306
fig. 54 – Pullman porter 326
fig. 55 – depot at Cisco, western summit, alt 5,900 ft. 336
fig. 56 – Observation lounge, *California Zephyr,* Oakland, '68 340
fig. 57 – Nevada, Truckee Meadows 349
fig. 58 – John Hogan as a conductor for *Southern Pacific* 350
fig. 59 – Dedication 351
fig. 60 – Southern Pacific engine 2372 352

a

b

John Hogan — (born 1928)

A Brakeman Tried and True

John builds steam locomotive models from scratch and from spare parts. He has ridden run-away boxcars down Coathanger Curve. He has been dragged beneath a train. He has been knocked off the top of boxcars. He has seen 90-ton cars flipping over and over like they were toys. He is a nice man and he is very good at playing cards in the caboose. He laughs a lot, and always has a good story to tell. Here are some of John's stories.

Sanitary Jake

Jake was an engineer. A hoghead. It seems he got that nickname, Sanitary Jake, because on a trip from San Francisco to Watsonville, he got in an argument with his fireman about how much water was back in the tender.

So as the engine is going down the track at 30 or 40 m.p.h. the fireman looked up, and looked over to the other side of the cabin, and there was no engineer there, the seat was vacant.

And here's the engine going along with no engineer.

Suddenly the engineer appeared from the back of the cab soaking wet, from his chest on down, and he said, "Now, gosh darn it, I told you there was enough water to make Gilroy!"

Right in front of the brakeman and the fireman, he was soakin' wet, 'cause he walked up and he climbed down, there was a ladder right down into the tender water tank and he went all the way down to the bottom of the water tank and used himself as a dipstick so he could show how much water there was.

And there are just so many people on the railroad like that.

"Were you a trouble shooter? Did you go out in case there was a need? What would you do on the train? If you went on as a brakeman, does that mean if something went wrong with a brake, you'd fix it?" I asked.

"Well, actually, that was a name that came about a long time ago, when the only brakes they had on the trains were on the engines. Because they had what was called a steam jam, and it was just straight air, and it would only apply on the engine, and when they were going down a hill to avoid a runaway, the engineer would signal with the whistle for the brakeman to start riding high, and turn 'em down," John said.

"What does riding high and turn 'em down mean?" I asked.

"Goin' on top of the car, and tyin' 'em down means cranking a handbrake," John said.

"You mean you had to do 'em by hand?!" I asked.

"Yeah. Oh sure. They were brakemen."

"If you had eight wheels on a locomotive, you had sixteen brakes to put on?" I asked.

"No. You'd break the locomotive by breakin' the freight cars. To stop the train or slow it down. And then of course, this was in the early days, when there was no brakes on the rolling cars. Air brakes start coming in the late 1880's, but they didn't really work good until the mid 1890's, when they were well developed," John said.

"But when you were working, you still had to be on brakes by hand?" I asked.

"Well, yeah. But for a different reason. The brakes are so sophisticated now. There's very little chance that anything could go wrong. It's letter-perfect now. The technology for brakes is plumb perfect. But when I hired out in '54, a lot of times I worked out of San Luis Obispo, and there's this big grade over San Margarita, and some of the conductor's wanted the brakemen to ride high just in case 'cause they'd done it for years and years — and trainmen were getting out of that practice. One brakeman would ride in the caboose, and the other in the engine, 'cause there's always two brakemen on a train," John said.

"If someone wanted to make sure there wouldn't be a runaway or if both the brakemen had to put brakes on one would start at the back and the other would start at the front, and put the brakes on, on individual cars?" I asked.

"Yeah. You had a big hickory club and you carried that with you always," John said.

"What was that for, leverage?" I asked.

"Yeah, 'cause you could stick it in that wheel and you could multiply the mechanical gain with a club enormously."

"How would you know when to stop? By the sound? Did the wheels start to screech?" I asked.

"Yeah. You could feel it when you got it up so tight, you can feel the drag."

"So there's no in between when you're supposed to put those on, you're supposed to put them on all the way?" I asked.

"Yes, depending upon the situation," John answered enthusiastically. Today, if the engineer needed brakes, then he's in big trouble, the whole train's in big trouble. You're gonna slide the wheels, 'cause you can actually slide the wheels by tying the handbrake down, it's got mechanical gain to it.

"But normally working out of San Luis Obispo, they'd used these retainers. It's a function of the air brakes, when the train starts down the grade, now the engineer in the cab can set a little air, then he releases, then he might have to set a little more air. Well if each car didn't have a retainer, he could lose his air. 'Cause he has to wait until the air pump on the engine recharges the line," John said.

"So he could be in a situation where it might be recharging?" I said.

"Right, so they have these retainers. Most of them were located right up near the brake wheel. There's a little lever, called a retainer. And the function of that is, when all the retainers on the whole train are up — every car has a retainer up — the engineer sets some air up in the cab, then they won't release so fast, they'll release a lot slower, so he can have more control of the train from up there, and the brakemen would go from car to car, setting these retainers — while the train was going up the hill. Then, when it started down, the engineer had a lot more control of the train. Then when they finally got down to level, the brakemen would have to go and knock each one down. And set each one on. There's no need for handbrakes nowadays," John said.

"But you used to carry a hickory club?" I asked.

"Yes. Just in case."

"Was there a time you needed it?" I asked.

"Yeah."

"Was that on a runaway?"

"No. But I have rode a runaway onetime. I wouldn't want to go

fig. 5 – Tuolomne, CA, 1952: West Side Lumber Company *'Climax Engine'*

through it again. I'll tell you that. On the Union Pacific. We were running from Green River, to Rollins Wyoming. About a one-hundred-ninety mile district, then we'd turn it over to another crew. It was on this local freight.

Runaway Boxcar

We were out on the main line. We're out on the desert, the prairie, so we're goin' along and the conductor backed a train in. We only had an engine, one car, and a caboose.

And so instead of cutting the caboose off and coming in with the engine, he just backed the whole train, the caboose and the one car and the engine, backed into the siding, and picked the other car up.

We picked up the car with the caboose, so it was now the rear car. And we pulled out onto the main line.

We went about two miles and we had to pick up another car, in an industry — I think it was a stock car, right out on the prairie. So instead of hangin' on to that car, and coming in with it too, he cut that car off, and left it on the main line. And we still came back into the siding with the caboose and the one car and the engine.

I had cut the car off to send the engine away, and as soon as the couplers let go, the air hoses popped, well the brakes are supposed to function automatically on every car. This was all downgrade, you see.

So the airhose popped, but the brakes didn't function. And the car started rolling back in the opposite direction we were going.

So the car start rolling back, and there's a brake on one end of the car, it was the far end. So I got on the car, and the brake's on the other end of the car, so I went over the top.

And meanwhile, that car's pickin' up speed. And down there, another thousand feet, there's a curve, called Coathanger Curve.

And this car is really picking up speed.

So I got to the handbrake.

And the harder I tugged on that brake, the faster that car went.

It was an impossible coincidence, that the air brakes didn't work, and the handbrake didn't work.

The conductor saw what was happening, so he cut the engine

off, and he came out with the engine to go down and chase me on the top of this runaway boxcar.

I'm comin' up to this curve.

It's goin' too fast to get off. You know, there's so many things, you might make the curve or you may not, if it rolls over, I don't know, but if I got off at that speed I'd a been unfortunate, so I stayed on the car.

That car leaned around that curve.

I don't know what held it on the track.

But when we made it around that curve, I could've kissed that boxcar.

Then it started rolling uphill.

I stayed on it after the curve, 'cause I knew it was going to go uphill, and I was looking for a big chunk of wood or something, because the minute it stops, you can put a chunk of wood under there, and it will stop it, but once it's moving, you'll never get it stopped. So the minute it stopped, I was off lookin', but I couldn't find anything, not even a rock.

So the boxcar stops, because it's rollin' up a hill.

Then it starts moving back the other way. It starts rollin' back.

Meanwhile, the engineer's coming flyin' down the track.

Well here they come down around the opposite way with the engine, and there was kind've a clump of trees, so they couldn't see what was happening. And here it comes rollin' back.

When it starts movin' back the other way, well you can't stop it. And I'm running down there trying to give them a stop sign, and I just couldn't get down there fast enough.

I knew what was going to happen next. I was runnin' down the track, about the same speed as the boxcar, tryin' to get down there to get them stopped.

And they came around the corner.

At that point they weren't coming fast enough to be hurt,

And BANG!

The engine and this car rammed into each other and derailed. Nobody got hurt.

I just sat down on the rail and calmed down for a while.

I could've been killed.

But a miss is as good as a mile.

Later Roy the engineer told me when they saw the boxcar go around that curve, he said, "I just couldn't believe it. We were waiting for it to see if it was layin' over on it's side with the wheels pointing up in the air or somethin', with you under it."

But it stayed on the rail.

But I tell you, that was somethin'.

I Saw Cars, Ninety Ton Cars, Just Flipping Over and Over Like Toys

We had half a train go on the ground.

It happened about five years ago (1985).

I was the conductor on this freight train. We left Fresno about three-thirty, four o'clock in the afternoon and were comin' to Richmond.

I got all my work done. I was sittin' up in the cupola of the caboose and watchin' the train over, and 'bout ten miles south of Merced we're coming along, goin' north.

Well there's this road that comes almost at right angles to the railroad, and I saw this automobile coming down this road and I said to myself, 'Man, that guy's sure going fast. I don't know if this guy's gonna stop or not.'

I'm sitting back there.

He didn't even slow down.

He ran right through the gates, right into the side of our train.

I'm flabbergasted. It was such a shock to me.

He hit between two boxcars; one of the boxcars just ran over his automobile and cut it in half.

There was a great big shower of sparks came up.

Part of his automobile got under one of the wheels of one of the freight cars, and it's gettin' dragged along — it derailed the boxcar.

Half his automobile was still back at the crossing, and this great big shower of sparks came up, and all I could say, to the brakeman sitting by me, was "Hang on!" I couldn't even hardly talk, just say, "Hang on!"

And the train approached a siding track. Well that boxcar was bouncin' along on the ties, and it decided to go one way, and the train another way.

It was helter skelter.

I saw cars, ninety ton cars, just flipping over and over just like toys. I was sittin' back there, and it was the most awesome sight I ever saw in my life.

Y'see, my life is on the line at that point too.

It's coming back to the caboose.

All the cars ahead of the caboose are turning over.

So I watched lots of cars in front of me coming derailed and flipping over, one at a time. It was like a slow motion movie. The cars had slid along on their sides, and as they slid you could smell the burning paint on the side of the boxcars.

And the only reason the caboose didn't turn over, was because the drawbars slid by and it came uncoupled when the car right in front of us flipped over.

The caboose was still moving, and we rammed into the bottom of the car that was ahead of the caboose, and we came to rough, but nice stop — we stayed on the track.

Oh Jeeze!

I sat there for a minute, and I said to the brakeman, "Are you okay?"

And he says, "Yeah, how about you?"

"I'm all right," I say.

We got down, and we walked around.

There was nineteen cars derailed.

So I had watched nineteen cars in front of me coming derailed and flipping over, one at a time. And there was a carload of plywood, well it went out in this field and hit this great big rock, and the car stopped, and the plywood just kept going. Another car had brand new refrigerators in it, and it twisted open just like a giant hand had twisted this car apart, and was throwing brand new refrigerators all over the rightaway.

Later on, when everything cleared, I went back to look at what was left of his car, and it was almost like it had gone through a saw. It was just unbelievable. Honest, my eyes were that big.

The tape in the engine later on showed we were goin' around 68 m.p.h. We're authorized 70 m.p.h.

So I got on the radio, and I called the dispatcher, and I said we had a serious derailment, and they wanted to know if anybody was hurt, and I said no, no one on the train.

After we talked for a while he asked, "What was the cause of it?"

I said, "I think somebody said we got hit by a car, and it

derailed us. Better get an ambulance at so & so crossing, for this guy." Well, they needed a hearse for him, really.

So anyway, the superintendent, who is a big official, he came out. A whole bunch of people started showing up, and this superintendent came up and he said, "How are you doin'?"

"Fine," I said sort of beneath my breath.

"It was quite a mess here, wasn't it?" He said. He asked us, "You must've been shaken up. Can you continue? You don't have to if you don't want." he said.

The brakeman, he was shaking so hard. I was too.

The train stopped about a quarter of a mile from the crossing, where this guy ran into us.

Later on I found out his BAC (blood alcohol level) was almost point 2. So he was ... a lot of people, couldn't even stand, having that much alcohol in their blood.

He paid the price for it.

You Don't Get Too Many Chances Like That

I knew this guy who was the engineer on a local freight, and we were sitting on a siding in the caboose one time, goin' to beans, and he told me the whole story.

This train originated in Los Angeles, and was on it's way from San Jose to San Francisco, a fast-mail train. Going through Mountain View, this gravel truck pulled out right in front of them.

The engineer put the brakes in emergency, but, y'know, it was like nothin' at that speed. Anyway, they plowed into the gravel truck, and just disintegrated the truck — it just exploded like a handgrenade — and the train continued on; but the engineer felt the engine really begin to bounce. And he assumed that the four-wheel pilot truck, (editor's note: in the front under the engine), was on the ground. Which it was. Then all of a sudden, the whole locomotive, over it went, on the hoghead's side. And he was in quite a shock as he watched the grass going by the side of his window as the train slid along on its side on the grass.

Then the fireman, who was on the other side of the engine cab, came tumbling down on top of him.

If a pipe had broken, it would have filled the cab full of super-

fig.6 — Mountain View, CA, 1951: engine ran into a gravel truck

heated steam, and they couldn't have got out.

There wasn't one steam pipe broke in the cab — not one.

The tender had come up against the cab, and trapped them in there. In fact, one of the baggage cars ended up on top of the tender. When the rescue crew finally got them out, they hugged each other, they made it!

You don't get too many chances like that.

The Time I Stuck My Foot On The Drawbar

I was just careless. There's no words for it.

It's a very bad commentary for somebody that's supposed to have a lot of experience.

We were riding on the end of a car, we weren't even coupled to another car. It was just the engine, and one car. And this drawbar slides in and out, even if nothin's on it. It takes all the shock out. Some cars are real rigid, the drawbars don't go in very much, or don't go out.

And you should not step on them. If you're going to ride in between the cars, you ride on the crossover walkway, not on the drawbar.

Well I decided that they don't know what they're talking about when they build these cars, and I know it all. See, it's a lot easier to stand on the drawbar housing. I was standing there, one foot was on the walkway, and the other foot was on the drawbar, and the engineer stopped, the drawbar went forward, the drawbar came together. It grabbed a hold of my foot, and tore the heel off my boot. And it was a heavy boot, too. It was just a few inches away from mangling my foot.

I told everyone, when I was walking along with my boot flip-flopping that loose heel and sole, and I just said that the heel came off. I got away with saying that, they're not going to challenge anyone with thirty-six years of seniority.

When you figure you know it all, that invites some incident to happen. I don't know why I ever did such a thing. It was just a few inches away from mangling my foot. I've had a few close calls, and somehow, maybe just dumb luck, I've come out of it. When you look back over time, luck has a lot to do with it.

The Grim Reaper

There was this guy, he had one of these harvesters, and he was moving it from one farm to another, and he had to cross the tracks, and right on the railroad track, the thing decided to quit. So he got out, and he had to walk about a half a mile to a telephone, and he called someone and said he needed a tow on his harvester.

He came back, and the thing was in shambles.

It was all turned over to one side, and when the tow truck showed up, they couldn't tow it, because the wheels were all busted. So the tow truck just turned around and went back.

And the train was standin' not far away. Everyone was all takin' notes down. And here this harvester was just a pile of junk.

This was down in the country, someplace around Merced or Madera. It was like a harvester for cotton, a big piece of machinery. It was just totaled, the whole thing, into Christmas tree ornaments.

Automobiles and trucks go up to the tracks, cross 'em, then you go down.

Vehicles usually stall goin' up, and get stuck on the tracks.

Old Timers

My personal experiences were just about average, but just listening to the old timers talk, was always kind of interesting to me. I didn't really take part in it, but just to listen, to hear somebody, with maybe a strange accent from another part of the country, I don't know, usually people were somewhat old, and interesting, and they would tell things like, there was a big superstition when the diesels started to show up, and the old engineers just couldn't get used to this new-fangled diesel.

There was all sorts of accusations that the new diesel would magnetize your watch, and they would effect your vision with magnetic waves, and electrical waves.

Well, none of that ever proved true.

They believed it, and it was an old superstition.

I used to love these old timers talking.

The diesel engine's running a big electric generator, and the electricity it produces goes to the traction motors. A steam engine was just simply a big coffee pot, and they were so used to the old, big, bouncing, swaying, belching, sooty engine, that now when all of a sudden they got into a nice, clean, shiny new diesel, and there was something they missed. They were so used to the roar of the exhaust. It wasn't as romantic.

But if the diesel hadn't shown up, there would be no railroads.

Steam engines were enormously expensive to operate. After World War II, there was inflation that set in all over the world, but in the United States, inflation, the cost of operating things, began to rise, and something as widespread as a railroad to operate, the owner certainly wanted to operate economically.

And not only that, the diesel was superior to a steam engine. The old timers hated to admit it, but the diesel was much more powerful. It could be used for weeks, they didn't shut them down for weeks, they'd run for weeks, day and night, twenty-four hours a day, they just didn't shut them off. And they worked just as well, and they were always ready for service.

Now a steam engine had to be taken out of service, and the boiler blown down, and this maintenance had to go on to it, then fire it up, and get it back on the line. And the diesel would just run, and run forever. Even sitting around in the round house, it would just run idling.

They do shut them down now, to cut down on pollution.

But they used to just run forever. And the old engineers, they just couldn't get used to this new-fangled diesel.

So, it was like that at first, then of course people got used to them. And they didn't magnetize your watch. And they didn't effect your vision, or your hearing, as they were purported to do. And they're a lot cleaner.

Sometimes the diesel engineer will wear slacks to work. It's just so much better.

Funeral Train

One time I was on a train in '57, that was a diesel train, and it was a funeral train. They had these old condemned steam engines, they were pulling old condemned steam engines.

And we went on the siding one time, to wait for another train, and the engineer went back, the first steam engine that was behind the diesel, that was condemned, he wanted to get some momento off that engine, because he said he made his date as a hoghead on that engine.

And here it was now going to be cut up into little pieces for the furnace. He was visibly upset.

Y'know, it was a good part of his life, that was going there.

Old Timers' Stories

When I was on the N.W.P., I remember an old engineer talking, about a story told a long time ago, it was early in the days of air brakes, when the train would have air brakes.

It seems they were going from Eureka to Willits with this train that was carrying big logs on flatcars. And just one car after another, just twenty or thirty flatcars with big logs them.

This brakeman was telling this story, they were coming down this hill, and the engineer was using too much air, and pretty soon he found himself in a situation where the air reservoir tank was almost depleted, and he had no air.

And they were free-wheeling.

And the engineer yelled over the roar of the engine to the brakeman, to go back and start tying them down.

And the brakeman looked back there, and the cars were swaying back and forth and back and forth, and every once in a while some of the logs would roll off the cars. And the brakeman said, "I ain't going back there."

And he told the engineer he wasn't going back there. 'Cause he would have had to walk over the logs to get back there, and he wouldn't do it. It'd be suicide.

So anyway, they came down this hill, and they were making miles an hour, expectin' the whole train to run off the track at any moment. But they made the bottom of the hill.

And then they started up again.

And of course, uphill, the engineer was able to control the train again. After they stopped, they looked back, and they saw the caboose coming down by itself, 'cause the other brakeman and the conductor had pulled the pin on the caboose, and they could control the caboose with a handbrake.

So when the two brakemen got together, the first brakemen told the other guy, "You sure weren't much help in trying to get the train stopped."

And the second brakemen answered, "If you were going to turn over, we weren't going to go with you."

When those things happen, everyone that's on the train knows what a dangerous situation like that, that's it's already past the danger point.

There wasn't much he could do, so he might just as well uncouple the caboose, and let the train go ahead.

Especially with those logs falling off in front of them.

Duke — the Dog of The Texas & New Orleans Railroad

On the Texas & New Orleans Railroad we're waiting to go out on a freight train, and this other freight trained pulled in the yard, coming from the East, and this old dog got off the caboose with the conductor and a brakeman.

There was quite a story about this dog, was that he was quite ... well, all the railroad men had really befriended this dog, and so when he was just a puppy, they decided to take him from El Paso to San Antonio.

And the dog apparently liked the trip, and the caboose, and so pretty soon, other crews were askin' if they could borrow the dog, and take him for a ride.

Cause it was a cute little dog.

And pretty soon, the whole railroad, they just let the dog wander around the railroad and ride the whole line, and the dog would decide where he wanted to go.

He'd sleep in the yard office, or if a train was ready, the crew would coax him up into either the engine or the caboose, and he used to ride all over.

And I remember seeing that dog gettin' out of the caboose.

He probably got more miles than I ever did.

The home terminal for that Texas & New Orleans Railroad line was El Paso.

Texas & New Orleans runs from El Paso to New Orleans, so that dog had probably been down in the French Quarter a hundred times, or in San Antonio watched the Alamo, he'd been all over. Probably went over to Juarez, across from El Paso, probably swam in the Rio Grande.

His name was Duke.

But everybody on the railroad, they'd always save something to feed old Duke.

And he was part of the employees.

There was a story, that somebody had even put his name on a time slip.

Cause the conductor's in charge of the crew, and he makes out the time slip.

I heard that another railroad, that they had a dog like that, and they just let him wander all over the railroad, they'd take him in the caboose, or in the engine, and he'd go for a ride.

Then he'd get off at the next terminal, he may stay on the caboose, or he may get off. He'd ride all over the railroad. All the railroad men knew him, and a lot of the other employees too, and they all vied for his attention. They always wanted him along for the ride.

"Let's take him to San Antone this time."

"Yeah!"

On this other railroad, the dog died eventually. It may have happened to Duke too.

And they buried him alongside the railroad track.

The Kid In The Wheelchair

When I was on the S.P., there's this old town of Atascadero right on the S.P. main line. Atascadero's just a real small little town. When I was down there, the tracks would go by this house that was maybe two or three hundred feet back from the railroad track, and there was always this kid on a wheelchair up on the front porch.

And he always waved to the crews, and the crews would wave back.

Pretty soon, he was obviously disabled, so the crews start throwing off comic books. And one thing led into another, and

fig. 7 – open observation platform; quite the cat's meow, w/deckchairs & awning   17

crews would throw candy off, and all sorts of stuff, in little packages, so it wouldn't get all busted up.

Anyway, apparently someone found out that the kid had incurable muscular dystrophy, is what I heard. I don't know if that's fatal or not. The kid was certainly in very poor shape, and he was just a favorite of the whole railroad, and all the crews knew him well, and he probably knew all the crews, caused they always tossed him stuff.

Well it seems, I didn't actually witness this, but it did happen, some of the crews got together with some of the officials, and one morning, The Great Daylight Limited slowed down and pulled to a stop in front of the kid's house. And the conductor and engineer and trainmaster all got off the train and other officials, and they walked over, and put him in his wheelchair up in the engine, and they took him all the way to Los Angeles. Riding up in the engine there.

And he got a bird's eye view of the whole trip.

So the crews, and I guess the S.P. paid to put him up in a hotel in Los Angeles.

The next morning they brought him back, and the Daylight stopped going northbound.

I remember when it happened. I didn't actually see it happen. But I know it happened. But I do remember seeing the kid out there.

And the kid died.

And there was more rails at the kid's funeral, then there was relatives, from what I heard.

It was quite a story.

And there was hardly anything in the newspaper about it. There was a little article in the company magazine. The company wasn't really tootin' their own horn, or anything.

It was pretty fantastic.

Old Ben

There was a switchman.

He was really a good-hearted guy. But he just didn't think about what he was doing.

One of the jobs we did in Richmond, as a switchman, we had

these twenty-two cars that were on maybe five different tracks in the yard, and we had to line the cars up in a certain order. Twenty-two cars, in a certain order.

Old Ben, he'd get out there, and it'd take him a long time to line up these cars. They had to go into this plant, and they were loaded according to their position on the track, so each car had to have a specific position in the track, and there was two tracks in the building, with eleven cars on each track.

It was like a puzzle. It took a lot of time, and it really took a lot of thought, how to do this.

Your cars are scattered all over the yard, and you have to start with the low numbers, and just keep adding on to them. You could make the job go for eight hours if you didn't know what you were doing.

But if you thought a little bit about how to line these cars up, you could do it in about an hour or so. Y'know. It was tough work.

But you'd think about how to get three car off the track here, and five off there, and six there, and they're all scattered. You might have the six spot ahead of the eight, then you got to get the seven in between, and stuff like that.

Well anyway, this one time Old Ben was switching all these cars around, and he got them all lined up, but they were backwards.

Took him two and a half hours to line all these cars up, twenty-two cars, and they're all backwards.

So rather than admit defeat, he took them around a Y-track to turn them around.

And everybody on the railroad got a big chuckle out of Ben Ryan having to go around the Y, so the cars would be turned around right.

That's not to say that I never made a mistake in linin' them up ... but to get them backwards.

And he'd been there for twenty-five or thirty years.

And he used to play pinochle. That's kind of a disease on the railroad. We'd sit around playing pinochle all the time. And Ben was about the worst pinochle player I ever saw in my life.

If you know something about the game, it's a bidding game, where you might outbid somebody else, to get the chance to lead.

Anyway he'd win the bid on an impossible hand, and then, when he saw what the widow was, he say, "Well, I know this is an impossible hand, but I'm going to play it anyway."

And it was impossible.

He'd lose.

The poor old guy.

I liked the guy. There's something, there's kind of a technical thing, it's sort of hard to explain. But he'd go out there in the switch engine, and pick up all these different industry cars, and he'd put them in a certain order — just to make a lot of work.

Or try to help the yardmaster or something, and the way he'd do it was so funny.

He lost his paycheck one time, playing pinochle.

Apparently the whole check or something, so his wife came down there, and she was trying to get the Santa Fe to give him another check.

I don't know what they told her, but I guess it was pretty plain.

Pappy Way

There was this old timer, his name was Pappy Way. And he was from Missouri. And he was one of those typical old time switchmen, bib overalls and everything.

I used to work with him on an afternoon job. Went to work at three o'clock in the afternoon. After we went to work, we'd get all these lists, things to do out in the yard, cars to line up and all that stuff, then after workin' for about two hours, the yardmaster would tell us to come in and get a cup of coffee, and we'd go back to the shanty on the switch engine.

Before Pappy Way went into the switchman's shanty, he'd take a little side trip to his car, where I guess he had a little snort, a drink of booze stashed-out someplace, see. He was perfectly okay when he came to work, but during coffee, he suffered a little bit.

So anyway, after a length of time, the yardmaster sent us out to do some more work, and after an hour and a half, or two hours, we'd come back for lunch, or as they say on the railroad, for beans, and so anyway, again, old Pappy'd make a side trip to his automobile, and come back.

And he was in pretty bad shape after that.

I remember this one night, he was, after beans, we went out to finish up the work, and we had to line up all these cars that this other guy I was telling you about, Old Ben, had lined up all mixed up. These twenty-two cars that were all goin' to this warehouse, and Pappy was just in no condition ... see, he was a foreman, and he's supposed to decide what to do. And he was just in no shape.

Anyway, I remember seeing him standing out by the bull-switch, it was pitch dark. He had the switch list about two inches from his nose, and he had his lantern pouring down on it.

And so the other switchman said to me, "Bring the engine over to track five, and we'll get eight cars, and we'll throw those out, and we'll shove some back, and we'll pull six track, and we'll double six to five. So anyway, we're working, lining all these cars up, and Pappy's just standing there weaving back and forth with this switch list about two inches from his nose, and cars are whizzin' by him, engine goin' down there and pullin' some more, and throwing some out, and doublin' over.

And so finally, we walked up to Pappy, and he put the list down, and he raised his finger, like he was going to say something. And this other switchman put his arm around Pappy, and he says quietly, "Pappy, don't worry. They're all lined up."

So Pappy got on the engine and we went out and we put the cars on a storage track and all came home.

It Brought A Tear To Pappy's Eye

I remember one time, it was a hot night, and the other switchman and myself were riding in the front of the engine, by the short cab. And it was a hot night, and the door was open on the engine, and the engineer and Pappy were in the cab of the engine, and we're goin' out someplace to do some work, and me and the switchman are just riding on the front of the engine there, and we heard this crash!

It sounded like a bottle breaking.
It was a bottle breaking.
Pappy had dropped his bottle.
And it fell on the steel floor of the cab.
And it just broke in a million pieces.
I think it brought a tear to Pappy's eye.

He was such a great guy. I always loved him. In spite of his penchant for John Barleycorn, he was a real good guy. You could never say that he didn't do his part. He really was a great guy. Unfortunately, he retired about, gosh, somewhere around 1980, and he didn't last too long. I always liked him. He was such a great guy. He was way overweight. He wore bib overalls, and had this old slouch hat on, and was just so typical with his watch chain coming out of his overalls. I just always liked to work with him. It's funny.

A Workingman's

I remember one time when just after I hired out on the Santa Fe, we bought this house up in the hills of El Cerrito. We were talkin' one time, and Pappy said, "I heard you bought a new house."

"Yeah," I said.

"Whereabouts is it?" he said.

"It's in the hills, in El Cerrito," I said.

Pappy looked at me and said, "A workin' man has no call to be livin' up there."

Like he just couldn't understand doin' something like that.

He was just so set in his ways.

But he had a heart as big as a boxcar.

He'd take his shirt off and give it to you, if you needed it.

He accidentally dropped his dentures down the urinal once.

That guy, he was something else.

There were so many around there, that were like that.

Am I an old timer now? I guess I am. See, when I first hired out on the railroad, they had a lot of steam engines. There were virtually no diesels at all. The last ten or fifteen years, engineers, young guys, come to work, and they want to know how it was to ride the steam engines. 'Cause the steam engines are simply gone. There's none of them left.

I'd say, 'They're dirty, and rough riding, and noisy, but they were really something. There was somethin' about them, those big monsters, puffin' black smoke and cinders and all that stuff. But there was a real charm to them.'

fig. 8 – *'Switch engine'* in Berkeley, CA, 1957

You can tell almost what engine it was, by the sound of it's whistle. There was different types. The bigger engines had these real, real mellow steam boat whistles on them, real low tone.

In fact, different railroads were known for their whistle.

It was kind of a trademark.

As a kid, I remember hearin' Western Pacific engines; they had an entirely different whistle from the Southern Pacific. On a hot summer night, I could hear the whistle way off in the distance. It was just really somethin'.

Even the diesel whistle, it's not quite the same as a steam engine's, but you can hear the whistle a long way off.

Some whistles stick in my mind.

Southern Pacific had these big steam engines, the last ones that they bought. I've got records of them I can play, records just of train whistles, ten or fifteen records of different railroads, the sounds of trains, not just the whistles, the sound of diesel and steam engines. The railroads have always kind of gotten into my blood, you might say.

Woman Hoghead

They hired this woman engineer, hoghead, and she goes back to Topeka to shake and bake hoghead school. So anyway she comes out, and it was over at China Basin.

And first day, she comes out, and she comes into the switchman shanty and we shake hands all around, and so anyway, the first thing she said to me, was, "I don't make drops."

A drop is a flying switch. That's when an engine pulls a car and it's got to pull way ahead and then the car goes down a different track, see.

It takes a little bit of coordination. It can really go wrong.

So the first thing she said to me, she had an attitude, and she said, "I don't make drops."

And I said, "Well Lady, I'm tellin' you this. I don't want to hear what you can't do. We're gonna go out there, and if I hang a sign on you, you better take it. If you don't, we're gonna come back to the shanty, and we're gonna find out who's right."

It just hit me the wrong way. She'd say that, y'know.

And we go out there, we make the drop, and it was just perfect, just like uptown.

It'd really bothered me, the first thing she said, was what she can't do.

I don't want to hear that.

If she didn't want to, then she should have hung up her gloves, and worked as a secretary, or somethin'.

From then on, we got along fine.

It was a bad introduction, really bad.

Woman Switchman

The was this woman switchman. Who held the switch open. Jeeze!

She got off the engine, see, they were on the road. And she's supposed to line this spring switch see. And they're really hard to move over. They aren't just like a regular switch, they're a spring switch so you can run through them in the opposite way, and you don't tear up the switches.

A switch has to be lined, normally, a switch has to be lined so movement can be made in either direction.

Well a spring switch, the train can go through it against the points, but it can't back up, 'cause the points keep coming back and forth. It can always go out of the switch.

So anyway, this gal, she was a real nice person, but sometimes, she didn't really understand what was going on.

So she gets off the engine, they gotta head into this siding, and she tries to line the switch on, but she can't get it all the way over.

So the fireman leans out the cab, and says, "You got it lined?"

She said, "Yeah."

And she's holding this switch.

And those cars are going by.

If she had just let off a little bit, the points would've opened up, and the car would've caught the point, and flew her into Napa County.

And she held the switch all the way over.

The rear brakeman gets off, he's going to line up behind, see. And she's standing down, she's still there. She should'a been on the engine, see. You line the switch, you get on the engine.

And the train pulls in, and the rear brakeman sees her still there, holding the switch, and he says, "What are you doing?!!!"

She says, "I'm holding the switch."

And the whole train went in the siding safely. There wasn't one wheel caught the point.

Because she held on to it.

It really took a lot of muscle.

She couldn't get it all the way over so the handle went down in the slot.

All these things that go on behind the scenes.

That's the way the railroad is.

Eve

I remember when the first woman came out.

The crew didn't know how to behave with a woman. And she came out. She was a student.

Y'know, when we get on the equipment, nobody stops for you, you never expect anybody to stop for you, it's ridiculous. I'd get on, everybody'd get on a rolling boxcar or an engine, just like getting into an automobile. It was just no problem at all, if you do it right.

So anyway, this gal came out, and they started from the shanty, the engineer comes out, he just keeps on going, and picks the crew up, and they all get on at the right time, on to the moving train.

But today, he stopped, for the lady to get on, and they went out in the yard, and he stopped for her to get off. It was so ridiculous. We got a lot of work done, then we all got back on the cab to go out to one of the industries, well, the fireman got up to give the gal his seat. The whole thing was so ridiculous.

From there we tried to outdo each other in decorum, and propriety.

There were so many jokes about that, because so many people were watching ... other crews saw the engine'd come up and stop by the shanty, and she got on, then they took off. And all the guys watchin' would go, 'Haw. Haw. Haw.'

When she learned later on that they don't stop for you, she must have thought we were a bunch of idiots.

Hoboes

I used to see hoboes all the time. You could always just about tell a real hobo from a bum. There's a big difference there.

A hobo has a pretty good outlook on life, they never work.

They don't ever bother anybody, they just want to travel. From time to time, I'd see hoboes get off the train in Richmond, and they wanted to get off in Stockton. See, Richmond's kind of a dead end, as far as transportation goes, 'cause Richmond is the end of the line.

But a lot of times, I've seen transients get off the train, wondering if this was Stockton.

And when I'd find them on the train, I'd talk to them. I didn't ever bother them or throw them off the trains, unless they got on the engine. I never threw 'em off, but I never let them ride on the engine, 'cause they might start foolin' around with the controls. And no one would tolerate that.

They'd get back on the second or third or fourth unit.

The railroad police, if they see them, they'll just get them off.

From time to time, the police will come down and go through the yard looking for someone who's obviously wanted by the authorities.

The story on it these days is that it's still not very hard for a hobo to catch a train; in fact, it's almost easier, with all these piggyback truck trailers on flatcars — that's a good place to ride. It's kind of breezy. But most of the boxcar doors are all sealed. They're closed when they are either empty or loaded. But there's still a lot of sliding door cars that hoboes can get in to.

They go in the empty cars.

"I met a guy once around the mid-seventies, who was a young guy, kind of a hippie," I said. "He used to like to catch a train somewhere north of here, and take it up to Oregon and pick apples. He'd follow the seasons around the northwest, and ride the train around. He said he'd ride up to Willamette, work in the orchards, then get back on the train and when they were finished and the early harvest season was changing, they'd get back on the train and go to the next orchard to pick a mid-season crop like the cherry trees. He'd say, 'You gotta leave here by this time to get to the cherry trees in pickin' season.' He had it all worked out. It sounded like a really nice thing to do."

"Some of the young brakemen, they used to take rides, go up to Oroville on the Western Pacific, or down to San Luis Obispo. They had plenty of money, and visible means of support, but they just wanted to ride on a freight train. They could go first class on a passenger train," John said.

The Hobo Capital Of The World

In Stockton, it's supposed to be the Hobo Capital of the World. It's in the newspaper once in a while. They have some kind of a hierarchy, a president of the Hoboes of America, or something. It's really amazing. They're really hoboes, they're not tramps, or bums, or anything like that. They're real hoboes.

They have a trestle, it's between the Western Pacific yard and the Southern Pacific yard, there's kind of a trestle, and I think that's where they meet. 'Cause there's always a gang of them around there.

They don't bother anybody. They never get in trouble. A lot of times, they'd mooch or somethin' — I've had them ask me for cigarettes, and I say, 'Yeah, sure. Okay.'

My attitude is they're very respectable people. That's the life they choose. To be always on the go. And Why Not?

Stanahan

There was so much stuff going on in China Basin.

There was this guy. He was an old time switchman, and he used to let us smoke cigars, see.

We're loading a barge to take cars over to Richmond, and he had the darndest time keepin' his cigar lit, see. And he was standin' on the apron of the dock ramp, that loads the cars onto the barge there, and he kept tryin' to light this cigar, and I guess he kinda got too close to the edge of the apron there.

And all of a sudden, he disappeared.

He fell in.

He'd took a nice little dive in the bay there.

fig. 9 – roundhouse *switch engine* & roundhouse in west Oakland

So everybody's running around looking for a life preserver.

Nobody could find a life preserver.

Well they didn't need one, 'cause here comes Stanahan up. Y'know, he got up one of the lines. He's soaking wet.

But he's got the bent cigar still in his mouth.

He was kind of embarrassed too.

He still had his lantern, and he still had his hat, I don't know how, and the cigar. I think he lost the matches.

One Night

There was so much stuff that happened over there.

They had this ramp. They had this street, mainly for trucks. And it used to go right down in kind of a cul-de-sac in the railroad yard, see. And this ramp had a nice little platform up there, that ended up on the railroad tracks, because they used to shove flatcars in there, see, and if they had a tractor, they could just drive it off onto this ramp.

And one night, we were out there switching cars, there was no cars in that ramp track, and we're out there switchin', and I saw a pair of these two lights goin' up in the air, then all of a sudden there was this big CRASH! And the lights went out.

So anyway, we went over there.

Some lady had come down there, figured she was driving on a street, she drove right up the ramp, and she had the biggest surprise for her because the ramp ended up in the air, and her automobile was airborne.

It came down, and the wheels were spread out flattened.

She was so upset. 'Cause she was afraid what her husband would say. She asked us if we could fix the automobile. But the wheels were bent out flattened.

"Nah, can't fix it. Let's bury the car here, and tell your husband somebody stole it," we told her.

Little Red and The Fuze-ies

And wild pinochle games, ah Jeeze. There was so much stuff going on at China Basin. It was really a busy place at one time.

They had three afternoon jobs, they had two daylight and three midnight jobs over there. And one of the jobs, we'd just go up Jackson Square. They'd go up there with twenty or fifty cars, every night, and they'd work all the industries up there. Jackson Square was kinda an industrial area, downtown San Francisco. I can't remember what streets they were.

There's all these different little sidings, and little warehouses, all had a track onto 'em, and you'd go down the street with the engine, with these cars, and you throw fuze-ies out, or flares — on the highway it's a flare, but to us it's a fuze-ie.

And we'd switch cars out different places.

And if you had one car out of place, it made the whole job so miserable, 'cause you had to peddle 'em, and some you'd peddle on the way going to Jackson Square, because you shove back in, and when you got to Jackson Square, some of them you'd start on the way back. And you had to know which way the cars went.

It would take you half an hour, forty minutes, just to line them up, so when you went out of the railroad yard to go down there, it would go smoothly.

There was this guy, they called him, Little Red.

He was always throwing fuze-ies out, ahead of the engine, see. And when you got to a street crossing, it would really light up the crossing.

This one night he tossed a fuze-ie out; it ended up on top of a building, see. And those things, they really burn with a very hot fire. And there was a chance he was gonna burn the whole building down.

So he start climbing up this drain pipe, and he almost got up to the top of it, and it broke. And it just folded up and he comes down on top of it.

So he just ended up calling the fire department to get out there, and said that there was a fire on this roof, and nobody knew how it got started. We want to report a fire.

Little Red

But old Little Red, he hated to see somebody eat more than him.

He thought he was something else.

And we used to go to lunch, or beans, over there, and there was a take-out restaurant that wasn't too far from the yard office.

And I don't care if you went into a restaurant with him, I don't care what you ordered, he had to order something more, see.

So anyway, the yardmaster told us to go to beans. Instead of taking two automobiles, the fireman said, "Well, let's go up to the restaurant." So the fireman drove us up there.

Little Red was going to get a hamburger or somethin'. The fireman ordered two hamburgers and two cokes and two orders of french fries.

So Stevenson, he had to order three of everything. So he gets three hamburgers, and three cokes, and three orders of fries, see.

We go drivin' back, and get back to the yard office, and Little Red discovers the fireman wasn't going to eat all the two orders of everything, he just bought an order for the engineer.

So here he was stuck with all this food. I think he threw half of it away.

We were all sittin' around sayin' to him, "Are you gonna eat all that stuff?"

And we shamed him into it, really.

Really Heavy Cars

We were at the Richmond docks loading the barges with trains one time. See, we'd put an engine, a locomotive, on the middle track, there was three tracks. And because it's the heaviest, it went on the barge first, on the middle track.

And then we're loading cars on the sides.

We loaded one side, and they were really heavy cars. They were cars of grain, and they were really heavy, they were ninety tons a car. And the engine weighed a hundred and fifty tons.

So we got the cars on one side, and start shoving cars on the other side, and the barge was tipping quite a bit in the water with all this weight on it.

The engine broke loose. And start coming.

I looked up.

I saw a blue flash coming.

It hit those freight cars.

And it just wedged right into them.

And Jim, this switchman, he just stepped aside just in time, or he would have been ... oh man, he would'a been ... .

Famous Curves Throughout the U.S.A.

There's the Horseshoe Turn at San Margarita, near San Luis Obispo. On the Texas & New Orleans Railroad, they start pullin' up this mountain, and if they have to head in this siding at the top of the mountain, the rear brakeman will get off the caboose and walk across a field about 400 feet, and he can get up to the switch before the train gets there.

He'll line the switch, the train'll pull in.

Then when the train gets all ready, he'll line it back and get on the caboose.

Usually it's the head brakeman who lines it, but the rear brakeman can be up there before him — that's Horseshoe, right out in the desert, between a place called Valentine, and Small, in Texas.

We had Coathanger Curve on the Union Pacific, near Green River, Wyoming — where I rode the runaway boxcar and almost cashed in my chips.

There's the Ketty Y.

Ketty Y — they put a Y in the middle of the air. It was the only place they could put it. One track goes east to Salt Lake City. The other track goes on The Great Northern to a place called Theber. During the Great Depression, that was a beautiful trestle; business was so bad that they pulled the rails up on the lead that went to The Great Northern, 'cause they didn't have enough business, and probably sold them for scrap. They were that poor. And so later on, when the Depression began to bounce back, they built it back.

On the Tucson Division of the S.P. between Hela Bend and a Place called Pacheco, is the longest continuous curve I know of in the world. For five miles, the train going east is making a left hand turn. For five miles. And then, you come off the curve, and it's the longest stretch of straight track in the United States — forty miles without a curve in it. And the longest piece of straight track in the world is in Australia, one-hundred-eighty-seven miles without a curve in the track. Just straight through the desert. But it's forty miles on the S.P. But what's so funny, is you get off this five mile curve, then you go straight. I don't know why they made that curve like that, I never did hear the explanation for it. Maybe it was to bypass a town that wouldn't buy railroad bonds in the 1880's.

Approaching Denver from the west at night by rail, you can look way down in the distance, and you can see the lights of Denver — way off in the distance. And you go through four complete switchbacks to drop down in elevation, you make four complete loops, so you don't have to go straight up on the way out; and that is completely spectacular. Every time, if you look out the left side windows, you can see the city, and then when you go around the first loop of course the city disappears 'cause it's on the other side. Then when you go around the next loop Denver's a little closer. And then you go around the third and fourth loop and it gets real close. It's so spectacular.

In The Desert

I used to see the guys out there in the desert, a track gang, drivin' spikes. It's 105 degrees out there. 'Awww,' I'd say to myself, "How are they doin' this?"

There's a real art to drivin' spikes.

These guys are swinging a spike maul in 105 degrees, sleeves rolled up, a hat on their head, bib overalls on, oh Jeeze!

It's killing me sitting up in the cab watching them. And I'm not doing anything.

Roasted Coal

A lot of times, out in Franklin Canyon, on Highway 4, not far from Martinez, the Santa Fe goes along Franklin Canyon, and they have this coke plant, where they make refractory coke, coke for steel making.

And that stuff, aw, is it terrible. I'd come home, after switchin' that plant, and stand in the shower, the water stays just black for

fig. 10 – erecting hall in Sacramento; engines under repair, 1946

five minutes. It's just terrible. Coke is roasted coal.

They ship it in covered hoppers, that are all sealed when they ship it, luckily. You go through town with a couple of those cars, if they weren't sealed, and it blew out the car, the whole town'd be black every place. But they seal them. Breathin' the stuff is not so good, either. I'd sure hate to work in that plant.

The Friendship Train

This was an interesting train. This engine was pulling what was called The Friendship Train.

After W.W.II, there was just absolute desolation and deprivation and so much hunger in Europe that a bunch of people got together and said, "If you've got a can of beans come on down to the depot, and throw it in the boxcar."

It was fantastic!

This was in addition to the Marshall Plan, which was rebuilding Europe and Asia economically.

Anyway, this Friendship Train was pretty interesting. They took ten boxcars and painted French and Italian and British national symbols on it; there was four trains started out, one from Seattle, Portland, Oakland, and Los Angeles. There was supposed to be ten cars apiece. Before the train left Oakland, they'd filled up the ten cars, and they were just using any old freight car because they didn't have time to repaint it. So the train left Oakland, with about twenty cars instead of ten. And the same thing in L.A. and up in Seattle.

When the trains got to New York and Wilmington, some of the trains were running in three sections, and there were about seventy cars for each section. And from each, Seattle, Portland, Oakland and L.A., they'd stop along the way, and say, "Hey, have you got a can of tomatoes or something?"

And the people would answer, "Yeah, yeah!"

It was just person to person. No governments involved. Or anything.

It was really magnanimous.

I saw the train. I was in the service. I'm sure my mother brought something to put in it. I can't remember if I brought anything or not. I was probably too interested in the engines.

fig. 11 — washing-out boiler; getting scale out; Oakland CA, 1943

My Personal Pullman Car

I have a car I bought. It was in Kansas City. Right now it's in Los Angeles. I had it moved from Kansas City to Los Angeles. It only cost about $120 to move it here. It's a Pullman Car. It has sleeper's in it, and drawing rooms instead of berths. I got it for $2,000. AMTRAK just turned it loose. They bought some new equipment. They were going to scrap this. This engineer I work with, he turned me on to it. He said, "Hey, you got an extra two thousand?"

"What do you got?" I said.

"I heard about this Pullman," He said.

Now I got it. It's in Los Angeles being stored at AMTRAK's yard.

This other guy, he has nine cars, if you can believe it.

Another guy has two.

I was a student instructor. For some reason, they asked me. They'd take a guy off the street, and they'd put him on a switch engine, and he was supposed to learn the job.

The fireman was too busy with the work, to deal with the student, and the pin-puller, and the field men, they didn't know anything anyway.

So the student was pretty much at the mercy of everyone ... it was kinda like when I made my student trips. I'd get on there, and the switchmen didn't hate students, they just didn't seen to have a use for them.

When I was beginning, they were so suspicious of students.

I was on this local freight for one week, and I didn't learn anything. I didn't even know what they were doing out there. And so the last day, the conductor, who was a real old man, he says, "Well, kid, you want to know anything, just ask me. Just ask me."

So I said, "Pappy, ..."

And he barked, "What do you want?!!!!"

He turned out, after I got through all my student trips and all that stuff, he turned out to be a pretty good guy. Y'know, he was just suspicious the front office had sent somebody down to spy on him.

Anyway, on the Santa Fe, they had bad luck with putting a guy on the switch engine when he was supposed to pick up all this

fig. 12

stuff, and so the superintendent came to me, and he said, "We're gonna try a new plan, and we want somebody, we want to have these students not more than eight at a time."

"Eight's too many. How about seven?" I said.

"Okay," he said.

And, anyway, we start in with having them in a conference room, and somebody to explain the job, and what a boxcar looks like, and what a railroad track looks like, just go start from the basics of it.

And so anyway, he said, "Do you want to be a part of this?"

And I said, "Sure."

So I suggested, "How about building a little model railroad?"

And he said, "That's a great idea."

They got some money together, and we got a big piece of plywood, and we build this model railroad. It was just two tracks, and a crossover, and a little spur into an industry.

And we set this thing up, and I had these student train workers come in Monday morning at eight o'clock in the morning, and I said, "I appreciate that you people know nothing about the railroad, and I knew nothing about it either until I started. Nobody expects you to know the innards of a whole new occupation." And so I went on and on.

Three days of talking, and movie films, and going through the rule book, and all this stuff, and then on the fourth day, we went to the car shops and the round house. They were in the process of fixing boxcars, freight cars, and you could see all the wheels, and the drive bar, and the air hoses, and all this stuff.

And the students aren't being pressured. The equipment's there, it's not moving, it's static.

And these people have got to get to know all these things, very well.

Then we go to the round house, and see what a live engine looks like.

It worked out real good.

It was somethin' I didn't have the advantage of having, when I started.

I sure would've liked to started that way.

Like I said, my first week, I didn't learn a thing.

I didn't even know what they were doing.

Out there movin' cars around, "Ohhh, did you see that?"

Then, the fifth day, the car got an extra engine, that means an engineer, I was in charge of the crew and the engineer, and we'd load all students on the engine, and we go down to a place in the yard that's not being used, and stay in the clear of any activity, and not bother anybody, and we'd pull some cars out on the track, and take turns, we'd kick the car, givin' the cars a shove, and somebody pulls a pin, and the engine will stop, and the car keeps on going.

You have to hold the pin up with your hand.

That way, you don't have to shove the car into a truck and have to go with the engine way down to the end of the track, all you have to do is give it a little ride down there.

And that's how we do a lot of switching that way.

That's according to the book.

That's acceptable.

We'd take turns, the student'd give a sign, a particular sign.

And students got to take part in a switching operation.

You could explain something like this until you're blue in the face. I wouldn't blame someone if they didn't understand what I'm talking about, y'know.

Each one took a different part.

They rode the car, and put on the brake after the car was cut loose from the others, and they rode the car onto a track and wound the handbrake down to get the feeling of it.

A million words would never describe it.

Most of 'em were young people and enthusiastic.

And most of them are there today.

I thought that was terrific.

You'd get to see the switches, get the feel of pulling a pin, get to give a sign to an engineer. How to give signs is very important. 'Cause the engine might be forty or fifty car lengths away. And if you give a little sign, he don't know what you're trying to do. And you're gonna be stopped 'til he gets the proper sign.

They really got a feel of what it was.

You're movin' real heavy pieces of equipment.

There's no room for accidents.

Accidents are always pretty bad.

I don't want to see any accidents.

You never turn your back on a moving piece of equipment.

You never, never turn your back on a moving piece of equipment. It'll mash you down into nothing.
Well, they had pretty good results from the training.
They used that course for four or five years.

I was a student instructor off and on for five years, 1976 to 1981. One day I got something in the mail, that I was named as a defendant in a class action suit.
'Well, what is this?!' I wondered.
So I called a trainmaster, and told him I got some sobering news in the mail. He said, "Here's the number of the legal department." So I called them.
They said, "Oh yeah, we were just going to get a hold of you. It seems that in your first class, there was a man who was taking student trips, and they disapproved his application before sixty days. See, he wasn't over what they call the D rail. For that first sixty days, the company reserves the right to sever anybody for any reason at all. Ordinarily, they don't hire people just to fire them.
Anyway, this person thought that he was being treated unfairly because they dismissed him before his sixty days were up. And he filed a class action suit against me and the railroad.
So the lawyer told me, "We want you to take a deposition about what you instructed the class at that time."
I had the class for five days, and I'm sure that I stated once every day at least, that the company reserves the right to dismiss you in that sixty day probationary period, for any reason whatsoever, and that's a fact, that I did.
They do not hire people just to fire them. They turned him on his record, apparently he had a bad record someplace. Maybe he was late for work more than once, or whatever.
I made a deposition as to my part in instructing the class, then I never heard any more about it. I guess they settled the thing one way or another.
The statue of limitation was seven years. And he waited six years before suing, so he could try to collect back pay for six years.

"What are the different kinds of rolling stock?" I asked.

"Boxcars, they can be called side-door pullmans, 'cause hoboes ride in that; there's a flatcar; a tank car; a hopper — that's a car they load from the top and the sides are slanted and all the commodity can be unloaded out through the bottom; a gondola car, which is just a open box, and it's loaded from the top; all types of flatcars. A long time ago there were refrigerator cars with ice in them, then they were replaced with mechanical refrigerators; special flatcars for carrying piggyback flats. Santa Fe even has some flatcars for carrying wrecked equipment — wrecked boxcars without the wheels, so you can set them down right on top of the flatcar, and the bolsters are adjusted to the length of the car they're gonna carry. Rolling stock could mean engines, too," John said.

A Humpyard

Argentine yard is a big Santa Fe yard in Texas. It was a humpyard, y'know, where they shove cars up on a hump, and let them go down by gravity, and they go onto maybe fifty different tracks.

They had another film on Barstow yard. That was even more modern than Argentina. It was incredible. They had computers that would determine not only how fast the car was rolling, but what it's rollability was — what it's acceleration was, and the computer would predict how far the car would roll down the track.

So they get these cars to go down the hump in cuts or by themselves, and the cars that they would want to go farthest down the tracks, they would want those to go the fastest so they would go way down into the track. Then, once they started to fill the cars up, they wanted the next cars to go slower. And this was all computerized.

The cars would couple together, and they would never couple at more than four miles an hour, 'cause this computer could figure all that out.

The Drop

(Editor's Note: a drop — when the engine's pulling a car, and let's it go, and a man has to ... see there's an interval, when the draw bars are stretched out when you're pulling, and the engine has to [hesitate], so the man can pull the pin, to release the knuckle, then the engine has to pull away, and he has to get out of the way; and between the time the engine gets over the switch, and before the car, or cars, arrive at the switch, a man has to line the switch, so the cars will go down a different track from the engine. It takes a little bit of coordination. It's usually the last car, or last string of cars, that gets dropped.)

If it was an easy place to make the drop, and the engineer knew what we were going to do, we used to have just one guy pull the pin then run over and line the switch; but we used to get a student on there, 'cause usually it's a three-man job. The foreman gives the signal; the pin-puller's riding the engine to get the pin; and the fieldman will get the switch, or ride the car over, or one of the two.

At this one place, me, as the foreman, or Joe, this other fellow, would just get up there and pull the pin, and the engineer would see what was going on, and he'd pull the engine down, and there'd be no one riding the car or anything; and the guy that pulled the pin would get on the fly, and line the switch over, and the car would go sailing down the opposite track.

The engineer would take the engine and go way down and sit on the crossing, so no car'd get hit, 'cause there was no one riding the cars. Normally you have somebody riding the cars, on the handbrake.

And the student's would go, "Hey, how'd that car get away from the engine onto that track over there?"

And I'd say, "Well, we made a drop."

Attila the Hun

I gotta tell you about this other conductor.
There was this old conductor.
I was on a certain pool job, and we'd go from Bayshore to Tracy, or we'd go from Bayshore to Roseville, or from Bayshore to Oakland, y'know, around the bay.
He had the loudest voice I think I've ever heard in my life.

He was a real nice guy, but he had a real fierce look, he kind of looked like Attila the Hun. And he had the voice for it too.

He was a jewel. A real nice guy.

Anyway, we went to Tracy. Usually it was overnight going to Tracy, 'cause we'd do a lot of workin'.

And we'd get to Tracy about eight o'clock in the morning, and would he go to bed? No. He'd go to the card houses in Tracy. And he was always pretty lucky, I guess.

So he'd stay up all night, going to work, getting to Tracy, then all day he was over in the card houses.

We'd get called seven or eight o'clock the next night, to come back to San Francisco. And he would spend all his time over at the card houses.

Anyway, the ritual was, we would leave Bayshore 'bout ten p.m., and we'd get to Redwood City and we had some work to do. Well I was on the job the longest, so I was the rear brakeman. Usually we had an extra brakeman, and he'd be the head brakeman. Normally it's the guy with the most seniority that's the rear brakeman. Get to stay in the caboose. And he'd do more work up at the head end.

Anyway, I was the rear brakeman. Most of the time I'd ride ahead, up on the engine, to help with the work, see. Don't leave the head brakeman to do it all.

So we'd do work in Redwood City, then we'd go over the Dumbarton Bridge and had some work in Newark, and then Niles, then after we left Niles, by Union City, at the foot of the grade. Leavin' Niles, I'd go back in the caboose, and we had nothin' to do until we got to Tracy.

And we had this old coal stove. And I'd fire that thing up, and put coffee on. We used to trade off buying a sack of donuts. So leavin' Niles, the coffee's ready, a great big pot of coffee on there, on that old coal stove, we had donuts or something, or danish, or something.

He'd sit at the conductor's desk, with this real neat kerosene lantern. Boy, those things were beautiful. I bet they'd go for five hundred dollars apiece. They were really neat. They had a rocker on them, so when the caboose moved, the lantern stayed level. They were all brass, real neat. A big lampshade, and a silk mantle, it was bright, you bet they were.

Well, old Pete'd sit at this conductor's desk, and spread his racing form out, and regular as clockwork, we'd leave Niles, I'd come out with a big pot of coffee, pour coffee, and I'd go up in the Cupola, and have coffee and chew on a donut.

Every night, the same thing.

Well, one night, we're all set, we left Niles, he's sitting at the desk reading his racing form, and I'm just ready to pour coffee, and the slack ran out, and dumped the whole coffee all over Pete. Just this hot, scalding coffee, and he jumps up, and there's coffee pouring off the tips of his fingers, and is he upset. Whoa!

Not because he got scalded.

But because I ruined his darn racing form.

What slack running out means, is that the engine either starts to pull faster because they're going into a dip or up a hill, and the engine's pulling faster than the cars behind it, then the engine slows down a little bit, and the boxcars slam into the engine.

Or, the engine might top the hill, and the engine starts to go faster than the cars coming up the hill, then it jerks against the cars.

And at the back, in the caboose, you're getting the whole thing, in both directions.

That's why you never want to be a caboose rocket.

You got to hang on all the time. You got to have your hand on something at all times. You just gotta hang on. That's all there is to it. Or you get your head banged, or get knocked down, you never know when it's coming. Even on the flats, there might be acceleration, or deceleration, that's right.

You get an inexperienced engineer or something, or some engineers are a little better than others, some can handle a train better, but you get this slack.

Pete

Pete was such a great guy. He was really an outstanding person. He was so rough, and had a real severe voice, "WELL!!" and like that. "WELL OKAY!!!" "I'LL LET YOU SLIDE, THIS TIME!!!"

What a voice.

One night I think we were just going around the bay over Dumbarton, just a short trip from Bayshore to Oakland, and we were riding back in the caboose there, and Pete says, "WELL BY THE WAY, ANY CHANCE OF YOU LENDING ME A TWENTY!"

"Ah gee, Pete, I'm close to the vest myself," I said.

"OKAY," he said.

"Well wait a minute, maybe I can go over to my mother's house and get twenty from her," I said.

"WELL I'D SURE APPRECIATE IT," Pete said. A real rough voice, y'know.

"Okay Pete, we'll figure on it," I said.

Anyway, we get to Oakland, and I had my car, so we drove over to San Francisco. My car was in Oakland, his car was in San Francisco. So we drove over there to get the train.

So anyway, we drive to my mother's house, and walked in.

Mother was playing whist, or bridge, or something, with three other ladies, that were neighbors.

And we come walkin' in there. Pete with his hat on.

And so I asked mother, "Let's go out in the kitchen." And we do. And I say, "Can you lend me a twenty, Pete's a little bit short?"

"Sure, sure," she said. She goes through her purse and comes out with a twenty.

We get back in the dining room, and Pete's sitting down with these ladies, showing them how to play poker.

"WELL LET'S SEE, I GOTTA PULL YOU, I GOT TWO OF A KIND; YOU'RE FADED; I FOLD; YOU FOLD."

And these ladies are having a heck of a time, just a wonderful time with Pete.

And so my mother sits down, and I sit down, and we start playing poker.

I don't know who won, but those ladies loved it.

Later on, a couple of weeks later, my mother said, "Where's Pete, all these ladies have been talking about him and askin' where Pete is, and his rough voice, and is his hat still on, and how every once in a while he'd adjust the brim."

Ah that guy was so great.

Such an outstanding person.

The first time I ever saw and heard him, I thought, "I'm not going to work with this fool!"

He was a big man, over six feet tall, and so severe, just a picture would frighten you away.

The Card Houses In Tracy

Pete used to go over to the card houses in Tracy.

We used to live in the caboose. We had bunks in the caboose, and I cooked in the caboose, y'know, not too good. But Pete used to go over to the card houses, and I'd go to bed.

Man, I was tired. I didn't want to play cards.

It was always the same thing. As soon he'd sign the register, boy, he'd jump off and go over, it was only about two blocks away.

I'd go to bed in the caboose, they'd put in on a caboose track.

So this one night, Cabury called, and said, "You're called for 4:02 to Oakland. By the way, do you know where the conductor is?"

"No. I don't know. You try the card houses?" I said.

"Well we tried that," he said.

They couldn't find him.

So the other brakeman and me, we waited around, and boy, this was getting serious.

You see, they give you a call time, and you better be there. The train's waiting, and you better be there.

We couldn't find Pete.

So we went down and checked every card house there was. There was just about one street. And he was not anyplace. He was gonna get the jackpot.

So we walked by this bar, and saw this guy slumped over the bar.

"Uh oh, it's Pete," I said.

That was the only time I ever seen him, y'know, what's the word, cabooshed.

"Hey Pete, we gotta go!", I said.

"Oh yeah, yeah," he said.

So anyway, this brakeman got on one side, and I got on the other side, and we kinda eased him out of the bar.

He was in no condition to be seen around the yard office, so we walked him way around, and we got him in the caboose, and got him to lay down, so we went over, and signed the register, and got the bills, and we signed everything ... the conductor's supposed to.

Anyway, everything was going along pretty good, and I got the bills, and we inspected the train, and pulled out, and I swung on the caboose, and we started to go.

Well, it had to be the night we had some young engineer sittin' up there, and the slack would run in, and I had to grab ahold of the table, and every time the slack would run out, old Pete would turn over, and mumble something. And the slack would run out, and he'd mumble something, "OHHHH SSSHHHOOTTT!" And the slack would run in again. And this kept us up. And we started up over Altamont, and man, the slack was a real good one, and it knocked old Pete off the bunk, and he waked up, and went over to the conductor's arm, and big holed the whole train, and it came to an emergency stop.

He grabbed the valve. There's also an air gauge up there, so you can tell how much air is left in the train. You can stop a train from the caboose. All you have to do is let the air out of the train line, and the brakes'll function.

"Well Pete, this air gauge, the air's not coming back," I said. We had broke in two. When he pulled the air, the train parted. So I walked up there, and about twenty cars ahead of the caboose, one of the drawbars, well, the knuckle was broken.

Luckily, it wasn't the whole draw bar, the whole works. It was just the knuckle, you can remove it.

And so I came back, and I says, "We got a knuckle, Pete."

And he says, "WELL DON'T STAND THERE, CARRY A KNUCKLE UP AND PUT IT IN THERE!"

They're about two feet across, and they weigh about eighty pounds. A whole new knuckle had to be put in, 'cause the old one broke.

"What do you mean me?! You pulled the darn air, you carry it up there!" I'm not going to carry it up there. Outside it's sloping on one side of the train, and straight up and down on the other side. "You carry it. I didn't pull the air."

So we were arguing back and forth, and we strung a flag stick in through a hole in the knuckle, and we both carried it up there.

And Pete kept slipping and falling down.

"Never mind, Pete. Go back to the caboose. I'll get it up there," I told him.

So I carried it up by myself.

I put it in. It was dark. I had my lantern. You gotta unbolt it and you can get it in. Pete was falling all over the place, so the other

fig. 13 – (b) 'Back-Up' Mallet; running model John made. fig. 14 – 4-6-2, 'milk bottle' boiler'

brakeman kept a watch on him. I could handle puttin' it in myself. It takes a little finessing, a little jiggling. But you can get it in. The train had parted when the knuckle broke. So I jiggled the broken knuckle out and put the new one in. Then when I was ready, I just backed 'em up into the rear portion of the train, into the new knuckle, and made the air. I put it in and turned the valve on the air hose, because the rest of the train has to have the proper pressure for the brakes to release.

I came back, and Pete was back asleep.

That was the only time I ever seen him drunk.

He woke up the next day.

"WELL, THAT WAS SOME TRIP!" he said.

Deadhead

They used to call us to deadhead from San Francisco to San Jose to work a freight train, and they had this conductor, and I thought he was smiling.

Deadhead means you ride the train free, 'cause of your job.

I had just hired out. So I get on the train and I'm a deadhead on this train. This guy comes along, pickin' up the tickets, and he says, smiling, "I want your ticket please." With a big smile.

"Well they pay me to ride these trains," I said.

"I want your ticket, or I'll put you off," he said. He kept smiling.

I had a heck of a time convincing him. So one of the other brakemen spoke up, and said, "Yeah, he's going to San Jose with us."

I guess that conductor had some trouble holding in his dentures, and I thought he was smiling.

Deadheading

A lot of times you deadhead to Santa Clara. They want you in a certain place, and you get on the train. Most of the conductor's know you, and normally they give you a trip pass, but they never did bother once they got to know you.

Anyway, I lived in Oakland, and a lot of times, they'd call you to deadhead to Santa Clara for a drag east, then go to Watsonville, then work down there, and then come back.

Well you'd kinda have to take a chance whether to take the train to Santa Clara, or drive down there.

If you drove down there to Santa Clara, to work a train, they may want you to work it up to the City, see. Then you're up in San Francisco, and your car is down in Santa Clara. So it was always a big hassle to decide. 'Should I drive down, or go on the train?'

If you took the train down, then you went to Watsonville and came back, they'd bust you out of bed in Watsonville at four o'clock in the morning. And then you're sittin' down there, there's no trains, and your car's up in San Francisco. So no matter what you decide to do, it was wrong.

So this one time, I decided I was going to drive down to catch the train in Santa Clara. Santa Clara's five miles this side of San Jose. So I drove down and caught the train and went to Watsonville. And then comin' back, we got to San Jose, they decided to run us through to San Francisco.

So I'm up in San Francisco, eight o'clock in the morning. I wait around for a train to go down to Santa Clara. I wait half an hour, an hour for a train, then I go down there. I fall asleep on the train, and woke up in the depot at San Jose, and I should've got off in Santa Clara.

Ah man.

So anyway. I wait around. I could've taken a city bus, but I thought, 'I'll just wait around.' So I got on the train to go back to Santa Clara. And I fell asleep on that train. And I ended up in Palo Alto.

Oh Jeeze.

I had to wait around for three hours for a train to go back. So finally I get down there, and get off the train, and get my car, and drive home, and I get home just in time to hear the phone ringing and now they called me to go back to work. I had been fooling around all day, and I was still tired.

I went round and round, and never got off at the right place.

When I first hired out on the Santa Fe — they'll go faster than most railroads with freight equipment. Freight train used to be limited to 55 m.p.h., passenger train to 80 m.p.h. But the Santa Fe, they have better roadbeds than most railroads. Most railroads have raised their speed limits anyway. Now it's 70 m.p.h. 70

m.p.h. boy, is fast. But the big diesel engine, what's weird, is the way, when you look back, the whole train, all of the cars, at that speed, are swaying back and forth at different rhythms.

It's safe.

It works all the time.

They have good roadbeds, that are maintained well.

And they get down to Fresno, 205 miles, in no time. The quickest legal time is three hours and fifty-five minutes. Going through towns sometimes you have to slow down. You can't do 70 m.p.h. all the way.

Stallin' Around

This one engineer, when I was conductor on this train, he always stalled around. Normally I wanted to get out and do the work. The quicker we got the work done, the quicker we'd go home. And it was a local freight train, and we'd always go to work at the same time, but we'd never get off at the same time. It would just depend on how much work there was.

This guy really used to annoy me, sometimes.

'Cause he'd stall around, gettin' the engine out of the roundhouse, and I'm all ready to go. He'd just really infuriate me and annoy me sometimes, because he'd horse around. He was a not-too-energetic kind of a person.

Dell

In fact, there was a brakeman, he wasn't really energetic either.

He used to annoy a lot of other people. He didn't really annoy me.

All the switch stands, they have the big round target on the switchstand, well I think every switchstand between here and Stockton says, 'Why is Dell always late?'

Every one of them.

Somebody wrote it in pencil, on just about every switchstand, a sign about Dell, and how lazy he was.

You couldn't read it unless you were standing right there, when it was in pencil.

He tried to erase them all.

So somebody got a marking stick and made it even bigger, so you could read it from the train.

Harold Clark

There was an engineer I used to work with on the Santa Fe, he died almost two years ago. I always like the guy. He was a neat guy, Harold Clark. He was an engineer, and he always used to work in the yard, workin' a switch engine.

We had more fun playin' pinochle together. He was always rollin' his own cigarettes, Bull Durham, and I guess he wouldn't get them too tight, because when he'd light up a cigarette, sparks would fall down on his shirt, and he was always beatin' out the sparks against his stomach. A shirt would only last him a couple of months, 'cause it would have too many holes in it.

He retired about eight or ten years ago. And I called him up once in a while. Everybody in the whole railroad liked him. He was such a likable guy. I called him up, and I said, "You still got holes in your shirts?"

"Oh yeah," he said.

He died. And it almost shut the railroad down, there was so many people wanted to go to his funeral. Somebody asked me if I wanted to be one of the pall bearers. I said, "Yeah."

He really was a wonderful guy.

His son is a conductor, and he's a real neat guy too, just like his dad.

I always had quite a lot of respect for Harry. He was quite a pinochle player.

I was playin' pinochle with him one time. There were four guys around the table. He was a real good pinochle player, he would take all my coins, all the time. He was always winnin'. He was so much fun playin' with, it was worth it. I remember one time, we were all sittin' around playin' pinochle, and this guy, I guess he worked in the office, he wasn't a rail, he came into the shanty. He was standin' around behind each guy, and he'd tiptoe around the table, and look at everyone's hand.

He come up behind Harry Clark and he says, "You ought to play that."

Harry turned around and raised his voice at him and said, "I'll play my own darn hand, if you don't mind!"

The guy took right off.

Beginner's Luck

This engineer, he'd never play cards.

Just sit around and watch. Somebody talked him into sittin' down, and wrote down a paper for him, y'know — a hundred aces, eighty kings, sixty queens, what a pinochle is, and double pinochle, and all this stuff. And so he sat down and started to play, and he won. He won a lot of money!

He thought, 'Oh you guys are so easy!'

It was just beginner's luck. He didn't know what he had, we told him what he had. So anyway, he got bit with the game, and then he start losin'.

But it was so much fun to be out playin', like with Harold Clark this guy who was always lightin' these Bull Durham cigarettes, always slapping the burning ashes and sparks out that fell on his stomach. The front of his shirt was always full of holes.

The Silver Lady & The California Zephyr

That's a picture of The Silver Lady, (which was) The California Zephyr. That was one of the most famous trains of all times. It ran between Oakland and Chicago. It was such a beautiful train. There was so much optimism when it started, in 1948. It replaced a train called The Scenic Limited, which was made up of old, heavyweight cars, that were not streamlined. Then Western Pacific, which was a very small railroad, bought The California Zephyr, in conjunction with two other railroads, and it was just such a beautiful train. I rode it about four times. In this particular photograph, me and the ex-wife were going to Connecticut, all by train. Anyway, we got back there, it was her friends, we went to a house party, and somebody asked, 'You from California, huh?' 'Yeah,' I said. They said, 'How'd you get here? You fly, or drive?' I said, 'No. We took the train.' 'All the way? You took the train all the way?' they said. They just could not believe somebody would

fig. 15 – running models John built, *GS-4* on the turntable

come from California all the way to Connecticut on the train. I rode that train four times. Each time, it was just like eatin' a piece of Chocolate cake. It's such a nice train. I always tried to hire out on the Western Pacific, but never made it.

I was always with a good group of people that I liked. There's a few real jerks, but very few, really very few.
Y'know, they're hard-headed. A lot of rails are hard-headed. But they're good people.
That was one thing that really impressed me, when I first went to work.
And every railroad's the same way.
You're depending on each other.
The man up there in the cab, it's your life, right in his hands up there. Y'know, if you're working between the cars, don't ever, ever, move the engine, until you get the proper sign.
So if someone's underneath the car making air hoses, or doing something, that man up there's got your life in his hands; and you've got his life, in this lantern in your hand, you've got his life; if you give a wrong signal, or not pay attention to what you're doing, you're gonna get him into a crash with another engine, or into some cars, or something.
So we're working together.
We're not working as individuals.
We're working together.
It's a team job.
Absolutely a team job.
Like if you're switching cars out, a whole cut of cars, fifty, sixty cars, and each man has his job to do, or nothing is going to get done.
Everybody has to know what is going on.
So nobody gets hurt.
Nobody gets in between the cars, when they shouldn't be.

The Time I Did Turn My Back

A freight car will go down the yard by itself, and it won't make a sound. It won't make a sound, that's right.
It's like it's on water.

fig. 16 – part of John's train board

But man, if you're in the way, it's all over.

You don't get a second chance.

One night I was on a midnight job, and I was switching on this job, and we kicked a tankcar down the track.

Tankcars are really odd cars, 'cause all that stuff starts surging back and forth, and the car will go down the track going real slow, then it will pick up, all by itself, then it will slow down, with the surge of all that liquid in there.

Anyway, sometimes, for some reason, the car will stop, and go the opposite way, it will come back down. It was because the way this yard was built in Richmond, on a real slight grade, to the west. The yard is basically east and west.

Anyway, it was midnight, three o'clock in the morning or something, kickin' these cars down, and he let this tankcar go, and I saw it go down, and disappear into the darkness.

I was wearing this peacoat, and, he kicked some cars down a different track, then he kicked another car down the track where the tankcar had gone in the first place.

And when he did, the drawbar was sideways, and it wouldn't make a proper coupling with the next car. So I stood right between the tracks, y'know, moving this great big piece of metal, and something touched the tip of the peacoat.

Now the peacoat kind of sticks out at the back.

Something touched that.

And automatically I got out of the way.

That tankcar had rolled back against the boxcar I was adjusting the knuckle on, and I just reflectively got out of the way. There was something there, don't worry about what it is, something's touching you, get out of the way!

And that car came in and coupled in to the boxcar, where I had been adjusting the knuckle.

I would have been part of both of those cars.

The tankcar had touched the back of my coat, it was that close.

Boy, I just sat down.

After a while, someone yelled, "Why you sittin' down for?"

I just said, "I'll be there in a minute."

Nobody knew.

I never said nothing to nobody about it.

Other people have had the same thing happen.

What could I say? I didn't get hurt. No one was derailed.

It's scary.

Every time, every railroad I worked for, you do not turn your back on equipment.

You do not turn your back on equipment.

Something's going on the track, you never turn your back on it.

Cause if you do, it's gonna be the car that you turned your back on, that's gonna get you.

And there's no second chance.

Just one wheel, a boxcar wheel, weighs 700 pounds, just one wheel. And if a car's rolling, it will just cut a path through a two by four, and you know, what are your bones going to do.

I've seen people run over, and boy, it's not a pretty sight at all.

Not A Pretty Sight

Basically the first one I ever saw was a lady, a nineteen year old girl, who wanted to commit suicide, and she just stood right out in front of the engine, and we hit her at 55 m.p.h.

It was one of those cab-forward Malleys. I was about five feet from her, and she turned, and she looked right at us, at 55 m.p.h., and we had ninety-nine cars on the train. When we stopped, I had just hired out after I had made my student trips, and this old engineer said, "Well, you better walk back and tell the conductor."

I said, "Couldn't you send the fireman?"

"No, you better go back," he said.

Man, that was terrible. Jeeze, what a mess that was.

Hitting Pedestrians

And then, other trains, down the peninsula there, that was just terrible for hitting pedestrians. Not the freight trains, the commute trains. One year we killed two.

I been on other trains, one time we hit a nine year old boy. Those things are just horrible. Accidents will happen. This poor kid was scrambling, they are all trying to get across the track in front of the train.

There's not enough time. Those things are movin'.
What is it, 60 m.p.h. you're going 88 feet per second. 88 feet is a long way, in one second.
If you're a hundred feet away from it, you wouldn't have time to get across, at 88 feet per second, it's only twelve feet to get across the track while the train's movin'... twelve feet? Un un.
Or automobiles drivin' around the gates. There's another thing, that's just crazy.
You swallow your heart every time.
You come up on the passenger side and people with their eyes as big as saucers, they just got across in time. It's crazy. It's really stupid.
I don't really feel sorry for a driver of an automobile that would do that, but I sure do ... for the passengers in the car, it's absolutely unthinkable.
For what?
With a hundred car train, you're gonna be on that crossing for forty-five or fifty seconds?
Is that all you're gonna save.
Aw Jeeze.
And it's so final.

We Hit This Car One Time

We hit it so hard that it was welded to the front of the engine.
Yeah.
They sent a tow truck out to get wreckage off the track, and they couldn't move the car. It was actually embedded in the front of the engine.
So they got a big chain around the car, and tied the chain off around a rail, then backed the train up. And it went SStriiing POW! It made this great big noise when it broke loose.
I'll tell you, there were two school teachers that were sure lucky that they got out of the car just before it hit.
They had missed a curve and driven onto the tracks.
This conductor and I were walking back and there was a trail of school books and papers, they were school teachers.
We were walking almost a mile.
Somebody saw our lanterns, and we heard this voice say,

"We're over here."
   The conductor says, "Where?"
   They were in a farm house. So we walked in.
   Apparently these two school teachers, the farmer's wife had just given them a cup of coffee, and they were shaking so bad, the coffee was spilling out of the cup.
   They'd made it, though.
   Pretty soon, the police showed up.
   This was just south of Salinas.
   These two school teachers missed a curve on the track and they ended up right in front of a passenger train.
   It really wasn't very good timing.
   But they got out of the car before it got hit.
   It was like hitting a fly with a baseball bat.
   It didn't even scratch the paint on the engine.
   It moved that car.
   It made a contour out of that car.
   It was a Buick, about a '59 Buick.

Not All Fun and Games Sometimes It's Not Very Pretty

   It hasn't all been fun and games.
   I remember when I first hired out in 1954 I had about two months seniority, and I was on this freight train coming from Watsonville, and we were going through Mountain View about 55 m.p.h., and this nineteen girl stepped right out in front of the engine. And we hit her.
   There was just absolutely no way we could stop.
   We had one-hundred-and-one cars on the freight train, and at 55 m.p.h, you can't stop.
   It was even goin' up hill a little bit, and we hit her. The headlight shown right on her. She was wearing a white robe.
   Boy, it was just more than I could handle.
   We hit her, and of course, the engineer had put the brakes in emergency, and tried to stop, but it was futile.
   After all the hissing, and the steam, and the squeal of the airbrakes stopped, we were up in the cab and everything was quiet, and I just remained in the seat.

And this old engineer said, "Well, I think you better walk back and tell the conductor."

I said, "Well couldn't you send the fireman back." I didn't want to go back.

And he said, "No, I think you better go on back yourself."

I start walkin' back. The track was perfectly straight, and as I was walkin' back, I was shining the lantern at the cars, lookin' the other way, 'cause I didn't want to see her.

So walkin' back, I could see a lantern comin' out of the caboose, way down ahead of me, and I knew it was a conductor. The way the train had stopped, he knew something was wrong, so he'd started walkin' up.

And then I seen his lantern stop, and then it went the other way. And I figured, 'He saw her. There's no sense in me ...' 'cause I just didn't want to see it. Then I figured, 'I better go back and tell them what happened, 'cause they'll be coming up to the engine sooner or later anyway.'

So I start walkin' back. There was one-hundred-and-one cars in the freight train, and I walked back, and under the seventieth car was a big ball of clothes.

And another three cars back, there she was.

Man, it was not a very nice sight.

I thought, 'If this is what it's going to be like, I'm gonna find myself another job.'

We Hit A Car One Time

We hit a car one time, it was Christmas Eve. We hit about the last four feet of the car, and the engine spun it around like a top. Then the first car behind the engine caught it again, and spun it back in to the side of the train. And the train kept rolling the car over and over like a log. There was Christmas presents and groceries all over the place. The lady went out through the windshield, then the car rolled over on top of her.

Oh man.

fig. 17 – a *'rear-ender'* near Pasa Robles in 1942

Hitting A Truck Full Of Potatoes

There was an engineer talkin' one time about hitting a truck full of potatoes.

It was more humorous that it was tragic. He said he never thought the potatoes would stop coming through the broken windshield into the engine. And there was sacks of potatoes, and individual potatoes. There was a cloud of potatoes.

Nobody ever got hurt. The truck driver got out.

That was on the Gulf, Mobil & Ohio Railroad. The engineer had a Southern accent, and the way he told it was so funny, "I n'eer thought them taters would settle down."

My Old Lantern

I've had this lantern for thirty-six years. I've used the same one. I've got other lanterns, but I've used the same one for thirty-six years — I don't know how I managed to hang onto it for thirty-six years. I could tell you where every dent came from.

I dropped this off a passenger train in the desert, that's this dent here. I dropped it off the passenger train as they were picking up speed. And I got off the train. Ran back and picked it up. Then, by the time I got back, I just barely got back on the train. I just couldn't go another step.

If I'd gotten left out there, I'd still be out there.

This is the lantern that was called a tomato can. It's got another dent over here, and a bunch over here, from dropping it, and hitting it against cars.

It lights up pretty far. It has two bulbs. One supposed to be more of a spotlight, and the other's for signaling. Or if one goes out, then you can use the other one.

You're really gonna be in a bad way if a light goes out on you.

You might give a hand sign, and if your lantern goes out, the engineer's not going to stop until he sees your 'STOP' sign. He should stop if the light goes out of his view.

There's years and years of dirt and grease on my lanterns. There's dust and grease all over the train, the wheels, dust, it is kind of a dirty job.

Another Dent In That Old Lantern

It turned out okay, but it was sure scary at the time.

It was on the Tucson Division. They have all these sidings, right out in the desert, at small copper deposits. From time to time, we'd go pick up certain cars at certain places.

So this one afternoon, we're goin' along, we had to pick these twelve cars up, full of copper ore. They're really heavy cars, loaded right up to the gunnels.

As the engine pulled by, the rear brakeman, who was riding the head, he dropped off, because he was going to start knocking off the handbrakes. It was a diesel, but we were using handbrakes because the cars were stored on the siding. Unfortunately, there's nothing flat around Tucson, and he was going to knock the handbrakes off on these twelve cars, and after I put the engine on, I was going to walk back and make all the air hoses.

And he was going to start at the rear on one side, and I was going to start at the head end on the other side — and somewhere in the middle we passed each other.

Every time he'd knock a handbrake off, the cars would lunge forward, 'cause they were on a slant.

I'd go between the cars. In a way I was placing myself in jeopardy. Every time you go between two cars, you're placing yourself in jeopardy. You should always be able to get out of there in an instant. One foot in and one foot out. I never put both feet inside the tracks.

You have to stoop down to make the air hoses. And I got almost to the last car. And I went between the cars, and I was just ready to make the air hose ... and the cars started to move.

I turned around to get out of there, but my coat caught on the angle cock of the air hose, and it pushed me down. And as I went down, I grabbed the pin lever, and now my feet are under the car, and they're bouncing along on the ties. I was just waitin' for my feet to get to a switch. When you go over a switch, there's a crossrail, a rail that crosses over, that would'a probably caught me. Unless you can hold your feet up, and that would be impossible to do. It would yank your foot right off when it hits the crossrail. And the switch is gonna pull you off, and then you get run over. There's no clearance under the cars. I was virtually all underneath the car; my heels bouncing along on the ties as we were goin' forward. If you fell off, the brake rigging is underneath the trucking, and it would rip you apart, if you didn't land on the rail. And it'd started getting dark, and luckily I had my lantern with me.

That old lantern.

I threw it out in the desert.

And the hoghead saw it.

Man, he stopped! I could hear the engine go into *big hole* from where I was riding.

And man oh man. The other brakeman came running back. He was as white as I was. He said, "What can I say?"

Well, nothin' happened, so I was lucky.

When I heard that engine go into big hole, boy was I relieved.

The other brakeman didn't look for me. The engineer, later on he said, "Well I thought you were gonna stay on the rear end of the car, so you would've been out of sight." And he couldn't see me. So the other brakeman had given a sign to go ahead — and forgot all about me. It's kind of hard to explain, really. He was upset over what happened. But the engineer, when he saw that lantern go out, he didn't even think twice.

It's normal for the engineer to be looking back for any sign, to make sure no cars are on the ground.

Then again he could'a been looking straight forward, looking ahead to the main line to stop. But he was watchin' all the time. He figured I was sittin' on the rear car someplace. He didn't see me. I was between them.

Boy, that was a close one.

I'd rather forget it than remember it.

So we're moving slow, but fast enough ...

It was a good thing both me and the engineer was on the same side of the train, and on the same side of the curve, when I threw my lantern out there, into the desert, into the dark.

The Story About The Private Car

When I was on the S.P., I caught the brakeman job on the Daylight Special, and we'd go down to San Luis Obispo on the Daylight, and the next evening we'd come back to San Francisco on The Lark.

This one evening, we were standing around the depot, waiting for The Lark to arrive, waiting to exchange crews — because there was a crew change at San Luis Obispo. The train pulled in, and as we were leaving, the conductor said the president of Southern Pacific's private car was on the rear end of the train, and he didn't know if the president was in it or not.

I was the rear brakeman on the train, and we got going, and of course, the rear brakeman doesn't ride on a private car, customarily, unless you're invited in there, you ride in the last coach before it — which was a lounge car.

So we got to King City, and on a train like that, the rear brakeman has to get out while the train is stopped, and stand behind the train with a lantern ... you're supposed to protect the rear end of the train.

So anyway, I'm standin' there, and the steward in the private car comes out and he starts talkin' to me, and I find out that the private car's not occupied, they're just deadheading it up to San Francisco.

Boy, it was cold that night. It was freezing.

So the steward said, "Would you like some coffee?"

I said, "Yeah!"

He said, "Okay, when the train gets goin', come on in."

So when the train started, I went through the rear of the lounge car which normally was the last car on the train, but this time, this business car was there, so anyway, the steward was going to open the front door on the business car, as I went through the door on the lounge car, which is not normally used, 'cause it's always the last car, so that door was never normally used for passing through.

Anyway, I went through the very end door to get on the business car. There's two doors. One with a safety catch on it, another outside door with these big brass handles, that you can only open from the inside.

So the steward opened the door, and he showed me through this real nice business car that belonged to the president of the Southern Pacific. So he fixed coffee. Then I said, I better get back. The steward was going to go to sleep. He said, "When you leave the private car, make sure the door slams and locks."

"Yeah," I said. I let myself out, and I slammed the door on the business car, then tried it, and it was locked. And I turned around to discover that the wind had blown the door to the lounge car closed. And one of the dogs had dropped down, and I couldn't open it from the outside. And we're sailing along at 70 m.p.h., at three o'clock in the morning, and there's icicles coming off my ears. And I turned around, and I was poundin' on the door of the business car to see if he'd let me in. But he'd went to sleep, and apparently he had turned the buzzer off, or something.

So I rode practically from King City to Salinas, between the two cars!

That wind, it was cold there.

When we got to Salinas, I had to squeeze between the striking plates to get outside, and I ripped my uniform, and there was dirt all over my face, 'cause I had to squeeze through there. All the porters were asleep. Nobody gets on at Salinas. We just virtually checked mail. And I come up there, and the conductor wants to know what happened to my uniform — I'd tore the coat, there's dirt smudges all over my face — and I couldn't explain it to him.

I couldn't go over the top, 'cause there's no roof walks on passenger cars. I was in between about an hour, an hour and a half. It was freezin', holy smoke.

It was just because I didn't check to see if the door was still open.

Weather — It doesn't have to be a bad storm when you're outside to get soaked to the skin. You just have to put up with it. Wear a raincoat or something. You're gonna get wet, no matter what; but it just goes with the job.

I've worked on top in the snow.

The grab bars, you can't touch them with your hand — your skin will stick to the metal. When it's really cold, and you touch a piece of metal, your skin's gonna stick to it like dry ice. I always had gloves on.

Whether it's hot or cold, you can't go out there with bare hands.

I've worked in places where the cars were so hot from the sun, you'd burn your hand if you tried to climb up a car, like in the desert.

The same way when it's cold — everything is just so slippery, you just have to pay attention every minute of the time.

Once you're inside the caboose, or inside the engine, it's a lot different, it's a nice place to be.

You get out there, and it's really nasty, workin' in the rain, and the cold, it's just miserable.

It's miserable enough at night, when you just have a lantern, and you have to look at your list, and read your list with the lantern, but when it's raining, you have all this rain gear on, and your arms are restricted with all this stuff on, and sometimes it gets really hot wearing all this rain gear. I've been on a job where it's pouring down rain and we had to spot these cars in an industry. You have a switch list with all the car numbers, so you know where the cars are going to go, and it was raining so hard, you watch the list begin to disappear. You have to go get another one, and try to cup it in your hands, so it doesn't come apart in the rain. Then you get out to the place where you're supposed to spot these cars.

Nobody Said Nothin'

I remember this one time, it was really rainin'. Part of the job is, when you're spotting cars, (editor's note: shoving cars into an industry), the crew has to spread out so they can pass signals to the engineer — you don't want the car to hit the bumper at the end of the track — you want to spot the car right. A lot of times the engineer can not see way back to the end of the train, 'cause it's around a curve, and so the switchmen all spread out where they can pass the signals.

This one time, we were spottin' this track, and the only place I could stand, where I could see the other switchman, and the engineer, was right under a downspout.

Water was just cascading down.

Y'know, you didn't want to miss the signal — you could damage equipment, or someone could get hurt.

And the only place I could stand was under this downspout. It was like a firehose comin' down.

The other guys didn't say anything, they were as wet as I was from the rain. Everyone was too wet to think it was funny.

fig. 18 – *The California Zephyr*, nicknamed *The Silver Lady;* departing Oakland, 1968.

Running Through The Fog In Fresno

In the fog, up in the cab in the engine, you can't see the rails.

We're running at speed. And you better know where the block signals are, and all the crossings — most of the engineers memorized them.

I was on one evening, the fog was so thick, the engineer asked me to stand behind him, so he wouldn't miss a signal, it comes up and goes by so fast. And in the fog, you can't see it very far away. And if you take your eyes away for an instant, it goes by, and you've missed it. And somethin's going to happen in a hurry.

So he asked me to stand behind him, and back him up with a second pair of eyes.

At first it bothered me, but I figured, 'Well, if the hoghead doesn't know what he's doing, then he's going to be as worse off as I am. And these guys are real experienced men, and that's got to count for something.'

Sixty miles per hour, in the fog, in the country, where people fool around with the crossings anyway.

"What is it like workin' in the rain," I said.

When I work in the rain or something like that, I'm just super safe. 'Cause I know, if you fall off the cars, there's no place you can land, where it's soft. You can break yourself up. An accident on the railroad, is not a nice thing.

It's darn slippery goin' over the top of cars.

When you go over the top of cars, you step over the top of 'em from one to another. The roofwalks were about three-foot apart. It's scary, no kiddin'.

Even gettin' on the engine standin' still, the steel plates have what's called safety tread, but it's notoriously slippery. And if there's a little bit of grease or oil on there, you just have to be careful.

"If you're in the caboose and you're hangin' on because of the slack comin' in and out, what are you doin' running across the top of the cars with slack?" I said.

You can hear the slack. You listen for it. It's kinda like thunder, subdued thunder.

If you're unlucky enough to be crossing between two cars and the slack runs out, oouuuu, just be careful.

Even at twenty-five miles an hour, walkin' over the top of the cars, the cars are really swaying back and forth, and you just have to be really careful.

There's no handrails, and except for goin' over a mountain there's no reason to be up there. Even then, because the diesel locomotive has regenerative braking, and when they start the downgrade, the engineer handles the lever and the traction motors become electric generators instead of motors, and so the train is impeded by the resistance of the motors creating electricity. And you don't wear out the brake shoes and the wheels don't get hot, and you don't need retainers. But they still put retainers on the cars, though.

Use to be the retainers were always located up near the handbrake, which is up at the top of the car; and the retainers and handbrakes just became redundant. Now there's a crossover platform on the end of the car, and the handbrakes are down there, and you just don't need to go up high anymore.

They took all the roof walks off anyway, in 1977.

They decided it was just too dangerous to have anybody up on top of cars, and they put out a prohibition against being on top of the cars anymore.

It was really dangerous up there.

I Got Knocked Off The Top Of A Car Once

I got knocked off the top of a car once, switching a lumber mill on the N.W.P., and they were doin' some construction and they put this scaffold over the track, and we came in there at night, and I hit that thing.

I went right over the side of the car.

Luckily I went right over the side of the car, into this great big pile of sawdust.

Boy, I'll tell you I was lucky.

We were going slow, but it could have been a lot worse that it was. It was just kind of a real surprise, you find yourself airborne. I got hit from the back, on the back of my head.

They apparently were really fined for putting a scaffolding over the tracks. They should not have put that up. It was impaired clearance on the railroad track. Nobody really thought a train was going to go in there. Just construction workers did it. It was a situation that they couldn't really appreciate, and then some train comes in there, and someone gets hurt. Luckily it was superficial injuries.

If that pile of sawdust hadn't of been there, I don't know what would have happened. It's a long way down.

Cars vary in height. A boxcar is twelve feet from the ground to the top, but they do vary. Then you're standing up, adding to the height of it, another six feet. There's a big difference between twelve feet and eighteen feet up.

Baptist Special

I only worked one job as a passenger conductor.

Most of it was just a lot of fun.

When I was on the S.P. I had so little seniority I could just work the extra board. I was a brakeman this one time.

I got a call for a Baptist Special.

The Black Baptists were gonna have a special train to go to L.A. to have this convention. I was called for this train at 7 p.m. at 3rd and Townsend. This nice shiny train, good equipment.

All these people start showing up. They were real, nice people. I don't know if all Baptists are good, but these people were, real nice.

My job was patrol the train, make sure everything was 'copasetic'.

Anyway, the train got underway, and I walk up and down the train, and if somebody wanted to move the seat, I'd help them.

It was their train.

So I was walking into the men's room, opened the curtain and walked in, and there was this guy with a collar, with a brown bag, and he saw me, and he pulled it down, and said, "Sorry, sorry."

"Hey. It's none of my business. Just carry on," I said.

It was a Black deacon or something, with a collar, and a bottle of Southern Comfort.

But it was the way he pulled the bag down, trying to hide it.

fig. 19 - job of a *Redcap* (fore- & background) is to load luggage on carts & train

Insurance Special

One time I was called for an insurance special.
Which was headed for an insurance convention in L.A. or someplace.
Like the other train, the Baptist special, we started out in San Francisco, and same thing, I was supposed to patrol the train, just walk up and down, and make sure everything was fine. If somebody wanted something, if you can, help them.
Before we got to San Luis Obispo, I bet there was eighty-five insurance policies taken out on me.
People start selling me insurance.

Celebrities

There was this other train that used to go to Monterey.
We stopped in Palo Alto one time.
This lady said, "Would you make sure my daughter got off at Del Monte, there was some kind of girl's school down there, or something.
And I said, "Sure." She had a name tag on her.
She was going to flip me a five.
I said, "No, we treat everybody the same."
"Ah c'mon, take it," she said.
"Okay, I'll take it," I said.
The train started.
The other brakeman came up to me and said, "Hey, do you know who you were just talking to?"
I said, "No. Who was it?"
"That was Shirley Temple," he said.
Their daughter was going to school in Del Monte, I guess.
Tennessee Ernie Ford used to ride that train.
Usually down to Monterey.
He lived on the peninsula someplace, probably Woodside.
They don't send trains down there anymore.
AMTRAK never picked up the Del Monte Express.
That was a great little train too.

Coachyard Johnny

There was a guy, a passenger, we called Coachyard Johnny.
He'd get in San Francisco, about ten o'clock at night, and soused?
He was a happy drunk. He'd get on and say, "Heyyy!"
He'd mind his own business, and fall asleep.
Every night, he was supposed to get off at Redwood City,
He was gone.
So we'd take him to San Jose.
And leave him to sleep in the coach yard, on the coach.
He was safe. And it was nice and warm in there.
We couldn't wake him up. He was like a dead body.
Every couple weeks, he'd come down there, same guy, drunk again, and we'd leave him to sleep.
He'd never say nothing about it.

Off The Record

This commute train we used to work, we used to trade off buying donuts, see?
We'd get down to San Jose, and we had a long layover down there, and instead of getting sick of looking at each other's face, why we'd get a big pot of coffee and a dozen donuts, for three of us.
And so we always used to stick the donuts up in the hat rack, in the last coach.
So this one night, we get to San Jose, the donuts are gone.
Somebody flinched the donuts.
So the next night, it was somebody else's turn to buy donuts. We get to San Jose. Darn! They're gone again.
Somebody did away with them.
The other brakeman's, or the conductor's brother was a doctor. And the story got around about somebody stealin' the donuts, and the doctor said, "There's one way of breaking somebody of doing that. And that's to get some powdered alum, and some epicache."
Now epicache is used in hospitals if somebody swallows a poison and they have to make them, vomit, quickly, I mean, in a

hurry. And you take that, and you shake it up in a sack of donuts.

And we got two sacks of donuts. And we put one up there, three or four donuts in there, and we took the other sack.

And we got to San Jose, and the sack was gone!

So we never ever established who the culprit was, but I'll tell you one thing, he never took three steps after he took a bite of one of those donuts.

The following week we put a sack of donuts up there, and they stayed all the way to San Jose.

The Daylight Special & The Coast Starline

The Daylight Special was just a beautiful train.

Cars were all sparkling orange and red, with black tops.

You know they put out the call about six-thirty, and I'd jump up, 'cause the train left at eight-fifteen in the morning.

The conductor would generally look the crew over, make sure you had a clean shirt on, and your uniform looked pretty good.

I remember one time I got over there, and forgot about my shoes. They were terrible.

The conductor barked at me, "Go in there, and get a shine!"

So I went in there and got a shine.

The Daylight Special ran from San Francisco down to L.A. But we only took it as far as San Luis Obispo. And another crew took it the rest of the way.

It was beautiful. We had commuters, businessmen, vacationers, the train was always pretty full.

That train went through San Margarita Mountains, then dropped down to San Luis Obispo, then passed Guadeloupe, it went right along the cliffs over the ocean, and what a beautiful sight.

It still goes today, but it's a different train. It's called The Coast Starline now.

It starts in Seattle, and runs all the way to Los Angeles.

It goes through Oakland. It doesn't go to San Francisco now, it goes to San Jose. You've got to catch a commute train from San Francisco to get it.

We went to Seattle on it in June. The two of us, me and my wife — course we had a bedroom, it was about six hundred dollars.

fig. 20

But it was worth it. And when you go first class, your meals are paid. You can order anything. Call AMTRAK 1-800-USA-Rail. Drum up a little business here.

The Time The Fireman Let The Tank Heater Overflow

The Great Daylight Limited was just the most spotless train in the world. Every time it came to one of the terminals in Los Angeles or San Francisco, it would have a whole crew of men out there cleaning the train. It was just absolutely spotless.

Anyway, it left San Francisco this one morning, as usual, on it's way to Los Angeles. Well, after leaving San Francisco, the first stop would be at San Jose.

It seems that they have a heater on the engine, to heat the bunker-sea oil, which is just like what comes out of the ground so it can go through the atomizer. It heats the oil so that the oil gets a lot thinner, and it burns easier.

Well anyway, the fireman had turned the tank heater on, and forgot it.

So the temperature of the oil kept going up and up and up, and pretty soon it started bubbling up out of the tender. And then, as the train was going 60 or 70 m.p.h., after enough of it got out, it started blowin' back on some of the coaches.

By the time the train got to San Jose, they had oil all over the head five cars.

It was just black, gooey stuff, on this beautiful train. 'Cause the fireman left the heater on.

The Daylight Special

The Daylight Special was a through passenger, and jobs are awarded on seniority. And so the only way you could pull that when you were starting, was to catch it off the extra board.

The youngest regular man was sixty years old.

You work all your life to build up seniority, and then you hold a job for two or three years before you retire.

That's just the way the Mercedes bends.

You get a person starting up, and you got to put up with getting cut off, displaced. Usually during the winter times, the railroad cuts back their operations. Then during the summer, things are going fast and you're meeting yourself going in and out of the front door, there's so much work.

In fact, a couple times, I've gone down to Fresno, and by the time you get down there, you're pretty hungry, and you go out and have dinner and go back to the motel, and you just get in bed and the phone rings to go back to work, and my boots are still warm.

If you get called one-thirty in the morning, y'know, you get down there, you work, you get up at one-thirty, most people are just getting their best sleep, you're at work, watch the sun come up, blinding in your eyes, your eyes sting, you get a mouth full of rocks, a bad taste in your mouth from working all night, and you get down to Fresno, and you can't sleep, 'cause it's during the daytime.

So you stay up and drink coffee, and stay up and drink coffee, then you're ready to sleep.

Then the phone rings again, to come back.

But then you get up here, and you got a day and a half, two days home, before the next call.

Y'know, you just can't have everything.

Two hundred and five miles to Fresno, and basic pay is one hundred miles, so you're getting little more than two days pay to go down to Fresno, then a little more than two days pay, to come back.

And you can't beat that.

For the time you're away from home.

I could put up with a lot of one-thirty calls, for money like that.

When I retired, I was on a local freight.

We just went to work every afternoon at the same time.

As soon as we got the work done, we'd come back to Richmond and tie up.

Maybe it'd be three or four hours, or it might be twelve. You never knew. It wasn't three or four hours often, but you got paid for eight, a basic day, a hundred miles.

So if you worked twelve hours, you got a day-and-a-half's pay, considering the overtime.

There's a hundred and fifty mile day. Y'know, that's not too bad either.

You know, when you're working the Fresno run, you can't plan anything.

You can say, "Today is Tuesday, I'll be gone tomorrow, I'll be back maybe Thursday or Friday, which works out that you get home Saturday night.

I found something that kinda suited me to a T. I feel somewhat lucky to work for a company that is responsive, Santa Fe. They're basically concerned. You should see all the stuff they gave us. If I started a list: thermos bottle, tote bag, fire extinguisher, car kit, five different hats, twenty-five dollar gift order to a restaurant, Black Angus, oh man. All the stuff they gave us. Little stuff, pocket knives, flashlights, you know, little things, but you know, I appreciated them.

One time this engineer, his son took his vehicle with authorization, his dad's car, and he turned it over and got killed. And he was a young man. And the superintendent heard about it, and they were going to fly this engineer back to the Bay Area, he was down in Fresno, he was on a run down in Fresno.

Y'know, you go to a lot of trouble to be a little considerate of employees, and they do a lot of stuff they don't really have]to, and you know, I think I was really pretty lucky.

When I was running that student instruction thing, they took me out to dinner one time, all these officials, they were going to make this thing system-wide, and they were going to set me up in it someplace, I don't know where. That's what this person said.

Then they had a hiring freeze.

The last time I did that job it was 1981.

They started it up again. But it had been such a long time since '81 to '89, and I was sick one day they were going to decide who they needed, but they carried the program on.

Mr. Lui

There was this superintendent.

He came up from the ranks.

He's the kind of guy that would drive by on Reem Avenue,

fig. 21 – the guy on the bottom is *'Blinky'; Blinky* was always blinking his eyes.

watching the trains come in, on his way to work. And he knew, from watching the speedometer in his car, and would hold his speed down to thirty, thirty-five miles per hour. And if a train passed him, he'd get on his radio, and say, "Observe the speed limit."

That was Mr. Lui.

He was the kind of guy you just couldn't bull.

He knew railroadin'.

And he was a real leader.

In fact, early on when he first came there, he had a lot of history to him. He was a real old railroader.

When he first came there, I was gone out on a switch engine. We go out to a certain part of the yard, a certain area where there's industry.

We derailed the engine, and three cars. It was nobody's fault. It was just the engine picked up the points of a switch, and at the speed we were going, the engine went sideways, and the cars turned crosswise. It turned out the point was chipped, and that's why we caught it. The flanges on the engine picked it up. So we went down the track one way, and the cars went the other way.

We weren't using any airbrakes, we didn't have any air on the car.

And I said, "Ahh, darn. Mr. Lui's gonna come out here, and the first thing he's gonna see, 'cause you just could not pull anything over on this guy, the first thing he's gonna see, is that the air hoses aren't coupled, and he's gonna say, 'How come you don't have any air?'"

So anyway, we decided to put a couple of air hoses together, but because the cars were turned sideways, we just couldn't link the air hoses up, so we hooked up a couple airhoses as jumpers.

We got air to 'em. Then, the engineer pumped on them. The engine's sideways.

Anyway, we got the engine and three cars all over the ground, not only that, but we're blocking Canal Blvd. with the cars that were still on the tracks.

Anyway, Mr. Lui insisted that we all use air.

So we were gonna get out, and we were gonna switch the cars without air. We could handle a train without air.

And so the cars were turned sideways, and we couldn't hook up the air hoses, so we got jumper airhoses. Then we got all the air together, so the engineer pumped on them. Then, when they were pumped up, he put the brake lever into emergency, and so when Mr. Lui came out, he could see the piston travel on the brakes. That's how thorough Mr. Lui is, see.

We went through all this trouble to get these air hoses out, and the engines turned sideways and all this stuff, and here comes Mr. Lui's car.

He pulls alongside, he jumps out.

First thing he says is, "Man, I've never seen a lantern like that in my life."

You see, I've got this old lantern, that I had.

And we talked for about thirty-five minutes, about this lantern.

"Now when I was switchin', we used to call them tomato cans, Mr. Lui said.

And I'll tell you, he jumped in his car, and took off.

Never said a thing about cars all over the tracks.

Here Comes Mr. Lui

One Sunday morning, coming into Richmond, on this freight train, the engine derailed. This great big real heavy diesel unit, this real big unit, totally derailed coming into Richmond. We were actually inside the yard, when this engine derailed, it was about ten o'clock in the morning.

We'd been all night coming from Fresno, and I said, "Awww, man. Look at that darn engine on the ground."

We were just coming in, and we called the yardmaster. "Well, we got these engines on the ground." These were the biggest engines the Santa Fe had.

It was a serious derailment. You can't move them. I'm tired, and I want to go to bed. I want to get out of here. It was all night from Fresno.

So we're sitting around, waiting for things to happen, and here comes Mr. Lui.

He's got a barbecue apron on.

He was at some barbecue, and they called him out cause they got these engines off.

He looked it over. This guy is real slick. He knows all the tricks of the trade, and I say, "Are we going to have to wait here till they get a crew out here?"

And he says, "Nah, go on home."

So he rode us all in his car, and he took us up to the little Java house.

Mr. Lui was in charge of the whole division. From Richmond, to Barstow.

This was a hot shot train. The other time, it was just a switch engine, and he was more interested in my tomato can, than seeing the cars all over the track. He was a real leader.

I'm probably prejudiced, but it always seemed like the railroad was so dynamic, and there was so much drama involved, and just so many things, because railroads mean an awful lot to me.

fig. 23 – Great Salt lake, north end at Monument Point

88 fig. 24 – bound for the mountains, 12-mile tangent, 4 miles from Sacramento

Dick Murdock — (born 1917)

A Fireman & Steam Engineer

A Determined 8-Year Old Kid Boosted Into The Cab of a Little Switch Engine 2900 (2948) 4-8-0 and Taken Through the Paces of Switching a Fruit and Vegetable Cannery in Los Gatos Decides from That Moment On that 'Someday I'm Going to Be a Southern Pacific Fireman; Someday I'm Going to Be a Southern Pacific Engineer; Someday I Am Going to Run Freight.' And He Does.

"What year were you born?" I asked.

"1917. That would make me seventy-three; I'll be seventy-four in May. I retired in March of '78, after thirty-seven years on the railroad," Dick said.

"There was telephones in 1917?" I asked.

"Oh yes," Dick said.

"There was electric lights?" I asked.

"Yes," Dick said.

"There were no more steam automobiles, but there were automobiles. There were no more electric automobiles then either. There was probably electric rails then," I said.

"Un huh," Dick said.

"But there certainly wasn't computers."

"No there wasn't."

There Was A Camaraderie Amongst The Men

I hired out in September the 6th, 1941 — that was the date I made as a fireman. Right away, quick, there was a camaraderie, amongst the men.

Now sometimes the engineers weren't too friendly to the firemen, until you were accepted; but generally, if you were really sincere, it didn't take long for the word to get around, and you were among the group then — and then you were respected, and yes, there was a real close-knit relationship between those you worked with and anybody else around there on the railroad. Yes there was.

"Do you think that was particular to the railroad at that time?" I said.

"I'd rather think that almost in any industry there was that to a certain degree; but in the transportation industry, like the railroad, I am quite sure that it was stronger than it was in other industries," Dick said.

"When you were a kid, did you play with trains?" I asked.

I Was Hooked At An Early Age

Absolutely. I did. I had little iron steam engines, and little iron cars; they used to be iron all of the time, you know. And yes, I'd pull them around the front room rug. I was interested in trains from the time that I saw the first one, I'm sure. I was a train nut.

I was born in Oakland, at home, and my parents were reasonably wealthy; so I was of a good family. I wasn't of a poor family. So I saw all the streetcars in Oakland, and all the Red trains in Oakland, all those things in Oakland. And I, as a little, tiny toddler, was absolutely fascinated by these trains.

"When was it you remembered riding your first train?" I asked.

Riding My First Train

I remember riding streetcars at a very early age. We had a governess who took care of my brother and I — he was four years older than I; he was born in 1913. We had a governess by the name of Ma Cole, and she took us on streetcars occasionally to see friends of hers. So I would say by age three, four and five, or around there, I had ridden quite a few of the old Yellow Key System cars, at that age.

"When was the first time you rode the train by yourself," I asked.

The Suntan Special In The

Old Santa Cruz Mountains

I was probably ten or eleven by that time. I did ride the train when I was in Los Gatos. I moved to Los Gatos in 1925; and at the time, you see, I would have been eight years old, and I did ride the train from Los Gatos to Santa Cruz and back, quite a few times, when I was about that age.

Those were steam engines. Oh yes, absolutely. And the line went from Los Gatos, right directly to Santa Cruz. That line is discontinued now. It was a wonderful line. They ran The Suntan Specials every Sunday. And they'd take long Harriman commute cars, and they'd put two 2300's on the point, and they'd run through all those tunnels.

It would take about an hour to go the twenty-five miles from Los Gatos to Santa Cruz, on The Suntan Special.

So they'd go through all those tunnels. And they had 2300's on there. And those 2300's would smoke the tunnels up pretty good; some of those tunnels were pretty long. And in those days, why yes, we did get smoke inside the passenger cars, but not to any great degree. But there was always a little oil smoke in those passenger cars when you went through those long tunnels. You could smell it very clearly. Those were the days when they used to go through and light the gas lights for you; you didn't have electricity on the coaches.

Then we'd go pull right on down to the waterfront in Santa Cruz, and let all the people out at the amusement park — that's where everyone was heading; to the boardwalk. And then they'd pick them all up when their train was to leave and take them all the way back.

"When did it first dawn on you that you might want to work on a railroad? Can you remember when the realization hit you" I asked.

"Well yes, I certainly can," Dick said.

Ray Barber

I had the desire to work on the railroad when I was eight years old, 1925-1926. In 1926 there used to be a freight train that came down to Hunt Brothers cannery at Los Gatos, where they packed peaches and tomatoes and that sort of thing in the summertime — the cannery was usually closed during the winter-time. But during the summer-time the cannery was open.

A little local freight would come down and switch the cannery. There was a fireman on that 2900, which was a little 4-8-0 job, 2948 was the engine, and the fireman's name was Ray Barber; and Ray Barber took a liking to my brother and I.

So he let us ride the engine.

So from that moment on, I said, 'Someday I'm going to be a Southern Pacific fireman. Someday I'm going to be a Southern Pacific engineer. Someday I am going to run freight.'

And the real catcher to this story is — years later, I was going between Oakland and Roseville in freight service, and the engineer kept lookin' at me, and lookin' at me, and lookin' at me. And he says, "I think I know you."

"Why?" I said.

"Did you ever live at Los Gatos?" He said.

"Yeah, I lived there in 1925," I said.

"You ever remember a local freight switchin' the Hunt Brothers cannery?" He said.

"'Yes. YOU'RE RAY BARBER!" I said.

So I fired for Ray.

I think he's probably dead now. But if not, he'd be in his nineties, and lives in San Jose.

"What sticks in your mind? Is there anything you want people to know, about railroading, in your life, that they never would've known, and that you think that you should know this," I asked.

It's A Rough Darn Life

You should know that it's a rough darn life.

Because you were subject to calls twenty-four hours a day — if you were on the extra board, and you didn't know what kind of a job you were going to get — and some of them with mean old guys, mean old engineers that were hard to get along with.

And it was a tough go. And a lot of times, you didn't have very much money yet. And it was a real tough life. And it was very, very cold in the wintertime, and very hot in the summertime. And you were subject to extremes.

I think that anybody should know that you were subject to extremes, when you hired out on the railroad.

It wasn't a normal life, by any stretch of the imagination.

And it was very, very hard on marriages. Women could not understand the fact, that their husband was subject to call twenty-four hours a day.

"Could we talk about some of these extremes, for a minute. The first one you mentioned was some of the old engineers — I guess, in 1940, if they were an old engineer, they must have been born in the 1890s," I said.

"That's right, absolutely," Dick said.

"Doesn't any thing stick in your mind? Did any of them give people a hard time?" I said.

"Well, yeah. There was Iron Mike Harold and Youngblood the Indian. I learned something from that one all right.

Iron Mike Harold & Youngblood the Indian

Anyway, there was a fellow by the name of Iron Mike Harold. All the railroads had their characters, and Iron Mike Harold was a character. A mean little guy. Well one time, the story goes, he got a fireman, by the name of Youngblood.

Youngblood was fresh off the Indian reservation.

And they were going down the old route, before they had the Shasta Dam — all the way down to Keswick, all the way on to Redding, down that way; and they had a Malley.

And Iron Mike, he didn't earn that name for nothing. He was a mean, old character. So he started in chewin' on Youngblood, right out of Dunsmuir,

"GIVE HER MORE BLOWER! CUT DOWN ON THE ATOMIZER! TURN ON THE INJECTOR! TURN OFF THE INJECTOR!" — and all this sort of stuff; just really nippin' on him.

This guy Youngblood, was a great big guy. Not Iron Mike, he

was just a little mean guy. But Youngblood the Indian, he's a great big hefty guy fresh off the reservation.

Youngblood didn't say anything.

Mike chewed on him all way down.

They finally put the engine to the house in Gerber, and they killed the fire.

And Mike says, "Let's go over and eat."

Mr. Youngblood goes over, and he grabs Iron Mike by the neck and the seat of the pants, and he drags him right back, and reaches down and opens the firebox door — the fire's still in there; and he puts Iron Mike's head right in there. His ears are all singed, and his hair is crinklin' and everything, and Youngblood pulls him out, puts him in again, and pulls him out.

And now, old Iron Mike is screamin' for his life, "Let me down! I'll fire you! I'll fire you!"

Youngblood says, "You do anything you want, Mr. Harold; but from now on, you are gonna treat me, like a gentleman. The book of rules explains that if I don't know proper, you are to instruct me properly, and you are going to live up to the book of rules. Now if you want to get me fired, you go right ahead. I've only made the one trip, it won't hurt me at all."

They went back to Dunsmuir, and Mr. Iron Mike was a gentleman all the way.

And Mr. Youngblood stayed on the railroad, for a long time.

So I made up my mind, when I saw what the situation was, I said to myself, 'I'm going to stay on this railroad. I love the railroad — even the rotten life involved. You got to sleep in rotten old hotels, and sometimes in cabooses, and terrible greasy spoons to eat in and all that — but the thrill of it, runnin' the engines, and firin' the engines, and doin' freight, and passenger and all that, was very, very fascinating.

"How would you describe that thrill to someone?" I asked.

Well, first you have to have a fascination for the locomotive itself. Just to hear the hissing of the steam, and the turning of the wheels, and the ringing of the bell, and the sound of it — a steam engine had an almost human response.

And you had to appreciate that response.

And you had to know the mechanics of the engine, and how it worked and what made it talk back to you.

"What do you mean? If you'd push it, it would push back? If you were nice to it, it would be nice back? What do you mean, it had a human response," I asked.

A Steam Engine Had An Almost Human Response

Talk back to you. Now all right.

A steam engine is run by a throttle, and the reverse lever, delicately balanced against each other. A reverse lever, as you pull it back, it cuts off the valve stroke, and eventually, if you pull it all the way back, it reverses the engine, and makes it go the other way.

But you never pull it all the way back, you just pick it up three or four or five notches, and you'll notice that the exhaust softens, and it makes it easier for the fireman to keep up the steam and keep water in the boiler. So the idea is to delicately balance the reverse lever and the throttle against each other in the proper manner. That made it easy on the fireman, and the engine would pick up speed, and have a tendency to kind of Chuckle back at you — Chhh sch sch, schhh sch sch, schhh sch sch — when it was balanced right.

An engineer could kill a fireman — even the best fireman in the world.

Once I learned this, it was very, very important; if that engineer left the reverse lever clear down in the corner, and pulled the throttle all the way over, then the valve strokes are working in such a way that the engine is fighting itself, and your steam is goin' down, and the water in the boiler is startin' to go down. That's when you had to get up, when you knew what you were doin', and walk across the cab, and say, 'How 'bout hookin' her up, Mr. Engineer; you're killin' me, and you know it. And you better turn on your injector because the water's getting lower and lower, and we'll BOTH blow up unless you get with it."

"Do you remember your first day on the job?" I said.

My first day on the job was a night, that was my first paid job on Southern Pacific as a locomotive fireman.

fig. 25 – *Engine 24* was a little *2-8-0, Sierra Railroad*, Tuolomne, CA

Orlin Gowey was the engineer that night, on No. 1250, an 0-6-0 oil-burning steam switch engine in the Oakland yard. What I was supposed to do as fireman was give the engineer a full head of steam, and keep water in the boiler at a safe level. By the next morning when I climbed down out of the cab, I was tired out. The engineer came over to me.

"I don't mind tellin' you, kid, you fired that engine as good as some guys who've been around here three months or longer. Keep it up. You'll be okay," he said.

Striking It Rich On My Last Student Trip

One of my last student trips was through Martinez at the Shell Oil Company. I was on an old Mogul 2-6-0, engine number 1769; it was a switching job.

Earl Fosgate was the engineer; Mel Griffin was the fireman. Mel was teaching me.

"You got to keep the tender oil hot enough to go to the firebox burner. Put the back of your hand against the tank — when it feels hot, it's hot enough. Get it too hot and boil it over the tank is the worst thing you can do," Mel said.

Right then a geyser of hot oil shot out of the dip-stick hole in the engine, and out of the hole where oil's put in over the top of the tank.

The engineer start laughing.

Griffin didn't laugh. Neither did I. I start cleaning it off with kerosene, and scrubbing it with sand and a scrub brush. Later they steam-hosed it off when the engine was at the roundhouse.

Jay Moss — Port Costa Winter of '42–'43

It was raining cats and dogs every day. The reservoir at Port Costa filled up. Then it overflowed down the main street in town.

It was raining so you couldn't even see. What happened was, the turntable pit filled up with water.

Old Jay Moss, a switchman, left out of the yardman's shanty and start walkin' to our engine carrying his lantern and lunch bucket. One minute he was there, and the next he wasn't! All I could see was Jay's head stickin' up out of the water; and his lantern and his lunch bucket he was holding up high — he'd stepped into the turntable pit!

We hauled him out. Jay didn't have much to say.

"I'm okay. Let's get back to work," he said.

"Well okay, Jay. Why don't you put some dry clothes on first?" I said.

Willie Marshal

Mel Griffin, the engineer, told me this one about Willie Marshal.

Willie was an engine watchman. He had a weakness for the bottle. He was a little guy. Everybody liked Willie. His job was to go through the roundhouse and keep fires lit in all the engines in there, to keep their steam pressure up.

Well one morning Mel was walking towards the Port Costa roundhouse, and he heard this big 'BOOOOM!'

Windows rattled all over, the buildings shook, and a small flock of sparrows that got scared flew up out of the eaves of the roundhouse, and big clouds of black smoke followed up after them.

Willie Marshall staggered out of the roundhouse over to Mel. Willie had a cocked grin on his face.

"Mel, y'know them sparrows?' Willie said.

"Sure," Mel said.

"Well, I just made blackbirds out of 'em, " Willie said.

Dorothy

About that time I started courting a clerk at Shell Oil — Dorothy was her name.

I was firin' for Ralph Hudson, and he had an idea for me to try out. So that night I explained it to Dorothy.

"Look Dorothy, you can see the trains out your window during the day a long ways off, and when you see three big black puffs of smoke come out of one of 'em, that'll be me signalin' hi to you," I said.

Well the next day I waited for our switch engine to be called out. There were five crews workin' switch engines, to the odds were one in five we'd get called. And sure as heck we did. So what I did was widen on the firing valve and let more oil into the firebox than it could burn, and I had more black smoke than ever.

Dorothy could see it from a half mile away. And when she did, she'd rush up to the top of the Shell office building, and start waving at me. I could see her, and I answered back with more black smoke.

So our romance flourished thanks to belching black smoke. We got married a few years later.

Dutchy Luhr

In summer of '45 I was firin' for W. C. 'Dutchy' Luhr, a skinny German man so proud of his German heritage that he always wore a German sailor's hat and the F.B.I. always followed him around 'cause he was German and it was World War II.

Dutchy was a good engineer, but he thought he was the best. He had a strange idea about sanding out an engine. He only let me use six scoops of sand.

For an engine to steam free the fireman has to keep the flues scoured out. You do this by scooping sand through a peephole in the firebox door when the engine's working hard. It makes a big draft then, and the draft sucks the sand across the firebox, through the flues and out the stack, taking all the built-up soot along with it. Each scoop of sand brings out a great big cloud of soot, until there is no more soot coming out, and that's when you stop sandin'.

Well old 2568, a fine old hog, needed more than six scoops to do the job. But for reasons of his own, Dutchy didn't allow it. Consequently, old 2568 wasn't the best steamer.

The work was tiresome, but the pay was good. And after lunch Dutchy would let me run the engine for a few hours — and he'd be the fireman.

This didn't always work out so well. Because when Dutchy was fireman, he'd fall asleep. And when you're asleep, you can't work the firing valve right. Well I smoked up Shell Point so bad I couldn't even see the brakemen trying to give me hand signals.

I had to wake Dutchy up.
"Hey! Dutchy!' Wake up! I said.
He jumped, shook his head and looked at me.
"I wasn't sleeping!" he said.

A Ride Dorothy Never Forgot

One night we had a short train goin' home, and Dorothy was just getting off her shift, so we decided to sneak her on board and give her a ride home to Port Costa, eight miles away. Dutchy was in a hurry that night, and he got old 2568 really movin'!

We kept Dorothy out of sight through Martinez, since it was against the rules for unauthorized people to be on board. She sat next to me on the seatbox by the firebox, and flames would shoot out at her through the peephole on the firebox door.

After we got through Martinez, she was leanin' out the cab window like an old pro. At Port Costa we sneaked her off the engine.

It's a night Dorothy never forgot.

The Gaudy Oilcloth

Back then it was the fad to keep your timetable covered up with a bright oilcloth, the brighter the better. One morning Pappy Ovelman, a switchman, came over to me and Dutchy and showed us a brand new timetable that he had wrapped up in the gaudiest oilcloth you can imagine. Pappy was happy about it.

"When I give a signal with this here oilcloth, everyone'll know it's me," Pappy said

We never could figure out just how it happened, but one time, old 52 came by, and Pappy was on the ground giving the passenger train a rolling inspections, as was required by the rules. Well the dust settled down, and there between the rails was a crumpled piece of oil cloth.

"Look, same design as mine!" Pappy said. Then his hand went to the right rear pocket of his overalls, the traditional place for carrying timetables. As he grabbed thin air his face got longer, and longer.

"That IS mine! ... That darn 52 ran over it!" Pappy said.

And there stood Pappy, shaking his fist at the passenger train as it disappeared in the distance.

"What were like some of your best moments on the railroad?" I said.

My Best Moments On The Railroad

Well the best moments I really enjoyed is when I was on Number 12 and 19; of course 12 was The Cascade Limited. And this was in the summer of 1953 or '54, when I was in Dunsmuir, in the Shasta Division.

And we'd go up on Number 12, at eleven o'clock, out of Dunsmuir, and we'd arrive in Klamath Falls about one or one-fifteen, and then go to the little shanty they had there for the engineer and the fireman.

But the next morning, we'd get called about seven, or seven-thirty in the morning for Number 19, which was The Klamath, and it still had the GS series of 4400s on it; and I was firing for a fellow by the name of Curly Robinson. I thought he was a real slick engineer. A super engineer.

And he thought I was a good fireman.

We got along just really great.

And I think the greatest moments of my life was the three months or so that I fired Number 12 and 19.

My Big Thrill Was Getting Called For Number 19

Now Number 12 was all dieselized, so I didn't have to do anything, really, except take care of what I had to take care of on the diesel locomotive, which wasn't anything near as much as on a steam locomotive.

My big thrill was getting called for Number 19, with a big 4400 on there; that was the last days of steam, just about 1954, up in the mountains there, just about the last summer they had steam. And the passenger trains were all dieselized then.

The most pleasure was from was firing Number 19 from Klamath Falls to Dunsmuir, in July of 1954.

It was just great.

Sandin' The Engine Out

I was firin' for a fellow by the name of Curly Robinson.

I thought he was the best engineer in the world. And I hope he thought I was the best fireman; I don't know if he did.

Anyway, I was on 12 and 19, between Dunsmuir and Klamath Falls and back. Number 12 was diesel powered; that was The Cascade, and it was out of Dunsmuir about eleven-thirty at night, and we got into Klamath Falls about one-thirty in the morning.

And they have a nice little shanty right there for the engineer and the fireman right beside the track. 'Cause we were going to get called the next morning for Number 19. Number 12 was diesel powered, and we just tore up there in two hours; it was a great trip. And we'd be in bed by one-thirty. Registry in by telephone, and pile right in to a couple of bunks.

Then the callboy'd come by and call you for 19 about seven-thirty in the morning. This was in July, of 1953; and they still had steam on Number 19, 4400.

So we'd go up and have breakfast and we'd be about eight o'clock out of Klamath Falls on Number 19.

Curly, he would never say anything at all; he was just a wonderful engineer.

He'd start out, leavin' Klamath Falls right on time, when we got the highball, and I'd sand her out right away; right there.

He'd widen on it, and I'd put the sand right through the flue. And boy, the big clouds of black smoke would go out, it was dirty flues. That's the way to do it. You had to have a good draft to drag that sand right all the way across the firebox, right out the flues, and take all the soot with it. So I'd give her about fifteen scoops of sand, until no more smoke came out. Then I'd turn on the injector, and wash down the deck.

Then Curly would go to work. Boy, he'd hook up that baby by sound. I don't think he ever looked at a back-pressure gauge, I think he did it all by ear.

He'd ease down on that throttle a little bit, 'till he felt that baby start to gallop, that's what he'd do; this guy was good. Then he'd notch her up a little bit, 'till she talked back to him, just beautiful.

What's the fireman do. He turns on feedwater pump, and he sets his fire accordingly, and the old steam gauge stays there right on the pin, right at 250 pounds — 300 pounds on the 4400, right up there, right close to the 300 pound mark, within three or four pounds. Boy, we'd go tearin' across that Butte Valley, I'll tell you. It was a real pleasure. I've always heard that old expression, 'Lean your head out the window and watch the drivers roll; well, you could do it, with an engineer like that. He knew what he was doing.

And I'd lean my head out the window, and watch those drivers roll.

Curly would widen on that throttle, and I'd put the sand through the flues, to keep the flues clean. When the flues were clean, the engine fired easier. If the flues got dirty, the heat wouldn't get through, and the steam would start to drop back — you'd want to put sand through it to clean the flues.

Now they use all sorts of chemicals to clean your chimney in your house. But in those days, that was the only way you could clean the flues on a locomotive, was to have the engine working real hard; and you'd put the sand through a peep hole in the firebox door. You'd put it through in scoops. And you had a sand box right behind the tender, and a scoop. So you'd open the peep hole door, and you'd scoop the sand, and you'd very gently pour the sand down. And the engineer'd be working the engine so hard, it would suck that sand right across, through the fire, through the flames, and it would hit those flues, and it would just suck right through there, and just pull all of that soot out in a big gob. And you just keep puttin' that sand through there until there was no more big gobs — till it was just clear; when the sand came through and out and there was no change in color, the flue was clear.

You've probably seen pictures of steam engines goin' down where there'd be a big glob of black, then another big glob of black. That's the guy sandin' the engine out.

You'd sand them out about every twenty or thirty miles, to keep those flues clean.

You Had To Be Careful In July

You had to be careful in July, where you sanded out the engine. Fire. You could start the whole desert on fire.

Because, when you take a whole big scoop full of sand and take that soot right out there with it, a lot of it's still live embers.

So if it comes right down right to make a fire, you'd have one all right.

We didn't sand them out in the forest.

We sanded them out in the desert.

You're sandin' 'em out when you're leavin' town, when there's nothin' around but other tracks.

And you'd watch the wind.

If the wind was blowin' real strong, it wasn't good either; it could take the cinders over on somebody's house or somethin'.

You had all these things to watch out for.

You Could See The Sparks Coming Out Of The Flue

I'll tell you a story about a fire from cleaning out the flue on a steam engine.

I remember the sparks fallin'. You could see them come down.

It would've happened on the Western Division.

We started a fire one time leavin' Tracy.

And those are all dry hills — where the great big wind mills are now — up in there.

Boy, you could start a fire there.

We had places to sand the engines out all right, but sometimes, you sanded them out when you needed to sand them out, 'cause you weren't gettin' the steam.

And we started fires in the Altamont Hills.

A lot of times.

It's pretty windy up there.

But after all, what is there to burn?

Only the dry grass.

Well sometimes these fires would burn hundreds of acres of dry grass.

— Who's gonna put it out? By the time the word gets out, and the hill's burning up there, and the county fire department gets out there, and that sort of thing.

'Course the S.P. gets billed for whatever it costs to put the fire out.

But it was a pretty sparsely populated area. And mostly farmland, and that sort of thing. But yes, we started lots of fires on the Altamont with steam engines.

Diesels Were Worse Than Steam Engines For Starting Fires

It was the same with diesels, later on.

You weren't sandin' out diesels; they just naturally started fires.

Diesels had to have spark arrestors on them; and they do have, up to this day. You don't see them, but they're supposed to have spark arrestors on them.

The spark arrestors got all clogged up, and they weren't arresting the sparks properly, and so sparks were getting through, and landing out haywire out there, on the old dry grass.

So, we had all those problems.

The Worst Experience I Ever Had

It was on a local freight, during the war.

And it was a miserable local freight, that switched at Port Chicago, where they had that tremendous explosion in 1944, July.

Well this would have been in January of 1942 or '43.

A local freight went to work at Port Costa at five o'clock in the night; worked all night long, and tied up about five o'clock in the morning.

Worked about twelve hours, switchin' ammunition at Port Chicago.

All right.

We had to take water on the engine.

It was a cold, cold night.

A fellow by the name of Lee Beecroft was the engineer, and he said, "Okay, we're on the spot." — meaning we're not moving right now. He said, "We're goin' in to get a new switch list, now's the time we take water."

So he pulled the 2300-class engine up there, to the water spout.

It was cold. It must have been about midnight, one o'clock in the morning. It was awfully cold, a cold wind blowin' off the bay; boy it was cold, maybe 30 or 40 degrees.

So I got up on the tender, and I pulled the tank around, using a tank hook. They got a little latch up there, and they got this big long iron thing with a hook on the end of it, and you pull that latch, then the spout swings around, over the tender, and you drop the spout, into a manhole on the tank. And the spout has a little step on it; so you step on that, and push that down in there, and then you pull the rope; that starts the water flowing.

And you better be standin' on that thing, because when that force of water hits that downspout, it has a tendency to want to jump out of the manhole — so your weight holds it down in there, when the water hits the curve in the pipe, so throw it right into the tank.

Well there's a chain that holds the delivery pipe from the fountain itself, from the stand itself; and that chain allows the delivery pipe to come down just far enough to get in the manhole.

The chain broke.

That end of the pipe dropped down.

Water hit me cold in the chest.

Full blast.

Almost knocked me off the tender.

I just grabbed the manhole cover.

It knocked me off my feet.

And just drenched me, full blast! That water!

Well that made me let go of the rope; and there was a spring-loaded thing that finally shut the water off. Thank God for that.

I hollered for the engineer, "Lee! Lee! I'm wet! I'm wet!"

Well he saw what the situation was, and that quite a bit of water had gone into the tank, enough for us to get by the night.

Lee said, "Don't worry about it. Don't worry about it."

So he called the guys up there, all the crew; they came out about that time, and he said, "The fireman is soaking wet. Now here's what we're gonna do. We're gonna strip him down completely, we're gonna shut this back curtain, we're gonna shut his window, he's gonna fire the engine in the nude. While his clothes dries over the boilerhead. Don't give any signals on his side. Give

fig. 26 – *Sierra Railroad*, west of Jamestown, CA

'em all on my side," Lee said.

So okay, I stripped right down naked, not a thing on, not a thing. Shut the back curtain, shut the side window, and it was toasty warm in there. And all I had to do was fire the engine, keep water in the boiler, and a nice toasty fire.

In about an hour they were all dry. And the traumatic experience was all over. And I put on all my clothes. And they started working on both sides.

Because they needed to give signals on both sides.

Lots of times, the curve was on the fireman's side when they were switchin', and they'd come over and give signals to me, that I'd relay to the engineer, for the movement.

So that was probably the worst experience I ever had.

When that ice-cold water hit me, it was like getting punched. 'Cause you didn't expect that chain to break; it's supposed to hold that end of the pipe right there against the water tank, it's supposed to hold that just exactly right. When that chain snapped, the water came directly out of the spout and hit me in the chest.

That was probably my worst experience in terms of discomfort, and really being scared. 'Cause I thought I was going to get knocked off. If I'd'a gotten knocked and dropped ten feet to the ground, undoubtedly I would have been injured; I could'a hit my head.

An Accident

On August the 2nd, 1943, we were switchin' daylight switch engines in Port Costa, and we'd gone in and picked up about twelve cars ahead of the engine, and we're backin' out through a link from one track to another. And over on one track, opposite where we were backin' out, they were workin' on one end, and they started to shove ahead to follow that link.

I was firin' the engine backwards. I was firin' for a fellow by the name of Ralph Hudson.

I looked and my eyes got about that big; I could see those cars were gonna foul us before we got through that link! I says, 'Here they come, Ralph! Jump!' And I cleared both main lines; I jumped right out the gangway, and I cleared both main lines, clear over them. That boxcar SP 69434, an all steel boxcar, crashed the whole length of the tender and crashed right into the cab of the engine; twisted the cab, and broke all of the steam pipes in the cab, and the whistle went on halfway — that made it sound real, real mournful, a dying wail.

But Hudson didn't come out of the engine! He didn't come out. 'Oh my,' I thought, 'Ralph Hudson's killed. — and he was the greatest guy in the world.

Pretty soon he does come out.

He slides down the grab-irons on the engineer's side of the cab.

He's not dead at all. But he's just white as a ghost. And I thought, 'Jeeze. I never seen a guy that white.'

Well you know what it was?

Powdered asbestos.

From the broken pipes.

It was a heck of a wreck.

2762 was the engine. It was a hog. And it had to go to the shop. You bet we didn't see that engine for another month.

And I had a pretty badly sprained ankle. But in those days, I came back to work the next day. You just didn't try to take the company, or anything like that.

It was during the war. And there was a big effort goin' on during the war.

But it was a heck of a wreck.

It sure ruined that engine.

But they fixed it all up. Put a new cab on it. And straightened out whatever they could. And we had it back in about a month.

Another Accident

One morning ... it was Friday the 13th, too. Out at Gerber, on the second Number 20, going north. Joe Milland was the engineer. And it was a troop train. And so we had a straight shot all the way nonstop from Gerber to Dunsmuir, one-hundred-and-one miles. Except we had to slow down to twenty miles an hour, going through Redding, about eight o'clock in the morning, nine o'clock in the morning; and it was raining.

And here comes this truck.

He decides he can beat us across the crossing.

We're only doing about fifteen or twenty miles an hour.

I yell, "Hold 'em Joe!"

We hit that guy, boy. It was a semi. We hit him right at the cab. And it spun the cab right around, clear. And it threw the driver out.

He lit out there.

But he got up! He lit on his hands and knees, and he got up, and started arunnin'.

Some guy from a warehouse went out and caught him. Some of his teeth were knocked out.

We only went about four car-lengths after we hit him, and it didn't even show a dent on the engine.

If it hadn't been wet, I'm sure it would have killed the guy. But it was wet; and everything just skidded around.

All the soldiers all got out of the train. There was a big crowd around; a newspaper guy takin' notes and all that sort of thing.

So there was a big long delay.

But it didn't hurt the engine at all.

And the guy wasn't seriously hurt. Just lost a few teeth.

The Shasta Daylight

But I did have an experience on Number 10. That was The Shasta Daylight — with diesel.

I was firin' for a fellow, Earl Creason, a real nice old guy, a fine old man.

When we left Dunsmuir about one o'clock out of Dunsmuir, for Klamath Falls, Number 10. And it had the three P.A., passenger alcove, units on it.

So here we go, headin' for old Shasta Springs; windin' up there 30 m.p.h. Old Earl, he was a good engineer.

We come around the curve, right by Mossbury Falls, and I say to myself, 'Lord, here we come.,'

Right in the middle of the track, was about a ten-ton boulder.

It was the biggest boulder I ever saw.

And it got bigger, as we got closer.

Well of course, Earl, he put the train in emergency immediately. So we must have been going about 28 when we hit it, instead of 30.

We hit that boulder, and it felt to me like that engine jumped up a foot or two off the rail — it felt very much like that.

But very fortunately for us, the train did not derail. And the boulder disintegrated; but great big chunks of it went back underneath and broke all the air hoses between every unit and what was left of the boulder lodged back under the cab of the third unit, the A unit, pointing the other way.

Earl Creason got on the telephone right away. But it seemed to me it wasn't even five minutes until everybody in Dunsmuir from the general office was there. Well I don't know how the word got out so fast. There was a big crowd of people. And Mossbury Falls is pretty remote, too. But they had the section gang there, and everybody was there.

And so we were able to put new air hoses on, and connect those up between the units. And they had steam boilers back there, to run the air conditioning equipment on the train back there, portable steam boilers. The first two were knocked out; but I was able to get the third one goin' again; so the passengers had their steam heat for their coffee, and also to run the air conditioning.

We lost about two hours.

It took a lot of guys, with great big crowbars, to bring the remnants of that rock from under the third unit, to finally get it clear.

And it really wrecked the front of that engine; they had to remove the pilot.

Therefore we had restricted speed we were under and all that.

But it had got out over the air, so after we were about three hours late into Klamath Falls — there were people all along the line lookin' at the train where we had hit the boulder.

"I did have a lot of experiences, that were pretty scary all right," Dick said.

"What about the funniest thing that ever happened?" I said.

"Well a lot of funny things happened, but right off the top of my head, no particular funny thing comes up. The people on the railroad always had good senses of humor. They always liked to tell stories. And we all had funny little things that happened. A lot of funny things happened, I'm sure, if I thought through the years, I could think of a lot of funny things that happened. Let me think now," said Dick. "I remember one that I always got a kick out of."

Forgiven Taxes

One year we had forgiven income tax.
Yeah, it was during the war, probably 1943, '44.

And we had made this helper trip over the hill, Martinez Bridge, the train had stopped on the bridge, and cut away from the helper, and gone on down, and we'd gone down, and crossed over to a town called Quebec, got permission, everything cleared, so we're coming back after we helped the guy six miles over the bridge, now we have to cross over on the westbound main line, and go back to Port Costa, and start switching cars again.

Of course, we wanted to go back very slowly, y'know. We didn't want to get back into the work too quickly.

So one guy says, "How do you figure that income tax that we got forgiven? I got a piece of chalk."

So they get up on the tender, and he's figuring out, 'This is the forgiven part; and this is the unforgiven part.'

And they're writin' on top of the tender.

Finally one guy says to me, "C'mere. Does that look right to you? Does that look like the forgiven part?"

And the engineer says to me, "Hey, you're a smarty. You know quite a bit, c'mon up here."

All four guys were up on the tender. Nobody was in the cab runnin' the train. We were all back there on top of the tender with a piece of chalk figurin' out the forgiven portion of our income tax.

Finally the engineer says, "Hey! We're comin' to Martinez. Somebody better be in the cab!"

And he went on in.

Water Fights

We used to have water fights a lot of times, y'know.
Hot days, y'know.
Helping guys get over the hill, and things like that.
So they had a water box there for drinkin' water. And they also had water in the tank, back there. And you also have a squirt hose.

fig. 27 – *The Race Track Special,* at Bay Meadows

Now when you turn on the injector in the engine, to put water in the boiler, there's a squirt hose there you can wash down the deck there after you sand the engine out — but that's hot water, and you kinda have to watch that. You don't want to burn anybody.

So what happened that time, was this guy, he starts the drinkin' water. He filled up a cup of water to drink, and then he threw it on me.

And I said, "What in the heck are you doing?"

And he says, "It's hot." And he throws one on top of the engineer.

So I say to myself, 'I better get the squirt hose after that guy.'

But I didn't want to burn him.

So I run up on the tank, and the water tank is still full enough, and I dip down into the tank with a great, big one gallon bucket, and come back to throw it on this switchman who started it all.

And put up his hands and said, "Wait a minute! Wait a minute! You got 6,000 gallons of water, and I only got three in the drinking water compartment! Don't throw it!"

So he talked me out of it, and we called a truce.

We didn't get real wet.

It was hotter than heck.

Two Great Big Guys And A Firehose

One other time, talk about startin' fires again.

We were on a helper engine, pushing a train over the Martinez Bridge. From Port Costa to Martinez is three miles, and it's all brushy on the hillside, and water on the left, and brushy hillside on the right.

Well, I sanded the engine out along there, and we started a fire up on the hill.

So when we came back, it was time to go home. And the yardmaster says, "You guys started this fire; get ahold of that water car."

Now they had this water car there; a great big tank car that was just to go put out fires along the rightaway. They had that thing there. And it had a pump on it, and you had to connect it to the engine; it was a steam-driven pump.

We had a couple of great, big colored guys there; they were real good guys. Worked on the section gang.

So we coupled on to the tank car, and we go up to where it's burning along the rightaway, and these great big hefty guys are all ready, and we hook up everything there, and they get down there with this great, big hose, and both of them are holding the hose, and one of them says, "Okay, turn 'er on!"

So we turn 'er on. And Plink.

One little drop of water came out of the hose.

The pump was defective. It wouldn't work.

Here were these two great big guys holding the hose, and one little drop came out.

So we just took that baby back.

And called the county.

And they put the fire out.

It Wasn't Funny At The Time

I was firin' for Iron Mike Harold, and we had a diesel, and we were on Number 19, which was probably in 1954, in the summer. And we were comin' in to Gerber.

About four or five miles from Gerber, there was a crossing.

Here was one of those little Richfield gasoline trucks, that serviced the various Richfield stations at that particular time.

This guy had this distributorship truck. And he took the gas and the grease around to different stations.

And he was stopped all right.

Then he decided to beat us.

And we were makin' 60 m.p.h. with this train, and he pulls onto the track with this gasoline truck. He stopped right there.

And Iron Mike puts the train into emergency, which is the right thing to do — we're gonna hit this guy, we're gonna kill him, and we're liable to get killed ourselves.

It was a passenger train, and we started to stop pretty fast, much faster than you would with a freight, because freights have all that weight back there, and we didn't have that much weight. We started to slow down pretty good.

And that driver put his truck into reverse, and got off of the tracks.

Just in time.

We missed him by a couple feet.

But the last car on the train blocked him from crossing the track.

And Mike says, "Hey, did we get stopped in time to block that guy?!"

I said, "Yeah, we did, Mike."

He said, "Run back and get his name!"

The engineer tells me to run back and get his name, I'm gonna run back and get his name.

There was about fourteen cars on 19, so it was a long walk back. So I walked and ran back to the guy, and I said, "Hey, you gave us an awful scare." He didn't say a heck of a lot. And I says, "The engineer says he wants your name, address, and license number."

The guy says, "All right. All right."

And his name was Daryl Stepp, in Gerber, California. And I got the license number off the truck. Then I went back.

When we started the train up, after we got all of this information, we only had six miles to go, I could hear the wheels — some of them had locked, and flattened, CCClu-unk, CCClu-unk, CCClu-unk, CCClu-unk. So Iron Mike said, "We'll just go in slow." So we went in about 10 m.p.h. because if the flat spot on the wheel is too great, say six inches long, that means every revolution when it hits the rail, it will break the rail at that point. It'll break the rail. The CCClu-unk will break the rail.

It all depends on the length of the flat spot.

'Course these weren't long enough for that. They were probably four, four and a half inches. But at 30 to 40 m.p.h. they would.

So we go on in there, and there's always a bunch of head-end cars, baggage cars, and mail cars on the head end of Number 19, then there'd only be maybe four or five coaches, and one pullman; but the first five or six cars were baggage cars.

One of those cars had the largest flat spots on it.

It had a bunch of guinea pigs on one end of the car.

And blueberries on the other end.

When we went into emergency, the blueberries hit the guinea pigs, and the guinea pigs got loose.

Well when we opened that door, boy there was a million guinea pigs runnin' all around. And they were just absolutely swamped in blueberries.

Well you talk about a bunch of funny guys running around Gerber trying to catch them darn Guinea pigs, and they're all dripping blue berries.

Took 'em a long time to inspect that train.

Then they put a 30 m.p.h. speed limit on it, from Gerber to Oakland.

The train went into Oakland four hours late.

Just because of a guy we did not hit.

"What were some of the saddest times?" I said.

"The saddest times are like when we run over the fellow that time in the Gerber Yard. I was in the engine when we hit the fellow, and it rolled him around. It was not good. You don't like to take anybody's life. And we hit a truck driver in Redding once.

Then there was old Bill Knapke.

Old Bill Knapke

He was born in 1870.

Bill Knapke, he was a fine old man, an exceptional old man.

He lived to be ninety-nine years old before he died in Tucson, Arizona, at the Veterans Hospital.

He was a boomer.

He jumped from one railroad to another in capacities ranging from section foreman of section gangs to superintendent. I knew him very well. I never worked with him. He was retired when I met him. But I knew him for a good many years, including his last years, from about 1957 to the time he died in 1969 — he was born in 1870. I knew him for about twelve years.

All of his railroad stuff is in a book called *The Railroad Caboose*, by William Knapke, and it's a good seller, you can still get that book.

He was born in east Saint Louis in 1870. He was sixteen when he started workin' on the railroad, since 1886; and he worked on all kinds of railroads.

I have some of his letters yet, and I'm sure there's a lot of stories in those letters. I'd have to look them up. They're in the file cabinet somewhere.

And yes, I can remember a lot of his stories.

He gave me a manuscript one time entitled *Rolling Wheels*, in which his entire biography was written ... some of his stories about East Saint Louis, and the first time he ever went on a local freight.

His father was involved on the railroad too, and all his uncles, and his relatives, they were all on the railroad too; they were all railroad people.

Hey, Billy

There was about five or six different railroads runnin' into east Saint Louis, and he was fifteen or sixteen years old when the yardmaster come out and come walkin' across the yard.

"Hey, Billy," the yardmaster says.

And Knapke turned around.

"Yes sir, what is it?" he said.

"Well one of the boys just lost his finger on a coupler link and pin, would you fill in for him, and go out on that local?" the yardmaster said.

So Billy did.

Knapke had all his fingers; but I don't see how he did. 'Cause it was really somethin' all right, there was no question about it. Almost all of his friends didn't. 'Cause that was one of the way they hired people. They wouldn't hire you if you had all your fingers. They wanted you to be an experienced railroad man. You'd hold up your hand, boy, and if there wasn't a couple fingers gone, Un uh, you're not an experienced brakeman — because those link and pins, you had a great big thing you lifted up the link and pin, and then you dropped the pin down through a slot and if you got a finger in there, it was gone. It was the old link and the pin days for coupling and uncoupling. And the question was to get the link and the pin lined up properly, before you dropped the pin; and it was a very ticklish job while you were foolin' around within inches of a great deal of weight. And almost everybody lost a finger. All the old head brakemen that I remember, all lost fingers in that sort of thing. It was really pretty tough. There's no question about it.

fig. 28 – 4-4-0 American-Type engine, c. 1875; fig. 29 – 4-6-0 Ten Wheeler, c. 1885

Bill Knapke Told So Many Stories

I guess it was 1893. They came in on this old wood burning locomotive, and the operator came out and stopped the train, and he says, "Fellas we're on strike."

And he handed them Gene Debse's famous train order, that told all the guys they were on strike against the Pullman company, and not to move any engines.

Bill Knapke was on the engine that stopped at this little out of the way place, and he was the one that went in and got the orders — Bill Knapke, in 1893.

He was an old head then; he was twenty-three.

Knapke Did Tell Me This One

He dropped off the caboose to line the switch back, and the caboose was movin' pretty fast. So when he hit the ground, he did a pirouette. He went around and around, trying to keep his footing, and around and around and around, and he finally grabbed the switch stand.

A little girl was standin' down beside there watchin' him.

"Mister, would you please do that again?" she said.

He always loved to tell that story.

Then There Was Another One, When They Were Building The Dam Up At Boulder Dam

Knapke said to the engineer, "Do you know where the end of the track is, up here where they're building Boulder Dam? We're taking some cars up there."

And the engineer said, "Yeah, I do. I know where it is."

So they kept barreling along up there, and the engine's going backwards all the time, they were pulling the cars up, four or five cars, and Knapke's in a baggage car, just ahead of the engine.

So they're going along there, and Knapke says to himself, 'Jeeze, we ought to be gettin' pretty close to the end of the track.'

Now the end of the track, went right over to the edge of the dam. And they'd go right over, if they didn't get stopped in time.

Knapke looks out, and he sees a great big chunk of granite, and he recognized that as being only about five car lengths from the end of the track.

He reaches up, and he pulls the emergency cord, and the train goes into emergency, and the last truck, was just about a foot from the end of that track.

And so Knapke gets down and he says to the engineer, "Just where did you think you were going?"

"To the end of the track, of course," the engineer says.

"Come down here a minute," Knapke says.

The hoghead climbs down, and goes around the back of the tender, and he takes a look, and his eyes get big as saucers.

"You were at the end of the track," Knapke says. And he pointed over the edge of the bank, to the river below them rushing by.

And the hoghead went pale, and didn't say a thing..

The track would have sent them right down into the river.

"The last time you saw Bill Knapke, is that when he asked you to scatter his ashes?" I asked.

"What happened was, there was this superintendent whose name was Mr. McCann. And Mrs. McCann's mother was goin' with Bill Knapke. She was a widow. He was a widower. And they were kind of goin' together," Dick said.

Tucson

So McCann got transferred to Tucson, from west Oakland. McCann was a heck of a good superintendent. I liked Mr. McCann very well. I thought he was a fair, good superintendent; and Knapke thought the same thing; but Knapke wasn't workin' then, he was of course retired. He's goin' with Mrs. Burdock, which was Mrs. McCann's mother.

So they all go to Tucson. Mrs. Burdock was down there; and Mrs. McCann and Mr. McCann — they all go to Tucson.

And old Bill Knapke, that's when I got to know him. He got lonesomer, and lonesomer, and lonesomer, because Mrs. Burdock was his constant companion.

So finally he came over one day. And I always had a bottle of whiskey there when he came over. And he'd have one shot, and that would be it, never touched any more. Just one shot, but it was a good one. Then he'd chase it with water.

Anyway, he came over, and he said, "I can't stand it any longer."

I says, "Well, what are you going to do?"

And he said, "Move to Tucson. I've got to be with Mrs. Burdock. That's all there is to it."

So I said, "Okay."

So he did. He drove down there, and he got there, and he set up not very far from her, and they would drive around every afternoon and all that.

Well, one time he sent me a letter, or he may have called me on the phone, I'm not sure, and he said, "Dick, I hate to ask you this, but I want you to send a letter to the Tucson paper, and tell them you know of an old railroader, with a colorful background, that's living at such and such an address, and that he's a writer, and that he's been published in lots of places. I know this sounds terrible, but I'm lonesome down here, and I don't see Mrs. Burdock all the time, and I'd like a little publicity. I'll be honest with you."

I wrote the letter to the paper. In no time at all, they sent out a reporter out there, and he got all kinds of publicity in the Tucson paper — because he was a famous old character. He'd written a lot of stories, and he had all the proof there when the reporter went out to him, so I did him a real, real great favor.

That was about the time he started researchin' for The Railroad Caboose.

The Railroad Caboose must have first come out ... he died in '69, the book must have come out three years before that, in '66. I had one copy that I loaned, and never got back.

I forget who I loaned it to.

But I can still get it. I see it still advertised in Express Stop Books, or one of those railroad book clubs.

The King of the Rails

I got one more for you from Knapke.

He's down at Los Angeles, he's working on the L.A. division down there.

Yardmaster calls him up, and he says, "Bill, looks like we're gonna need a conductor on the local tonight. You gonna be able to make it?"

And Bill says, "If you call me before the last streetcar runs, I can make it." 'Cause he was goin' to work by streetcar then. Twelve miles, by streetcar.

"Well, we may not need you," the yardmaster says.

"Well, just remember if you do, to call me before the last streetcar's gone. 'Cause if the last streetcar's gone, I can't get there and go out on that local," Bill says.

Pretty soon the telephone rings.

"Yeah, we need you for that local I was tellin' you about," the yardmaster says.

"I think that streetcar's gone. Hold the phone a minute," Bill says. And he runs out and runs down the street, and sees here's the last markers twinkling the streetcar's gone. He runs back, "Sorry. The whole deal is off. I can't go. I haven't any other way to get there, I don't drive an automobile," Bill says. This was several years ago, of course.

"Oh, you put me in an awful spot," the yardmaster said.

"No, you put me in a spot. I told you very clearly, very very clearly, that if the streetcar was gone, then it was too late. If you wanted me for the job, you had to call me before the last streetcar left," Bill said.

"If I send a switch engine out there to get you, will you go to work then?" The yardmaster said.

"You're not going to send a yard engine out over those streetcar tracks, all the way to get me, are you?" Bill said.

"Yes. I'll send it out right away, soon as that streetcar clears the track, we'll send the switch steam engine out to get you," the yardmaster said.

So the yardmaster sent the yard goat out, and when they got there, the engineer gets down, and he takes off his hat, the fireman gets down, and he takes off his hat, and they say, "Get up there, Mr. Knapke. Anybody that can get a goat to go twelve miles out to pick him up to go to work, has to be the king of the rails.

"I didn't know you could run a yard engine on a streetcar track," I said.

"Well sure, as long as it's the same gauge, no problem at all,"

Dick said.

"Is that how they were made, the same gauge, on purpose?" I asked.

"Oh yeah, they were all four foot, eight and a half inches, you bet, sure," Dick said.

"Wasn't that unusual, or was it the same yard," I said.

"You bet it was unusual, to send the goat out."

"Well how'd they get the yard goat on that same set of tracks?" I asked.

"Interchange. There was a natural interchange there. A lot of times, there was an interchange. A lot of times, the streetcars were owned by the railroad," Dick said.

"Oh. And also so you could make drops, they kept the track all the same so they could use the same track," I said.

"Absolutely," Dick said.

"I had no idea," I said.

"Take the electrics for instance, in Los Angeles. What'd they do? They ran their local freights at night, when there was no streetcars. When the last streetcar was done, why then the local freight goes out on the track. Sure. Absolutely ... So they ran the switch engine out there. That's very unusual. And of course, the yardmaster made all the arrangements, so their wasn't any danger of any sort of thing. He got a hold of the electrics, and he said something like, 'Is that last streetcar there now? I have to use your track out there. We're gonna go out and pick up a guy, y'know.'

"That's amazing," I said. "When did Bill Knapke ask you to make those arrangements with his ashes?"

"That was when he went to Tucson," Dick said.

While The Angel Watched

Bill Knapke said to me, "Now, if anything happens to me, Mrs. McCann will make sure that you get my ashes. Now you know Bill Genner from Los Angeles, and I know Bill Genner from Los Angeles."

Now Bill Genner was an old military man, a great guy, he looked just like Douglas MacArthur — acted like Douglas MacArthur; stood at attention like Douglas MacArthur; had a strong jaw like Douglas MacArthur; and I think he talked more

fig. 30 — *4-8-2 Mountain-Type*, 1934; fig. 31 — *El Governor*, *4-10-0*, 1860-1903

than Douglas MacArthur.

Anyway, why sure enough, here comes a telegram one day — Knapke passed away last night, Veterans Hospital, ashes comin' under separate cover — something like that.

So it isn't too long until, sure enough, here come the ashes.

The funny part about it is, and the glorious part about it in a way was, apparently, at the crematorium, they didn't use enough atomizer to actually make them ashes — there was pieces of bone, rattlin' in this tin. About a time and a half bigger than a cigar box ... take a cigar box and make it half again as big, and that was filled with ashes, and they rattled, they rattled.

And I was married to Dorothy then, my ex-wife, Dorothy didn't think we should have ashes around.

I tried to hide the ashes in the linen closet, and I heard her scream one day, so I had to move the ashes. She'd found them under a pile of sheets; and she failed to have a sense of humor on that one. So we lost that one.

So then I hid them out in the garage; and she found them out there. Then I hid them around.

But the idea was, that Mr. Bill Genner and I were to go, where Bill Knapke had this experience, where he saved a train in 1915 from a terrible collision down there, at a place called Garnet; used to be old Palm Springs siding, but now its Garnet siding. And it's down there not very far from Palm Springs.

What happened was, Bill was on the local freight, and some cars got away, and were running down the hill, and they were goin' down in the face of a passenger train.

And so he chased them down with his local freight engine, and caught the cars, brought them back up, and shoved them in the siding just before the passenger train, come roarin' by.

So he went in to talk to the operator at that particular station, Garnet, or Palm Springs.

"I'm going to take this to heaven with me ... ... We just saved a train, and stopped a major, major disaster ... I'm gonna take this to heaven with me," Knapke said.

Now, over in those mountains, the San Jacinto Mountains, when this one crevice filled up with snow, it looked like an angel, with her arms spread. So, it had all happened, while the angel watched, Bill would say.

Anyway, Bill Genner and I drove out there one day in May,

1969; 'cause Knapke had died in February of '69, so it was in May of '69 that we drove out there with the ashes.

And it was blowin' like the devil.

Here we are in May. And the night before that, a freak storm come along. And by golly, old Genner, he points like old MacArthur, he points over there, and he says, "Take a look at that. Look at that. The angel's watchin'. Just like Knapke said — 'While the angel watched'."

The angel was watching the night Bill Knapke went down and got those runaway cars and pulled them in the clear before the passenger train came along.

So it was the same situation.

"Okay Bill, let's spread these ashes," I says.

"Well, okay," Genner says.

So we unwrap the box, and the tin box is soldered shut.

"Well how we gonna spread these ashes?" I said.

"First, let's have a beer … … … To our old friend, Bill Knapke," Genner said.

"Now, how do we get the box open?" I say.

So he goes along the siding there, and finally comes back, and holds something up in his hand

"Railroad spike," Genner says.

And using the railroad spike, we were able to break the solder joints.

"Where should we scatter him," I said.

"Well, we're in the siding right now, where Knapke brought the cars back, and pushed them in the clear in time for the passenger train to roar by. So why don't you scatter them from here, about 200 yards right down to the main line switch. That should do it," Genner says.

"Bill, the wind is blowing very hard. Do you think that Bill Knapke will be here very long when we get all these ashes spread?" I said.

And he takes the box and shakes it, and we hear, Rattle rattle rattle …

"Some of him will," Genner says.

So we went along, and when the box was open, we went along and scattered him, just shook the box a little, tilted it a little, shook it, and I walked the whole 200 yards.

Bill Knapke's still there.

I'll tell you, there was very, very, very few fine ashes ... most of them were joints — bones, and that sort of thing.

So Bill Knapke is there.

While the angel watched.

And at the exact location he saved the train by grabbin' the runaway cars and pushin' them into the siding — in 1916.

"You must have been cryin' your eyes out," I said.

"Awww, it was a sad deal, it was a sad deal. But we wanted Knapke where he wanted to be, and with his two friends. Because he liked this Bill Genner fella; and I liked him too. Bill Genner was a walking encyclopedia. I felt like an idiot around the fella, he knew so much. And he could go back and he could quote things from the Bible, he could quote things from the classics, that I hadn't even read in my lifetime. But he was still a lot of fun to be around, and a real good Joe, and he had a good sense of humor; and he and Knapke had hit it off great — when they were alive; and they saw each other quite often.

"Can I ask you two questions real quick?" I said.

"Sure," Dick said.

"These two runaway boxcars were going down the hill, and he was in back of them, up the hill?" I said.

"He was up the hill when they got away."

"How did he get them?"

"Chase them down the hill."

"Did they stop, and then he moved them?"

"No. He coupled on to them on the fly."

"That's what I want to hear about," I said.

"He coupled on to them on the fly, and then he stopped the engine," Dick said.

"So the couplings were open?"

"Well, one of them has to be open; they don't both have to be open. The idea is, the joint was made. You could've kept hittin' 'em, and pushin' em and makin' 'em go faster and faster — if the joint didn't make; but the joint made.

"He caught the cars; they were gondolas."

"Well then he must have caught up to them, then accelerated from a ways back?" I said.

"He hit them and coupled them; then he stopped; then he

reversed the train, pulled 'em back up the hill; then shoved them into the siding, before the passenger train roared by.

"Now as I recall that was non-block territory, so it wasn't governed by block signals yet — they came under, what was called, train-order territory. So the passenger train had no indication that the main line was blocked. So the idea was to get those cars in the clear before the passenger train was due — and he was very close to due.

"As a matter of fact, as I think I recall him tellin' me the story, when they shoved the cars onto the siding, the headlight of the passenger train came into view down the line. So he was close.

"That's why he wanted to take that story to heaven with him.

"He wanted the Lord to see what he had done.

"So, he did. He got to take it with him," Dick said.

"That was really nice of you to do that. It was probably one of the more holier moments in your life, I bet," I said.

"Yes it was. Because we had to go all the way to Los Angeles to do that. He'd died in February, and we didn't get down there till late May, May the 28th or 29th — I'm not sure, the afternoon that we did that.

"The sort of mystic thing about the whole thing, that gives you a feeling of reverence, was the fact that the angel had dusted herself with snow, so you could see her.

"While the angel watched.

"She was just as pretty as she could be.

"That crevice was just as pretty as we could see.

"I have a picture somewhere, that Knapke gave me, about that."

One of the Prettiest Curves

One of the curves that's the prettiest is comin' west out of Dunsmuir and down the hill into Redding.

There's a high trestle at Redding, a real high trestle on the approach.

And as you come down, the curve is to the left, goin' west towards Redding and Red Bluff, and the latter part of that trestle is on a curve.

Below you, is the Sacramento River.

It's just beautiful.
Below you is a nice big recreational park.
The trestle is at least a half a mile long.
Big long trestle with a sweeping left curve.
Then you come right in to Redding just so nice.
It's really a beautiful curve.
I always liked that curve, very very well.
It's impressive right there.

The Curve at Lake Shasta in the Moonlight

Another curve that I liked really well, was at Lakehead, California.

Lakehead, is at the head of Lake Shasta.

Going north, or east as it would be, railroad east — but actually north, comin' in to Lakehead, you have a beautiful curve that crosses the Sacramento River arm of Shasta Lake.

Nice big sweeping curve, coming in there, that I always liked.

And it's very good coming the other way too.

It was pretty exciting. The lake was right there. We'd watch the level of Shasta Lake.

Most of the time we'd come through at night, a lot of times in moonlight.

More About The Old Days

They always ran more freight trains at night than anything you know, not too many during the day. They had to stay in the clear of the passenger trains. The passenger trains were supposed to have priority — that priority kind of slipped away during the years; 'cause the freight trains is where the revenue is. And a lot of the time, they put the passenger trains into the siding, y'know, but that was at the end. In the old days, when the first class trains were first class trains, they had the freight trains in the clear, and the passenger trains made their schedule.

That was in the days when there was a good rapport between the working people and the officers of the railroad.

It was really wonderful in those days. I think that the officers

fig. 32 — 4-6-6-4, used in Nevada flatlands; fig. 33 — 2-8-8-2, as big as they get 131

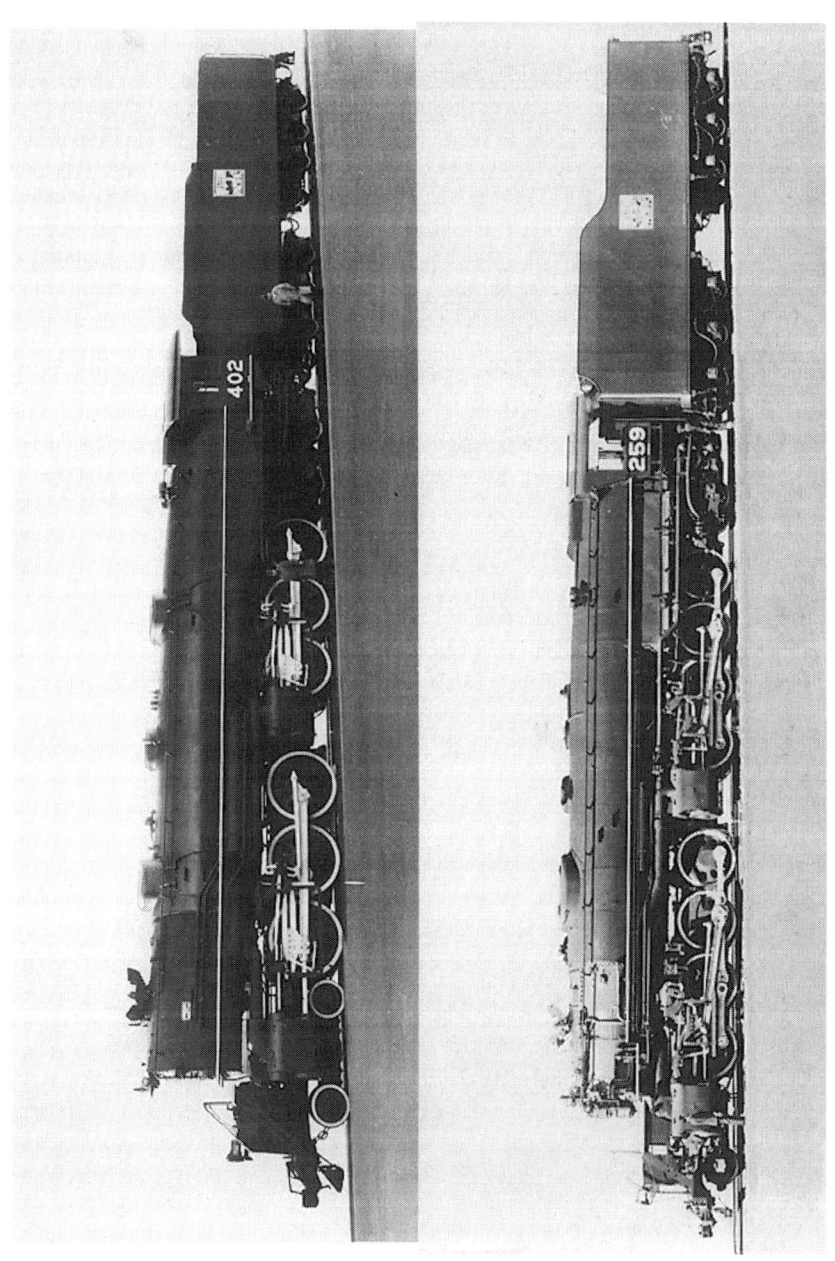

were very very important. The psychological gap between labor and management wasn't very wide at that time. A lot of the officers had come up through the ranks. And they knew what the railroad men were up against. And they knew how tough it was sometimes, and how easy it was to get into a situation, or to get into trouble.

Fellows like Max Howard, from Port Costa. Now he's still alive, Max is. But he was a great officer; 'cause he was a conductor first, then he finally became an assistant trainmaster, and then a trainmaster. And as a trainmaster, he could tell, just by talking to you, what the heck happened. And he was very tolerant.

He'd cover for you if he could. If he could. If he couldn't cover for you, 'cause the accident was too bad, or the derailment was too bad, why then he wouldn't. He'd say, "I can't. There'll be an investigation. We'll get you the best representative we can, and we'll go as easy on you as we can. But this time I can't cover for you. You know, when I can cover for you, I do."

Max Howard

Now this one time, I was with Max Howard out at Avon.
Somebody had thrown a switch, and forgot to throw it back.
So when we started to leave town, all the cars went all over the ground — about five or six heavy oil tankcars were derailed on the main line at Avon.

Well it wasn't my fault, because I hadn't known someone'd thrown the switch and forgot to throw the switch back. And we were all lined up on the main line to go, and the switch was wrong, so half the train started up the siding, and the other half went down the main line — that puts cars on the ground.

"Well wait a minute now. How could you, if the switch was already thrown, I mean, you started over it, and somebody threw it in the middle ... I mean, if you were already goin' one way, what was it, was the switch just bouncin' back and forth, and it decided to set the other way, is that what happened?" I said.

"Yes, that's what happened. About three or four cars and the engine were on the main line past the switch. And the switch was lined so when the train started to move, the switch was lined for the siding, and those cars that were behind that point, started to go up the siding, while the engine and the three cars were okay. So what do you do? — you pull the train apart; and it derailed the cars started up the siding," Dick said.

"You mean you were already parked there, and somebody threw it?" I said.

"Oh yeah. We were all ready to go, waiting for train orders."

"So somebody threw it in the middle of the train?"

"I don't know how the switch got thrown in the middle of the train; but it was. 'Cause we were stopped on the main line, had our air tested and everything, time to go back to Pittsburg and tie up. We started to move, and there was a big rumpus back there.

"Max Howard came out there, and we all got together, and we got those cars re-railed and everything, and he said, 'Don't worry about the switch. I'll get a guy out here to fix the switch' and everything. And there'll be nothin' said about it.'

I should've gotten fired; or somebody would'a gotten fired.

There would have been a big investigation.

He was able to cover it all up."

"What was it like when diesel started taking over steam?" I said.

1948

By 1948 we were aware of changes beginning on the railroad. The first freight diesels were arriving. S.P. like many roads, considered diesels superior. There was great savings in water and maintenance and manpower. Steam engines needed soft water to be most efficient — it was a constant battle to keep the boilers clean. A big steamer could boil away up to 20,000 gallons of water in a hundred miles; more in the mountains. Diesels, like automobiles, needed no additional water once their radiators were full. And whereas a train requiring six or eight steam engines needed an engineer and a fireman for each train, diesels could run in series, with up to six or eight units electrically connected together to respond to the touch of a single engineer in the cab of the lead unit. S.P. had purchased their final steam locomotive four years earlier, a cab-first Mallet 4294 — it's on display at the

California State Railroad Museum in Sacramento.

In the early '50s the phasing-out of steam power was in full swing. As more and more shiny new diesels appeared, fewer steamers were seen. Those that were still in use were patched up just to get by until they'd be replaced. There was an all-out campaign to get rid of firemen, because diesels "... had no fires to tend." Firemen with low seniority lost more and more job security every day. Those who stayed start showin' up to work wearing slacks instead of overalls — diesels were much cleaner.

Los Medanos siding east of Pittsburg was in the late '50s a collecting track for retired steam locomotives. They were sold to U.S. Steel for scrap. I was sad to see those old freight and passenger engines doomed to the cutting torch.

It had been the job of both hoghead and fireman to get their trains over the road fast and safe. It was a sign of disgrace to be hauled in by another engine. If there were breakdowns, we made emergency repairs on the road. Such pride was inherent in steam, and was not transferable to diesel.

Black Widows in the March of '51

I traded seniority rights with a Shasta Division fireman and moved to Dunsmuir Even though new 4-unit EMD 'Black Widows' came in ever day, there was still a lot of big steam power around. I was firing freight and passenger. My first winter there I took a hostling job and then I got to handle the Mallets, and the Decapods, the Mikados, Pacifics, Consolidations, Mountain-Type 4300's, General Service 4-8-4's, and 3-cylinder 5000's. After five years, Dunsmuir was completely dieselized. I had to leave Dunsmuir, and returned to the Western Division. At that time there still was steam at Oakland, Port Costa and Pittsburg ... that means I had to watch steam fade into history twice on the same railroad.

Between 1955 and 1960 I ran my last steam engines; and suddenly they were all gone. The only places you could find 'em were in city parks. Old Port Costa was closed down as a switching yard; the roundhouse and the other buildings were torn down; the water tanks were removed; and the turntable pit was filled in with dirt and concrete.

With my seniority I could work the engineer's extra list out of West Oakland during the summer. Other times I fired local freights in and around Pittsburg. On- and off-duty times were changed and work was shifted to get the most out of existing crews.

Soon firemen were all but eliminated. There were lots of experienced men, who would've been engineers later down the line, who got ruthlessly swept aside. Since then S.P. needed to backtrack and recruit people for their locomotive simulator training program.

With diesels you got longer, heavier trains, one-hundred-forty cars or more. This made some traffic problems at crossings in busy areas all over the U.S. There was a compounded delay when if, for reasons unknown, there was an emergency application of air brakes. Rules require that the brakemen walk the entire length of the train and inspect the cars; and if it's one-hundred-sixty cars, they can stretch for two miles, across many a crossing. Even with lots of automobile drivers honking, you can't move that train one inch until the train is inspected and the air is restored, and everyone's in the clear and you get the brakemen's signals to move.

My railroad career ended Memorial Day 1978. I made what might have been the shortest run in history — one hour and twenty-five minutes — we covered a hundred feet! We had ten SD-45 diesels and a caboose ready to leave the West Oakland diesel shop, but we couldn't, because there was a railroad wreck up the line.

I climbed down out of the cab. I looked back up at the crew I was leavin' behind.

"I'm retirin'," I said.

"If you had to do it all over again, would you change anything?" I said.

Dick replied. "Nothing on the railroad. I wish the railroad hadn't changed, as it had changed. I wished that steam engines would've lasted longer, 'cause I loved those much better than the diesels, much better. Diesels were warmer, they were cleaner, they were a Godsend to those engineers who were not good engineers; steam engines really bothered 'em. But to us people, to us who really loved steam engines, and loved to have them talk back

to us, we hated to see the demise of the steam engine.
"To this day, I resent that demise."

◊   ◊   ◊

Dick Murdock Talkin' Shop To The Western Pacific Railroad Club

Here's the gist of a short talk by Dick Murdock with some comments from his friend, a fellow steam and diesel engineer, Bob Moulton, followed by a question and answer period with some of the members of the Western Pacific Railroad Club of Northern California.

I did have a great deal of experience on steam locomotives. I hired out as a fireman September 6, 1941, in Oakland. I got promoted to an engineer, December 6, 1952. But I never really got to runnin' steam until I came back to the Western Division, the Shasta Division. And I did a lot of runnin' steam right up to its demise, in 1957.

In 1941, when I hired out, I stayed on the Western Division until 1951. Then I went to Dunsmuir, and I had a wonderful time. And while I was in California I was firing passenger and freight trains between Oakland and Roseville and Oakland and San Francisco, and Oakland to Gerber in passenger.

I was on the Port Costa switch engine for a long time.

I gathered a bunch of stuff from the old switchmen; they had worked when the train ferry boats were there — between Benicia and Port Costa, before they built the bridge in 1930. And so those old guys, there were when-the-boats-were-here-men.

"Say an engine goes in the round house for a day; and then it comes out at night. How long can you leave an engine — do you keep it warm?"

"All right. Hostler puts it in there and kills the fire. Then they've got a fire-lighter around. And if you've got a lot of engines in the roundhouse, he'll go around and watch every one of them. When the steam gets down around 80 or 90 pounds, he'll usually build the fire up, and get it right up to poppin'; then close her down again, and she'll stay for another five, six, seven hours depending what shape the engine's in and how bad it's leakin'," Dick said.

"Then if you've got an eight hour or twelve hour gap, you'd never let them cool down?"

"Not completely. That's what the firelighter's for at the roundhouse, to keep 'em goin'. 'Cause they have steam lines to 'em, even if they did go dead. In Dunsmuir they had a fire-lighter, and he kept the steam up in all of the engines.

"In terms of the ride that you get in the cab, how much of it is the locomotive, and how much of it is the track bed you're running over?"

"I found out that the locomotives had personalities, and if they came out of the shop as a rough rider, they were a rough rider. And if the track was bad, and if you got the combination together, boy, you had a rough ride — when you got in, you were just beat to pieces. Other engines seemed to hold their original riding qualities, even if they went into the back shop and came out again, they seemed to maintain their original riding qualities — maybe it had to do with the manufacturer of the frame and boxes and all that; but they seemed to do that. Now let's take the 4218 — now that was a good-ridin' cab-first Malley. Everybody wanted to catch the 4218; it steamed easy; it rode good; it didn't pound at high speeds like some of them did; it seemed to keep that personality regardless of the shape it was in. Everybody wanted the 4218, 'Oh boy, we got the 4218.' It was a nice ridin' engine, all the way to Gerber.

"Not so with the 4294 though — she was a rough ridin' devil from the word go. I never had a good ride on the 4294. Every time I caught the 4294, I thought, 'Oh boy, my guts are gonna ache when I get to Dunsmuir; and they did," Dick said.

"Every engine had its own individuality. Some fired differently. Some rode differently. You got to know their characteristics, and as soon as you found out, you were all right. But some of those engines, they never did ride smooth. They'd knock you off the seat box," Bob said.

"Those little consolidations, the 2-8-0's; they were not good ridin', they went *Chunn Chunnn Chunn Chunn*.

"Did you have any derailments or accidents in your days?"

"I'll let you take that one, Bob," Dick said.

"On the road I was fortunate. I never scattered 'em on the road. Many fellas did. Burnt journals, or something like that. But I just considered myself lucky, that's all. As a matter of fact, I was on a hot shot one night goin' east; it was a pig train. And fortunately, the operator at Stockton, the foreman, was on the job. The pigs, all of them, had journal bearings on 'em. But this particular car, was bouncin' pretty bad. And he got on the radio, and he said, 'Bob, you better stop. You got trouble back there.' That car wouldn't gone another mile. As a matter of fact, when the brakey set the car out, he was afraid to shove it over the turnout, there was so much lateral movement in the wheel. A good journal is on the average about six inches thick — this journal was about two inches thick, just ready to break.

"That's how fortunate I was.

"But some of the other guys weren't.

"One guy told me one time, 'I had a set-out the other day.'

I said, 'Why the heck don't you do it where there's a siding?'

— he'd set out about twenty cars over the bank, because of a burnt journal. One of 'em had burnt out, right in the middle of the train.

"And it's no fun if you're draggin' a-hundred-and-fifty cars when you can't see down the valley fog," Bob said.

"Did you ever have anybody in a caboose that was quite a ways back that got knocked on his can on a long train, unexpectedly?" a club member said.

"Was there ever a trip you didn't?" Dick said.

"How come they didn't put the crew up closer to the front?"

"Well the idea was to watch the train. That's what the caboose was for. Those guys, every time you had to stop, they had to walk forward the length of the train, and the head man had to walk it back. It was just a protective measure," Dick said.

"Did it ever happen say when you're coming down a grade, say, cars are together; then you start up a grade, and catch a guy unawares?"

Deadheadin' In The Caboose While Drifting Through a Place Called Escolat

We were deadheadin' back there in the caboose, and this particular conductor we had, he was a noisy guy, talked all the time.

We were about sixty cars back.

He was complaining about the rough handling and everything else.

Well the ride was all right, the hoghead was a good hoghead, the ride was smooth; me and the other deadheads, we didn't see anything wrong with it.

Well we headed into a siding, at a place called Escolat; and we were just drifting through at about three or four miles an hour. And all of a sudden, the slack came in — and this conductor was busy spoutin' off.

Well that slack hit and just flipped him off his feet, and upside-down.

Then he got up on his feet and he said, Darn it! See what I mean?!'

"Doesn't the slack hitting ever tear a car apart?"
"Sure. It'll pull cars apart, easy."

"Respirators. Bob, did you have respirators," Dick said.
"Sometimes we wish when we got those 1600's and the 900 class up there for helpers, we wished we had; because they were big boilin' affairs ... they filled the tunnel — there was no room for smoke or anything; there was no room for air. The cabs would fill up with smoke. We used to come out of those tunnels just ringing wet," Bob said.
"Oh absolutely, absolutely," Dick said.
"Where was that, up in Dunsmuir," a club member asked.
"Over at Twin Frazier, across the bay here. Out of Richmond," Bob said.

"Well if you're goin' through a long tunnel, and you only have on like one Malley, doesn't it help 'cause the cab's in the front, and the smoke stack is in the back," a ten year old member said, who had come with his father.

"Oh it does, absolutely. That's why they put the cab up front, and you didn't have anything to worry about. If you had a seventy-four car freight train, with just one Malley, why there was nothin' to worry about; all the smoke's behind you.

"That's one of the reasons they put the cab in front," Dick said.

"When the smoke came in the cab, after you closed the windows, did the same thing happen to the passengers," the ten year old member said.

"If they don't have their windows closed. Yes, sometimes smoke would get in the passenger cars. But generally speaking, no. Because the passenger trains moved fast enough, and all the windows were closed, and the air conditioning's on the train. Like on the Shasta Daylight, you wouldn't have no problems with smoke, they was diesels anyway, Dick said.

"How come they didn't put the cabs in front sooner; when did they do that?" an older club member said.

"1910 was the first one, on the S.P. They started out with some 3900's, that didn't have the cab in front. Then they let the employees vote on whether or not they wanted to try a cab first, so they did. And it worked out so well, that they had a whole slug of them by the time they got through," Dick said.

"So they kept them where there was big tunnels and stuff," a member said.

"Yeah. That was one of the reasons for them; that's why Sacramento Division had most of the cab-firsts.

"What they'd do, is they had a situation where they ran from Roseville, to Dunsmuir, and they would use Sacramento Division Malleys; but they couldn't use those Malleys, those cab-firsts, beyond Dunsmuir; they had some that belonged to the Shasta Division that could go up to Grass Lake and up to Klamath Falls. But anyone that was assigned to the Sacramento Division, could only go as far as Dunsmuir.

Archy Livingston

There was a fella up there with the name of Archy Livingston. He was a nice guy. Everybody loved him.

But he was a terrible engineer in the mountains. Old Archy Livingston, he was afraid of his own shadow, and he couldn't handle a train good.

And old Jack Peterson, the road foreman of engines, he was a mean old guy, and he felt like, 'Boy, I'm going to get rid of that Archy Livingston.'

He rode that guy — he was climbin' on the engines at the darndest times; he was eatin' on Archy's tailbone all the time.

Finally poor old Archy had enough of that.

So he went in one day, he went in and he rapped at the road foreman's place to see Jack Peterson; and Jack Peterson was there. Archy said, "Mr. Peterson, I'd like to talk to you."

And Jack said, "Well what is it now Archy?!!! What did you do now?!!!"

And Archy says, "Well, I've had enough. You're on my back all the time. You're ridin' me, you get on in the night, I can't make a good trip because I'm always afraid you're gonna get on. I can't take it any more. Here's my rule book. Here's my switch key. I quit."

Old Jack sat there for a long time, and finally he looked at him and said, "I won't bother you any more. Maybe that's the trouble, maybe that's the trouble. You just try a little harder, pick up that rule book, pick up those keys, and I won't bother you any more."

By golly, he didn't.

So Archy got a little better. And he got by all through the years after that.

That poor old guy was just ready to throw in the sponge.

Dunsmuir In Tunnels Full Of Smoke

Up in Dunsmuir, Number 20 needed a helper. They sent him down from Dunsmuir to Redding; and they'd usually put the helper on the point. So if they put the helper on the point, and I was the regular fireman on Number 20, then that meant that I was on the 4400 — second out.

We had a 3700 on the point and a 4400 and a twelve or fourteen car old heavy equipment train. Okay. There's a lot of tunnels from Gray Rock, where you cross Shasta Lake, all the way to Dunsmuir — about thirteen tunnels; some of them may have been daylighted by now, but back then they were fast track all right.

But, boy oh boy, those tunnels — the smoke you'd get from both engines, right back into the cab. So what do you do?

When you're comin' to a tunnel, the first thing you do, say if it's a hot summer day, you take off your jacket, and you take it over to the water box, and you wet the jacket down all over real real good. Wet the jacket down. Then you had a respirator; it looked like a funnel. And it came directly from the air, and it had a sponge in it. You'd wet that little sponge on the respirator, and then you had an air valve, and you'd turn the air on, and it would sprinkle that water in your face — when you held it over your face.

Okay. When you came to the tunnel, you'd shut the cab windows, and you'd shut the storm curtain in the back, close up the cab as tight as you could, to keep that hot smoke out of there if you possibly could.

Adjust your fire. Adjust everything, before the tunnel.

Then you'd get down off the seat, and you'd sit on the floor, on the deck; and you'd put this wet coat over your head, and you'd turn on the respirator ... and you'd pray.

And your ears would get hot.

And your neck would get hot.

And you'd start sweatin'.

And you'd get the claustrophobia.

And if you screamed, it wouldn't make no difference, you couldn't hear yourself scream anyway.

And then, okay, it's just a short distance between one tunnel and the next. So what do you do? You throw the coat off, wet it down real quick, turn the respirator off, open the window, gasp the fresh air, 'Ahhh! Ahhhh! Ahhh!' — then comes the tunnel! — Shut the window, wet the coat, put the coat back on, get down on the floor!!! ... You do that thirteen times, by the time you got to Dunsmuir, your ears were singed, and your face was black, and you were as tired as heck, and you were ready for bed."

It sounds funny, but it wasn't.

The second locomotive got it worse than the first.

And I was in the second one! 'Cause they put the helper on the front. The 3700, they put him on the front, and we were the second engine.

It wasn't as bad if there was just one locomotive ... you could make it through without goin' through all that; but suppose you're in freight service — the train's slower, heavier, and longer; then it takes you longer to get through the tunnel.

That's for sure. Boy, there's a couple of tunnels ...

If you ever stalled, then there's only one thing you can do. And that's to get down low on your hands and knees, and try to crawl out of the tunnel — if you ever stalled in there.

Get down where the fresh air is, if there is any at all, it's down there on the ground, as close as you can get. That never happened to me.

But it had happened to quite a few guys up there in Dunsmuir. I came very close, with a cab-first one time; but that isn't so bad. For one reason, because the cab is in the front. So you had the fresh air in front of you. But the poor guy in the second engine, if you're behind a cab-first, and you're the second engine, and you've got a boiler engine, then you're gettin' smoke from both of them in that one.

It's tough. It was really tough.

The engineer gets down the same way as the fireman; you'd have the engineer and fireman both gettin' down the same way.

You bet, boy. He'd have the throttle set and everything. He wasn't going to sit up in that seat box — you couldn't see anything in the cab anyway, except the lights were on. But smoke got in and filled up the cab anyway. You kept out all that you could possibly keep out; but it got hotter than heck in there. The reason the engineer got down was because he wanted to get his head protected too. So he had a wet coat over his head too. And he had his respirator on too.

So those tunnels were a real toughie. You didn't look forward to havin' to go through all of those tunnels, using that respirator; and some of those tunnels weren't very far apart. You just had time to manipulate the valves, wet the coat down, and to do it again. This was in '51 to '55.

At The Old Rails Club in Oakland

The other day I was down to the Old Rails Club, in Oakland. Bob's been down there several times. We meet on the second Tuesday of every month. A fellow by the name of Dave Steph was down there. He's a retired man out of the diesel shop.

And he says, "Hey! Look at this old magazine."

And he had a railroad magazine there from May of 1952.

He says, "Boy oh boy, there's one of the best stories in here. It's really good."

And he opens the magazine, and shows it to me and says, "It's called Mountain Hogger, it's really good, you ought to read it sometime."

I said, "Well, who wrote it?"

And he said, "YOU DID!"

I thought he was going to fall off the stool.

He went clear around the room sayin', 'Hey! This guy wrote this in 1952!'

It was called Mountain Hogger; it was about a guy who trained in the mountains.

It was autobiographical, a lot of it. I must have sold about thirty stories to railroad magazine, over the years, before its demise.

Grant Allen — (born 1897)

The Oldest Living Rail & Last Of The Old Time Boomers

Started Out in 1915 as a Telegraphing Dispatcher for the Atchison, Topeka and Santa Fe Railway and Finished Up 50 Years Later as Superintendent of Transportation of Western Pacific Railway, 1952-1963

During a 50-Year Railroad Career A Telegrapher Who is a Boomer Cut Off About Six Times a Year for Ten Years Also Works as a Car Distributor, Train Dispatcher, Track Gang Laborer, Inspector, Timekeeper, Brakeman, Trainmaster and Raises the Ante as Chief Dispatcher, Trainmaster and Assistant Superintendent for the Six Companies Railroad Building Boulder Dam, then as Superintendent of the Indian Valley Railroad, then as Superintendent of Transportation for Western Pacific Railroad.

The Work Record of Grant Sherwood Allen

"Gosh. Look at all these jobs you've had; telegrapher, car distributor, dispatcher; assistant trainmaster, chief trainmaster; assistant superintendent; superintendent; you've had a lot of responsibility," I said.

"Yep ... ... I think one of the things you might be most interested in, is my work record," said Grant Allen.

"1913? Is that when you started," I said.

"Yeah. Seventeen years old," Grant said.

"How old are you now?"

"Ninety-three. I was born December 9, 1897, in Indiana."

"My grandfather was a captain in General Grant's army; and my grandfather's the one who gave me my name, 'Grant.'

"My dad started to teach me to telegraph when I was seven years old. So by the time I was seventeen, I was a first-class telegrapher, sendin' telegraph, for the railroad.

"Yes. I'm a telegrapher — Morse, sendin' from station to station, from one office to another.

"That's right.

"Then I became a train dispatcher.

"Those initials in my work record by the name of the divisions is the office calls," Grant said.

"It looks like from when you were seventeen, in 1915, for about four years, at Atchison, Topeka and Santa Fe, you were sendin' telegraph," I said.

"I started working in Illinois, in 1913. That was on the Illinois Division of the Atchison, Topeka and Santa Fe. The first place where I went to work, was Cole City, Illinois. About fifty-nine miles southwest of Chicago."

"What kind of engines did they use?"

"All steam. I remember a lot of the Atlantic types, 4-4-2's; there was going to be a lot of years before they got diesels." Grant said.

"Do you any photographs of yourself at different jobs in your career, trains, or anything, a collection, or anything like that?" I said.

"Well, let's see. I think so," Grant said.

"Maybe you'd let me use a couple of them."

"Yeah. That's right. Sure."

"On your work history, where you have like the 'Z' Galveston, is that the name of the train or something?"

"No. That's the call of the telegraph office at that place. That's the call ... . If you are in Topeka — 'GO'; and you want to call Galveston, you call 'Z' — that's Galveston. And of course, those calls answer, down there, see?

"I was chief telegrapher."

1918 or 1919

"I met my first wife, at a station twenty-four miles east of Needles. And she had gone to telegraph school in Los Angeles; and learned to handle train orders, over the telegraph. So there were two girls workin' out at this place, and for kicks, I used to go out on the motorcar, with the lineman.

And they gave us some lunch, and when we got up to leave, I had my hand on the motorcar; she reached over and squeezed

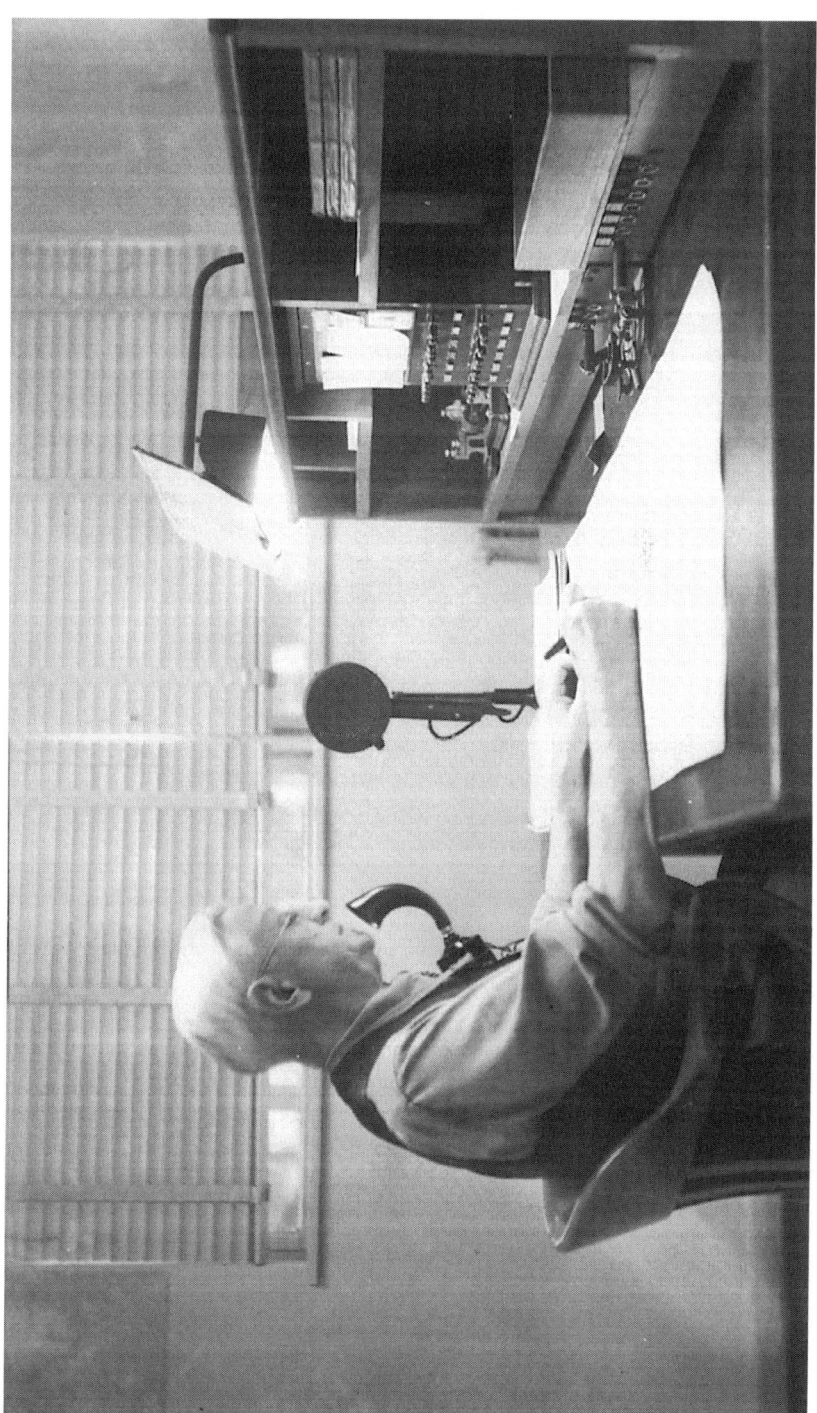
fig. 34 – a dispatcher's centralized traffic control board for a 119-mile subdivision

my hand, and that did it.

"When you said you used to ride around on a motorcar, you mean an automobile?" I said.

"No, no, no. A track motorcar!

"What's that?"

"It had four wheels on it, and a motor, and you could ride on the tracks, sure; it operated on the tracks," Grant said.

"A little gasoline engine?"

"That's right."

"I don't know if I've ever seen one of those. Did you used to examine the track on those?" I said.

"No. It was the lineman, he was checking the telegraph line. And I just rode with him," Grant said.

"Oh. I see. 'Cause sometimes the lines wouldn't work? Or they were down?"

"Oh yeah. They had broken insulators, or something like that; he'd have to fix 'em; stop and fix 'em."

"Must be hard to find them, to spot 'em," I said.

"Well he could spot 'em. That was his business," Grant said. "But anyway, you see, what happened was, my wife was not a full-time telegrapher yet. I helped her with that. But anyway, there was two jobs came open at Gadpie, end of the double-track out of Silligman, and I talked with the chief dispatcher.

'Can me and my wife have those two jobs?' I said.

'Ecch! No. You're too good an operator to waste on a job like that,' he says.

'Well you're going to get along without this very good operator, because we're leavin',' I said.

"And the reason we went to Salt Lake, was there was contracts — and if you bid a job in, why, then, you got it," Grant said.

"So you were in Salt Lake. According to your work history, you were twenty," I said.

"Uh huh."

"So then you moved to Salt Lake. In 1919. That's a pretty big move, isn't it, from Illinois to Utah?"

"Yeah."

"How come? How come you moved?"

"Because the Santa Fe was an unfair railroad," Grant said.

"It was?"

"Yeah ... you had to sign a Yellow Dog contract. So if you

belonged to a union, you're gonna get fired."

This is the story no boomer can match. I got cut off one job every winter, and I found another job to get that was by the border oil boom near Amarillo, Texas.

I got that job down there, so I worked my last day here from midnight to eight o'clock in the morning — I left Salt Lake in the morning; to get to Amarillo, I had to go from Salt Lake City to Barstow, and from Barstow, to Amarillo, on the Santa Fe.

I left Salt Lake on December 29, got to Barstow, got on Number 22, and I borrowed a rulebook from a friend of mine in Winslow, I got into Amarillo at 3:05 in the afternoon.

The assistant superintendent said, "We're awfully glad to see you. When can you go to work?"

"I could go to work this afternoon, if you can fix it," I said.

So he called the yardmaster and did what he had to do, and I had to go down to the courthouse to get my application notarized; and while I was hurrying down there, a great big fat cop with a big star on stopped me.

"Where are you goin' so fast?" he said.

"I don't know that it's any of your business," I said. I got on the cab, and I went down there to work at four o'clock.

I was between jobs, see, but all I lost was one day's pay. The last day I'd worked up there at Salt Lake, was the 29th; and I started my new job on the 31st. Lost just one day.

Now there's no boomer can match that one.

"Then you went back to Salt Lake City, then to Dodge City, Kansas; then back to Salt Lake. You're moving around like crazy, every five weeks or so," I said.

"Um hm," Grant said.

"Now here's something interesting, happening, here. 1915 to 1930 you were dispatching, so you did that for fifteen years. What kind of pay did you start at?" I said.

"Hm?"

"What kind of pay did you start at, at your first job. What was the pay like in those days?" I said.

"Oh. The first job I had was, $62.50 a month."

"A month. That's two bucks a day. Could you buy anything with two dollars a day then?"

"Sure as heck could. Why, operators in Topeka, Kansas, they got $85.00 a month and raised families on that. When my wife and I were both workin', we got four dollars a day," Grant said. "When I was in Salt Lake, I got cut off every winter, I had to find other jobs; that's how I went to Amarillo in the first place. I got called back by the general superintendent of the L.A. & S.L. to a job in Las Vegas, a regular job.

"So I went down there because I had worked Needles, and I was used to the hot weather; and that job lasted from 1928 to 1931 — of course I had a few months of other dispatching jobs in the middle of it.

But on April 30, 1931, then I was cut off completely.

Las Vegas

I went to Vegas in 1928 ... they built the railroad through there in 1906; so Vegas was only twenty-two years old then.

They put the railroad through, and then they built the town.

Back then Las Vegas was all of five square blocks — the company built it. And the company could sell these houses to employees at 1% interest.

Vegas started as a company town. Built around the railroad.

"Right next to the depot. Southeast of the depot. And anybody who wanted to buy a home at 1% interest, the rent was reasonable, they got their electricity from the icing dock; and also their ice, and people bought their water there too. It was a well-run, company town.

That's how the town of Las Vegas started.

The railroad built it. It was just a five-block square town, first of all. Then it grew out, and expanded around there. And they had these two gambling joints ... ... have you ever watched that t.v. show, Vegas; and those two gambling joints it shows there; that's the same ones that were there then. They always had their doors opening on the south side of the street; and that kept that side of the building cool. Then they had a whorehouse, in Block 16. They had a police station. And Nevada didn't have any state prohibition law; it was only the federal law.

And these bootleggers that had been divvying up to the police, the police notified them when the feds would be around. Those who weren't divvying up to the police weren't notified, and the ones who weren't payin' up to the police were the ones that the federal marshals always knocked over.

I guess there must be pretty much a million people living in Vegas now,

"Yeah, it's a big place now. They put that nuclear test grounds out there. Did you ever freight atom bombs to the nuclear test grounds? They're only sixty miles out of town," I said.

"No. They didn't have a railroad out there. They took the bombs out there by truck.

"Before the first World War, there was a railroad built from Las Vegas to Tonapah. Tonapah is southeast of Reno," Grant said.

"It says on your work history that you were a laborer once on the Los Angeles and Salt Lake Railroad — Union Pacific system."

"Right."

"What were you doin'?" I said.

"I lost my job as a train dispatcher — it had paid $265.00 a month — I got cut off, and I had to work as a day laborer.

How A Cut Off Dispatcher Ended Up Supervising The Six Companies Railroad

So I was cut off from my dispatcher job in Las Vegas for Union Pacific in November of 1930.

About a month later I got a job as a day laborer for 75¢ an hour for Union Pacific checking out material in the yard at Las Vegas; we unloaded rails and ties off the train, then trucked them to sites where they were buildin' forty-two frame bridges on the Boulder City branch.

One day I noticed the work train engine in from Boulder Junction was gone an awful lot — since it moved on the main line, it had to get work orders ... but sometimes it would be gone so long, and of course while it was gone, we couldn't unload rails or ties from it.

After thirty days, not much had got done except two legs of a 'Y', and a spur, and a siding.

They needed to get more work out of the work train.

So the chief construction engineer from Omaha come out and

talked to the project construction engineer.

"You better put somebody dispatchin' that work train who can get some work out of them!" he said.

"I got a layed-off train dispatcher in the labor gang that might do the trick," Mr. Weinstock, the project foreman said. He pointed his finger at me.

The job paid $175.00 a month; when I told my wife, she cried she was so happy, and we had be having such a hard time.

The first day on the job I rode the work train to Boulder Junction. The train wasn't made up right — there had been no instructions to the yardmaster at Las Vegas what order to put the cars in. The conductor told me that there were twenty-five partially-loaded cars on the siding. I decided there was enough material to make a train for the next day. When we got to Las Vegas, I put out instructions to the yardmaster, the chief dispatcher and the truck dispatchers, as to what time the train was going to be called.

When we got back to Boulder Junction, we set out the train on the siding; then we laid a mile of track a day until we reached Boulder City.

We Layed The Track & We Built The Yard Then I Was Out of A Job, Again

When it was time to put ballast under the ties on the track, I put on two work trains. The ballast was used to go under the ties to form a solid base under the track and hold the track in line. One work train would return a train of empties to Hoya Pit and leave the empties there for filling, and pick up the loaded train waiting there all ready to go. After we laid track all the way to Boulder City, a 500 car yard needed to be built. Six Companies Railroad already had a warehouse built; with a tent city to the south of the depot and yard. The warehouse was receiving shipments while we were building the yard.

The man in charge of the warehouse was a Mr. Weinstock. Every once in a while he needed some cars switched, so I'd cut off the engine and give him a switch. When the yard was done, it was going to be the interchange point with Six Companies Railroad

fig. 35 —dispatcher for Feather River Canyon & two maintenance men, just after WWII   153

and Union Pacific.
   We finished the yard.
   And I was out of a job again.

Workin' Again

On May 7, 1931 I hired out to Six Companies as a laborer at $4.00 a day. At least it paid twelve-and-a-half cents more than I had made on the Union Pacific doing the same work.

The six companies that were the contractors who formed The Six Companies company, were: Bechtel-Kaiser out of Oakland, California, who owned 30%; Utah Construction Company out of Ogden, that owned 20%; McDonald Kahn out of Los Angeles, that owned 20%; Morrison Knudsen out of Boise, for 10%; and J.F. Seah, and Pacific Bridge, both out of Portland, and both at 10% each.

My first assignment was to work with a gang using crowbars to unload heavy timbers from a flat car, for others to carry over to a stock pile. This was still in the time of the Depression, and among the seventy-five of us on the crew — including four bank presidents — I was the only one who'd ever worked a day in his life as a day laborer.

There was lots of odd jobs, such as hauling dynamite around, and tamping down concrete for the mess hall.

I Get A Break

One day Mr. Weinstock happened by and saw me. "What are you doing here?" he said.

"I did my job so good at Union Pacific we finished and I put myself out of a job," I said.

"Do you want to work for me?" He said.

"Sure," I said.

He went right away and had me transferred to the warehouse by the next day.

In the warehouse he showed me where there were a lot of broken nuts and bolts scattered in piles all over the floor.

"I want you to take care of these nuts and bolts and get 'em into the bins, so they can be inventoried," Mr. Weinstock said.

"Mr. Weinstock, you got the best little old nut and bolt sorter you ever saw," I said.

A few days later, the head timekeeper came up to me.

"Do you want to be a timekeeper?" he said.

My Time In The Timekeeper's Office

On the hill above the river was two or three bunkhouses, a dining room, and a new timekeeper's office.

I was put in charge of this office.

I had two helpers.

They checked when the men were on the job, and I posted that information on the men's time sheets.

It was so hot that some of the day laborers died of heart failure — 130 degrees every day for the whole month of July, 1931. After that there was a physical examination before a man was hired, and men with heart trouble were not hired.

After a couple months they consolidated all the timekeepers and I was sent to the main office in Boulder City.

In addition to my payroll work, and because I had worked in the canyon and was familiar with the different phases of each job, and because I kept the phases recorded along with the time worked on each man's payroll card ... I was assigned to account the distribution of labor costs and manhours on the different phases.

The job paid $175.00 a month.

That's Show Business

The contract for running the dining rooms were contracted to the Anderson Brothers, whose experience had been with movie people on location. They did a first class job — eight men sat at each table, and when the food platters were empty, they were refilled.

The only thing was, you tell what day of the week it was, by what they were serving that day.

But, so what?

Shovelling Out The Shovel Runners

The men who operated the big steam shovels that loaded material onto the railroad cars, or into trucks, were called shovel runners.

One day they went to see the general superintendent of the Six Companies Railroad, who's name was Mr. Crowe.

"We want a raise," they told him.

"Come back tomorrow morning; I'll give you my answer," Mr. Crowe said.

The next morning the men came to see Mr. Crowe.

Mr. Crowe gave them all a very short speech.

"You're all fired," he said.

He handed them their checks.

What Goes Around Comes Around

But the thing was, everyone working in the camp was paid off, and fired.

The Secretary of the Interior set up a reservation, and put a gate across the highway between Railroad Pass and Boulder City.

All of us had to hire out again, and be rehired — by a man called McAdams; then we were given identification badges.

Of course, none of the shovel runners were rehired.

The Icing On The Cake

The Reclamation Commissioner forced everyone who had been living alongside the river, to get out of the reservation. These people had to go to Las Vegas, and live in cardboard shacks, and get their water from a fire hydrant.

Meanwhile, some housing was built in Boulder City, and everyone working at Boulder City had to move out of their places in Las Vegas, to move into this housing.

'Saint Peter Don't You Call Me 'Cause I Can't Go —

I Owe My Soul To The Company Store'

Everyone working for Six Companies Railroad was supposed to buy from the company store.

Workers could buy anything in the company store. And the amount would be deducted from their payroll.

Anyone who didn't, got the stub of their payroll check stamped — and they had to go see McAdams and explain.

A Big Change For Me

What I did as a time keeper, was I distributed the labor — in other words, each job had a different job number, and I charged each man's labor, to the appropriate job number.

One December 15, 1931, the company comptroller, J. F. Reis came to me and said, "Can you set up a system of accounting like you've done so far, to cover the whole railroad project?"

"Yes," I said.

"Okay. I'm putting you in charge of the railroad project. I'm raising your salary to $200.00 a month after the first of the year," he said.

They set up an office for me in the gravel plant.

That raise never happened during the whole three-and-a-half-years I was on that job and the dam was finished.

Johnny & Paul Do It Their Way

When I took over we had four Plymouth gasoline powered locomotives, four wheelers that hauled material from Boulder City to the gravel plant. The gravel plant was on a 4% grade.

It took them six hours to haul back six empties to the gravel plant.

One day there was a carload of timbers, that somewhere had gotten a real hard coupling, because the load had shifted against a partially-set hand brake.

Crews on these locomotives were an engineer and a conductor. Johnny Sukulyn was the conductor, and Paul Richards was the engineer.

"Move the engine close enough to the car to connect the air hoses and pump up the air, so the car wouldn't get away from you — just in case the coupling won't drop into place right. That way the air brakes will stop the car and prevent a runaway," I told them.

But they didn't do what I told 'em.

Instead they tried to couple onto the car without the air pumped up into to — and the coupler did not drop into place and the car started to roll away.

The car headed off downhill toward a crew building a pile-driven bridge over the Colorado River.

I was frantic.

I got on the phone and rang the crew working on the end of the line out on the bridge.

They didn't answer for what seemed a very long time.

When they did answer, I told them about the runaway car, then they hung up.

They called back after a while, and asked me for the number of the car.

I told 'em the number.

Then they said that the car had stopped right in front of them, because there was rise in the track just short of the bridge enough to stop it.

After they heard what I had to say to them, there was no further trouble getting them to answer the phone in a timely manner from then on.

Needless to say, Johnny and Paul were no longer employed.

The Old Number 8 from the Mount Tamalpais & Muir Woods Railway

Another incident happened one day when the plant got a rush order.

It was for a certain size gravel.

There were steep grades, one-and-seven-tenths grades between the plant and the pit; so we could have ten loaded cars with a Mikado engine — that's what we did.

Up at the plant, they had four sizes of rocks, and they had a

fig. 36 – 1919, Grant Allen on 'one of those track motorcars'

rush order come in, for a certain size of rock, and this man that was handling this Shay engine, loading the cars with the rock, was not a mainline engineer, he was a construction man.

He was loading these cars at the plant, and there were four sets of tracks according to size of the trains for spurs to put them on.

He was using a 'Shay,' which is a 'geared engine,' for this job.

"Send that man down in the Shay with the ten cars of gravel," my boss said.

"The Shay won't make that 4% grade, with that load," I said.

"Do it. Send him down anyway," my boss said.

I talked to the conductor.

"You better ride on the rear steps of the rear car, if he lets that train get away from him, you jump off," I said.

"Okay," the conductor said.

Sure enough, the engineer lost control of the train, by improper handling of the air brakes; and the train was a runaway down that 4% grade, right to the edge of the river.

And that train ran so fast, that it stripped all of the gears and side-rods and everything else on that engine, and completely ruined it — made a wreck out of it.

And the engine had to be scrapped.

It was the old Number 8 from the Mount Tamalpais and Muir Wood Railway, in Marin, California.

The company later bought a very large Shay locomotive from a mining company in Montana.

Yep.

The superintendent was the aggregate man — aggregate's the stuff you make concrete out of; that's how he had charge of the railroad. I was workin' under him, you see.

"You'll have to run the railroad. I don't know anything about a railroad, except how to buy a ticket," he said.

He didn't disagree with me again.

We had a mountain railroad, and I wouldn't hire any man unless he had experience on a mountain railroad. 'Cause we had to use retainers a lot of the time, and all that sort of thing, and 4% grades.

4% grade is every mile you climb four feet.

'Here I go again,' I thought.

We started experimenting as to what engine would be best to handle the train through the whole trip from the gravel pit to Boulder City and back.

I was new runnin' the office. These two permanent officers of the Six Companies came in one day to talk to me, these two wiseguys come down there, to tell me how I should be runnin' a railroad.

You see, when the train comes in from the pit, if the plant can handle it, it goes into the plant. If the plant can't handle it, it pulls down to the other end of the yard and goes out and backs up on two stock pile tracks.

So this one guy, he recommended we buy second-hand Pacific Electric engines; he even had the telephone lines from there to the pit set close enough to hang trolley lines on the telephone poles.

"I want to use electric trains. I've got some from the Pacific Electric Railroad. I already set the telephone poles close enough to the track so trolley lines can be hung up," one officer said.

"No. It won't work. We'll lose time — Because if the plant isn't ready to take the train, then the train has to go to the stockpile, and then I'd have to meet the electric train with a steam engine, and then we'd need to use the steam engine to take the electric train to the stock pile. I can't tolerate that loss of time," I said.

The other guy, he'd gotten a line on six Malley engines, from Baltimore Locomotive Works, that some railroad had ordered then gone bankrupt, and couldn't buy them.

"That's right ... y'know, I've got the answer. I've got a sweet deal set up where I can buy six Malleys from a bankrupt railroad, for only $6,000.00 each," the other guy said.

"No. It won't work. We'll lose time. Those are big, heavy trains, you see. Then if the plant can't take the train, then a smaller steam engine would have to handle the train to the stockpile. I don't want that loss of time. That's great having those big, heavy trains, as long as the train is only at the pit, but if you get one of those babies outside at the stockpile, with only eight ties to a rail, there won't be enough derricks in Las Vegas to get the son of a gun back on the track. Forget it." I said.

There was only eight ties to the rail, because there was nothin' on them, except cars; 'cause we kept movin' the track over all the time, see. The stockpile would keep movin' this way and that way. And we'd move the rails after it and follow it. You build the lines differently if you're gonna move 'em all the time, and only put eight ties per rail — instead of eighteen to twenty-four.

So both men were frustrated. They threw their hands up and walked out.

Well I killed the schemes both these guys had.

I felt like I gained their ill will.

'Course they didn't know anything about runnin' a railroad, anyway.

They might have been pretty good at whatever it was they did, but they didn't know squat about running a railroad.

Then Warren Bechtel came to see me. "What's wrong with the railroad?" he said.

"Nothin's wrong, if you get your officers to leave us alone," I said.

"I'm gettin' someone to come in here and check out your operation," he said.

Well Bechtel-Kaiser had an aggregate plant at Oroville, and they furnished ballast from an old gold mine dredging dump, for the Western Pacific's Feather River Canyon line — and they knew the trainmaster for the Western Pacific, one J. P. McSweeney.

So Warren Bechtel had E. W. Mason, the general manager of the Western Pacific, give this J. P. McSweeney a thirty day leave, to come to Boulder City, and check up on me.

It all started one morning when I saw the superintendent of the gravel plant, Mr. Price, walking with another man, this, J. P. McSweeney, right over to where I was working in the dispatcher's office.

'Here I go again,' I thought.

The Key To Successful Operation Was The Men

The key to successful operation was the men. I would not hire anybody that did not have experience workin' on a mountain railroad — since we had 4% grades.

I hired men as they came along.

Most of them were train and engine men from the Union Pacific at Las Vegas.

Of course, I knew all of them personally, 'cause I had worked at Las Vegas as a train dispatcher.

The Lousy Dispatcher

While I was assistant superintendent on The Six Companies Railroad at Boulder City, a fireman came in who wanted a job.

"Where'd you work?" I said.

"Shasta Division of S.P.; I was cut off when the new line was cut in by Klamath Falls," he said.

"I was a dispatcher on that Division," I said.

"Y'know, there was a lousy dispatcher there who didn't know what he was doing and I didn't like him — I never met him in person; he got me outside at 1 o'clock in the morning in the rain and snow changin' indicator lights, to get these helpers on the siding out of there behind the scheduled trains. He was a louse to make us go out in the cold like that," he said.

"I was that dispatcher. But I'll give you a job anyway," I said.

The Wolf

Conductors and engineers got $6.00 a day. Firemen and brakemen got $5.00 a day.

It wasn't the most money in the world.

But it wasn't the least, either.

But it was the Depression.

And that money kept the wolf away from the door for many families.

Train Sheet Of A Single Day's Work On The Six Companies Railroad

"Yep. I'm the one who organized and ran the Six Companies Railroad. I was the only railroad operating person in the whole Six Companies organization. This was the railroad that serviced the building of Boulder Dam. The railroad was the main supplier of all the construction materials. I'll show you a train sheet. We had to get these printed, and the printer didn't have sheets of paper big enough; so I taped them together so it would be about five feet long, and two feet high. This a record of the trains; the names of the crews and everything; where the train left and where it went to; the times and everything," Grant said. The total loads handled, it says here, was 540; total empties handled, was 592; total tonnage handled, 64,578 tons.

"Holy cow! Was this just one day? 540 cars a day?!" I said.

"Yes. Just one day. You see, we ran ten-car trains out of the gravel pit, loaded, one an hour, twenty-four hours a day. And we took the empties going back. That's forty-eight trains right there. Then you hauled it up to the plant, they made the finished powder; then you had to haul it for the rest of the job, see. It was a main line operation, on a construction job. We were haulin' mostly cement, and gravel, haulin' the cement in; and haulin' it around where they needed it. 'Course, like I say, this was a slow day; there was only ninety-eight trains. It got up to a hundred-and-twenty, some days," Grant said.

"Really? It must have been pretty hard to keep track of them," I said.

"No. Un un. Not for a train dispatcher," Grant said.

"You're not tellin' me that this sheet of paper stretched out over your dining room table, is just one day's record?" I said.

"That's right This is one day's record," Grant said.

"Well, you were workin' sixteen-hour days, anyway, weren't you?" I said.

"No. I worked the day shift. We had a man on swing. And a man on graveyard. Train dispatchers. That was our business. That's how we worked on the main line, see."

"Let me look at this. You had columns for hours worked, engine failures, men deadheading, daily performance tally of all the cars, the engine number, the conductor, the brakemen, the time everyone worked the different stations on the way; you got to know everything ... " I said.

"It was a company record, of the day's business On this list of stations, from here, down to the gravel pit, was a branch, and here was a branch that run up to the top of the dam, at Himix. They had a minin' plant up on top; and you had to haul the gravel

fig. 37 – Margarite, 1918; Grant's wife at Montebello out of Ogden on the S.P. goin' west

and cement up there," Grant said.

"There's all the mileage between the stations. This is pretty impressive. But it was just business-as-usual for you, every day," I said.

"Yeah. Heck. Probably was the busiest little railroad, in the whole United States, in those days, 1931. The Depression. 'Specially, since it was only nineteen miles of railroad ... ... It was all single track. All the trains ran as extras, 'cause there was no scheduled trains on there," Grant said.

"Holy cow ... ... Ninety-eight trains all on single track; on three eight-hour shifts, twenty-four hours a day ... ... This is almost a five-foot long train sheet," I said.

"We patched them together; the printer couldn't get any bigger paper. `You read this schedule from the middle. This right side, is westward trains, and this left side, is eastward trains,' Grant said.

"This sheet has a title written on top: Dispatcher's record of movement of trains; Six Companies Railroad — Builders of Boulder Dam," I said.

"Yeah. I had to go down there, and finish building it. And organized the whole railroadin' side of that business. There was nobody but me, knew how to do it. And I'm the only one who can tell the story, today ... ... That was in 1931. It is now, 1991 ... I'm gonna have a drink; you want one?" Grant said.

And Cut Off Again

Some of the figures of tonnage hauled by our little twenty-nine mile long railroad are quite impressive.

We hauled 138,000 cars, containing 9,000,000 tons of gravel.

560,000,000 ton miles were hauled.

The railroad enabled the whole Boulder Dam project to run smoothly.

During peak operations we had seventeen crews working on each of three shifts on the main line; and all main line trains were handled with written train orders.

This wasn't counting the switching crews in the yard.

I feel fortunate that I was part of this monumental project.

And you know, I was the only operating railroad man in the organization.

That gave me an opportunity to use my organizing ability to put it all together. And that's what I did. And I did it so well, we finished the project ...

But I was out of a job, again.

Startin' Seniority Someplace

Then I wanted to get out someplace, and start some seniority on a mainline railroad.

'Cause this contracting business, it was feast or famine; when the job was done, I'd have nothing.

I needed to start my seniority someplace on a mainline railroad.

Which I did do.

On The Afternoon of September 21, 1934, I received a Western Union telegram from J. P. McSweeney.

'I'm gonna start hirin' brakemen tomorrow morning. Go see the trainmaster up at Portola,' the telegram said.

I reached over and took my papers out of a file. My relief man was watchin' me.

"So long, Jeff. I don't know if I'll ever see you again," I told him.

I drove all night long to Portola, all the way up to the top of the Feather River Canyon.

The next morning, I was the first brakeman hired by Western Pacific after the crash of '29 and the great Depression.

Not only that, but that job started my seniority on a main line railroad.

Superintendent of the Indian Valley Railroad

And that brakeman job at Portola didn't last very long. It was only during fruit season.

Maybe three or four weeks, or something like that.

And I was gettin' ready to go back to Boulder City.

I couldn't have my old job back; but I could run an engine. I'd learned to run a steam engine at Portola, and be a conductor.

But anyway, this man drove up in front of the camp I was stayin' in, and he come up.

"I'm lookin' for a man to be superintendent of the Indian Valley Railroad — you've been recommended to me," he said.

So I got that job.

That job lasted until they passed the Railroad Retirement Act — and my seniority on the railroad as a brakeman, from that little job at Portola, soared sky-high; see, I never was cut off as a brakeman in terms of seniority.

So that's how come I worked for Western Pacific as a brakeman until they could use me in the dispatcher's office. After that I worked for twenty-nine years on the Western Pacific.

The last eleven years I was superintendent of transportation for Western Pacific ... doin' the same job on a main line railroad, that I had done for the Six Companies Railroad.

"When you were working as a superintendent of Indian Valley Railroad, what were your job responsibilities?" I asked.

"Well I had charge of the whole railroad," Grant said.

"You did?!"

"Yeah. It was only a nineteen-mile railroad," Grant said.

"What a great opportunity!" I said.

"Oh yes, it was. Anyway, I had to send in all the reports to interstate commerce places, and the big railroads, and that sort of thing. I was the agent at Paxton, and the agent at Cresent Mills. If I had a pick-up at Cresent Mills, I'd go be the agent; then I'd come back to Paxton, and be the agent there; and also the superintendent," Grant said.

"The agent, does he book all the orders? What does the agent do?" I asked.

"The agent handles the shipments — people ship packages or whatever it is; and that's what the agent handles. Working for the railroad, dealin' with these customers who want to ship something; or if something came in for 'em, you checked it out to them ... individual packages for residents, or carloads of coal or whatever for companies," Grant said.

"That must have been a great opportunity to do that. You must have been so delighted."

"Oh yeah. Bein' a brakeman was pretty tough for a guy who's always worked in an office. In bad weather you had to climb up on the cars and turn down the retainers, and all of that. And turn up the retainers going uphill, and turn 'em down going downhill, climbin' up and down the ladders. When it got cold and rainy, that was pretty tough," Grant said.

"Yeah. If you were used to workin' office jobs, to go outside like that," I said.

"That's right."

"You were pretty determined to survive, weren't you?"

"I always was.

"I'm a pretty healthy person. I had my physical examination about two months ago. My blood pressure's one-hundred-twelve over seventy; my cholesterol is one-hundred-twenty-four.

'You must be doin' somethin' right. Come back and see me next year,' my doctor said.

"I'm ninety-three," Grant said.

Assistant Trainmaster at Tobin

I was sent up on a job up at Tobin, as an assistant trainmaster. What they had up there, was P.G.&E. wanted to build two dams, up in the Feather River; one at Cresta ... and one at Rock Creek.

The right-away was built on decomposed granite — with hard places stickin' out, see.

So this job was haulin' this rip rap from the quarry pits, seven miles downstream, and they had dug these soft spots out beside the river, and you'd dump the rock in there, to build up the track bed, and go back and get some more.

And finally, we got the job done.

We were haulin' rock, to fill in those soft spots, for the track bed for the railroad tracks; fillin' in between these hard places.

Because the rise of the water, would keep nibblin' away at the soft spots, see. So we had to put rock in there see, so it wouldn't bother the right-away.

P.G.&E. had to pay for it, 'cause they were building the power plants.

Mile Post 253 in the Feather River Canyon

I was appointed Assistant Trainmaster at Tobin, California at Mile Post 253 in the Feather River Canyon, on the Western Pacific

Railroad on September 1, 1948. I had previously been their dispatcher at Sacramento since 1943. The reason for putting me in charge of the project was due to my experience running the Six Companies Railroad.

P. G. & E. decided to build the Cresta and Rock Creek powerhouses, with diversion dams about seven miles upstream from the powerhouse construction sites. The Cresta Dam was at Mile Post 247 just west of Merlin. The Rock Creek Dam was at Mile Post 257.

Since the Western Pacific has right-of-way, and because the right-of-way had been made on decomposed granite fill, we had to stabilize this fill with rip-rap for one mile upstream from each dam. This way we could keep the rise and fall of water from eroding the right-of-way fill.

We got the rip rap from a quarry at Tobin.

Therefore, a camp was built at Tobin. Morrison and Knudson contractors broke down and loaded the rip rap on air dump cars. The Western Pacific train and engine crews hauled the rip rap and dumped it at the two dam sites.

We had two twenty-car trains, and about ten spare cars. Each train had a Jordan spreader.

We dumped about 6,000 carloads of rip rap at each dam site. Some days, we loaded, hauled and dumped 100 carloads — all with little or no interference from main line trains.

We housed the personnel working on the project in cabooses and outfit cars. There was a longer spur nearby where the cabooses and outfit cars were where the two train and engine crews, the car repairers, the engine watchman, and the laborers lived. And at the end of that spur was a cook car, and a dining car — on the upstream end of this track.

Me and my wife had a living car on a short spur by the river. It had two bedrooms, one on each end, and a living room in the middle. The water department piped in water from Jackass Creek and there was a shower bath installed in our car, and also in some of the other cars. Next to our car there was another car that was used for the telegraph office; and that's where the trainmaster's clerk lived. And a telegrapher lived in there too.

The Tobin Crapper at Jackass Creek*. (* Crapper was the name of the English plumber who invented the flush toilet.) Originally we were told that we were going to have a flush toilet in our car.

fig. 38 —Grant Allen lived here one winter when he was layed-off

But it was not put in, because the company figured that then they'd have to put flush toilets into the other cars too. There was one Chic Salon for general use outside. The trainmaster wanted another one for his use. The Bridge Building Department sent a crane car to Altamont and loaded a two-holer onto a flat car, and shipped it to Tobin and installed it close to our car. They set up a lattice screen around it. P. G. & E. got a bill for $450.00. We could have built two of 'em new for that kind of money.

Twenty-two years later, in March of 1970, me and my wife rode the last trip of the California Zephyr, and when we went through Tobin, the better part of that Chic Salon was still standing.

"What's the assistant superintendent of transportation job in San Francisco for Western Pacific?" I asked.

"The superintendent of transportation has charge of all the activities on the railroad.

"He was the top dog," Grant said.

"You were? In San Francisco?" I said.

"For Western Pacific Railroad," Grant said.

"So you were on the top of the ladder?" I said.

"In that department. There was a president; a vice-president-general-manager; and I was superintendent of transportation — that's third in line."

Superintendent Of Transportation for Western Pacific

I was superintendent of transportation for Western Pacific.

I had the use of a business car. I did a lot of traveling.

It was the happiest eleven years of my whole life.

I had complete charge of buildin' The Six Companies Railroad; but this time I had complete charge of running the same kind of a job, on a mainline railroad. And the vice-president-general-manager come to me; and he called me to his office.

"I come out of the engineering department of the Milwaukee Railroad, and I don't know too much about operating. So you run this darn railroad just the way you see fit. As long as you tell me what you're doing, I'll back you up," he said.

fig. 39 – Ten Wheeler No. 77 (oo000), Western Pacific, Sacramento, Aug. 1941

That's how much confidence he had in me.

"You said you were there for eleven years ... what would one of your days be like? What would it be like if I followed you to work for a week?" I said.

Those Eleven Years Were The Happiest Years Of My Life

Well, I had charge of the operation of all of the trains. I figured out the schedules. We were operating the California Zephyr at that time; and there wasn't much I could do about that except find out what the delays were, if they got delayed.

And I figured out the schedules for all of the freight trains.

And the expense of running a railroad, is how many trains you run. And if you can keep the operation of freight trains down, and still serve the customers, that's where you save money.

And I was pretty darn good at it.

All the time I was there, we made a little money.

My predecessor didn't do that; and my successor couldn't do that.

I was in better with the customers than some of those other fellas were, see. If the customers had any complaints about anything, they'd always come to me, instead of the traffic man, see. So I worked pretty good with them; 'specially California Packing Company — that was our main freight hauler; canned goods.

We were at 5th and Mission in San Francisco.

California Packing Company had several canneries all over the state; they were Del Monte brand. And the old guy who ran it, they just thought I was great; because they could always get a hold of me, if they had a complaint — they didn't go through the traffic man. That made traffic madder than heck — they didn't want me talkin' to the customers.

The customers came to me.

They might want to know where their cars were. The clerk in my office always knew where their cars were, 'cause he had track of the car numbers.

"That's a big job, to keep track of everything like that," I said.

"Well, that's all I've done, all my life; is transportation. In transportation, anyway, even when I started as a telegraph operator," Grant said.

"Did you say that they gave you a car; and you traveled around in a private car," I asked.

"Yes," Grant said.

The Private Business Car

There was a business car, assigned to the officers of the railroad — from president on down. I had the use of it.

This car we had, it used to belong to Doris Duke, the tobacco heiress; and even the silverware in there, had Doris on the silverware.

And there would be a kitchen; sleeping quarters for the porter and the cook; and the porter would serve the meals; we could have the fanciest kinds of meals on there, that there was — if you wanted to entertain customers. And there was separate bedrooms on there.

"Like you said this tobacco heiress has a private car; was it usual, or unusual for people to have their private cars? Was that pretty common?" I said.

"Oh yes. There's a lot of people, at least a thousand people, who own their own private cars — even today."

"Today?!"

"That's right."

"What do they do with them?

"There's a book out on 'em, called 'Mansions on Wheels,' Grant said.

"Mansions on wheels," I said, looking at pictures in the book. "There's a pump organ in there. Look how beautiful those cars are done up. They're very elegant; they're beautiful, they must have cost a fortune, just like real mansions," I said.

"Darn right," Grant said.

"So people would have all these beautiful private cars, and they'd travel, not by air, but by railroad?" I said.

"That's right. And they have them stored, where they can be taken care of; and when they wanted to take it out, I'd have a man down in San Diego that had the privilege of assigning them; pick out what they want — and the railroad takes it out. Of course, they'd have to pay the railroad for haulin' it around for them."

"How much would that cost?" I said.

"Oh I haven't any idea ... . There's a whole bunch of them, down there in Florida," Grant said.

"So people still do that today? That must be fun."

"Oh yeah. Sure."

"Here's a picture of a guy with his Rolls Royce and his Jaguar automobiles parked by his private car; and it's overlooking the ocean — is on a siding of his own?" I said.

"He's probably got it set on the ground ... no, he's got it on tracks," Grant said. "I'm a railroad historian. That what all these bookshelves are about. I get inquiries all the time from people about this and that and the other thing. And I can tell the answer.

"I retired in 1963," Grant said.

"You must have known a whole lot of people," I said.

"Oh yes. I had a retirement party here, and people came from as far away as Chicago to see me — other transportation officers," Grant said.

"That's wonderful," I said.

"... That's right," Grant said.

"The girls just loved me in the office. I saw a few tears, back there, when I left. You see, my predecessor, and the guy that was supposed to be his successor, if one of these women would fit in the job, why, he'd disqualify her for the job, because she was a woman. That was common then, for the men to not hire the women. The way I felt, was if they had seniority enough to get the job, they got the job. And they worked out all right, better than a lot of men used to work it," Grant said.

"So you were being fair."

"Yeah. Sure. That's right. I've put in fifty years of railroading, from 1913, to 1963. Today is the second week of January, of a new year, 1991," Grant said.

"You must have seen an awful lot of changes on the trains," I said.

"Oh yes. Sure.

"I am ninety-three years old.

"I am the last of the old-time boomers.

"The only thing about being so old, is that you outlive all

fig. 40 – Southern Pacific coachyard, San Francisco, 1959

your friends.

"Well, railroads have been my whole life. Y'know, I learned to run a steam engine. When I was off duty, I'd go out there, and the guys would teach me how to run a steam engine, air brakes, and everything, the whole works. When I went to San Francisco, I was put on a rail-dowsting job out of Winnemukka. And by that time we had diesels. So, I learned to run a diesel. There's a pair of tracks from Winnemukka to Wesso — W.P. eastbound; and S.P. westbound. And we'd be working out near Bealoma, and we'd just cross over there and go come in on the westbound; instead of getting orders against the eastbound trains on our own railroad.

"Then I'd get up and run the diesel engine home, while the guy's rested in the caboose. I ran 'em from Beawally to Winnemukka; that's about forty-five miles.

"The air is the same on diesels and steam, see, it's just learnin' the throttle; airbrakes are the same. Anybody can start a steam engine or a diesel; it takes somebody that knows how to stop it. And when you get on a passenger train, the man handlin' the engine's got to stop so there's no jarring, and he has to start so there's no jarring — either steam, or diesel. And they do not jar, you'd never know you was moving. The first thing you know, you look out, and you see you're moving. You don't feel it.

"For a train dispatcher, I learned a lot of things out on the road, didn't I?

Bill Millard — (born 1912)

#1-Priority Steam Engineer

Followed In His Grandfather's & Father's Footsteps & After Workin' Summer Jobs in the Roundhouse, Checking Cars in the Yard, Calling Crews, & a Firin' Apprenticeship, Was Promoted To Engineer.

"When were you born?" I said.
"1912. I belonged to Engineers' Union forty-five years," Bill said.
"When did you start working on the railroad?" I said.
"1929. On summer vacations and stuff. I was seventeen," Bill said.
"What did you do?" I said.
"I helped at the roundhouse. I called crews. I'd check cars in the yard. It was kind of a summer job. And then, I finally went firing in '37 — that was the first opportunity I ever had to go firing.

"And I never worked a full year, 'till 1940. And then, from then on, I was working.

My Grandfather, My Father, & I Were All Steam Engineers

My grandfather went to work, on the Rock Island, in engine service, far as I can go back, is in 1871. He joined the Engineers in 1881. And my father joined the Engineers in 1902. And I joined the Engineers in 1943.

I remember my grandfather had a 50-year button when I was a kid, going to high school.

My father had a 40-year button when he retired.

I had a 35-year button when I retired.

Pride in Belonging to the Engineers

I was kinda, well ... there was a pride in belonging to the Engineers — the way I felt about it, at least. It wasn't that I had to be an Engineer or anything. I could'a stayed in the Fireman, I belonged to the Fireman from the time I went to work, in 1937 ... 'till I got promoted.

The Deep Freeze

Off-and-on for the railroad. What happened, was we had kind of a boom in '37. And in 1938 it kinda died out, '39 it kinda died out. And it picked up again in '40.

And the sad part of it was, up in the area where I was working — if you worked for the railroad, and were cut off, or terminated for seniority purposes, or for lack of business, then nobody wanted to hire you; 'cause they knew that just as soon as you got squared around again, you'd go right back to work on the railroad.

From 1940 on, I was all right, as far as workin' the railroad ... ... there was several times I could'a worked before then, but I had a job that I didn't want to turn loose. 'Cause by the time I turned loose, if I did, when I'd come back for work at that job again, then I'd be out of a job again.

And I remember talking to one fella, and he said, "Bill, it's a shame we can't put these jobs in the deep freeze, and thaw them out when we need them."

That was in Dunsmuir, on the Shasta Division.

That's where I was made.

That's where I started out.

1871

My grandfather retired in 1917, off Rock Island.

He told me he was on construction between Chicago and Kansas City, when they built that railroad in 1871. Prior to that, he worked for his uncle, as a brakeman, in Wisconsin. They would go on the train to Wisconsin with merchandise.

fig. 42 – Pinochle, switchman's shanty, John (r), Harold Clark (l), Pappy Way (t)

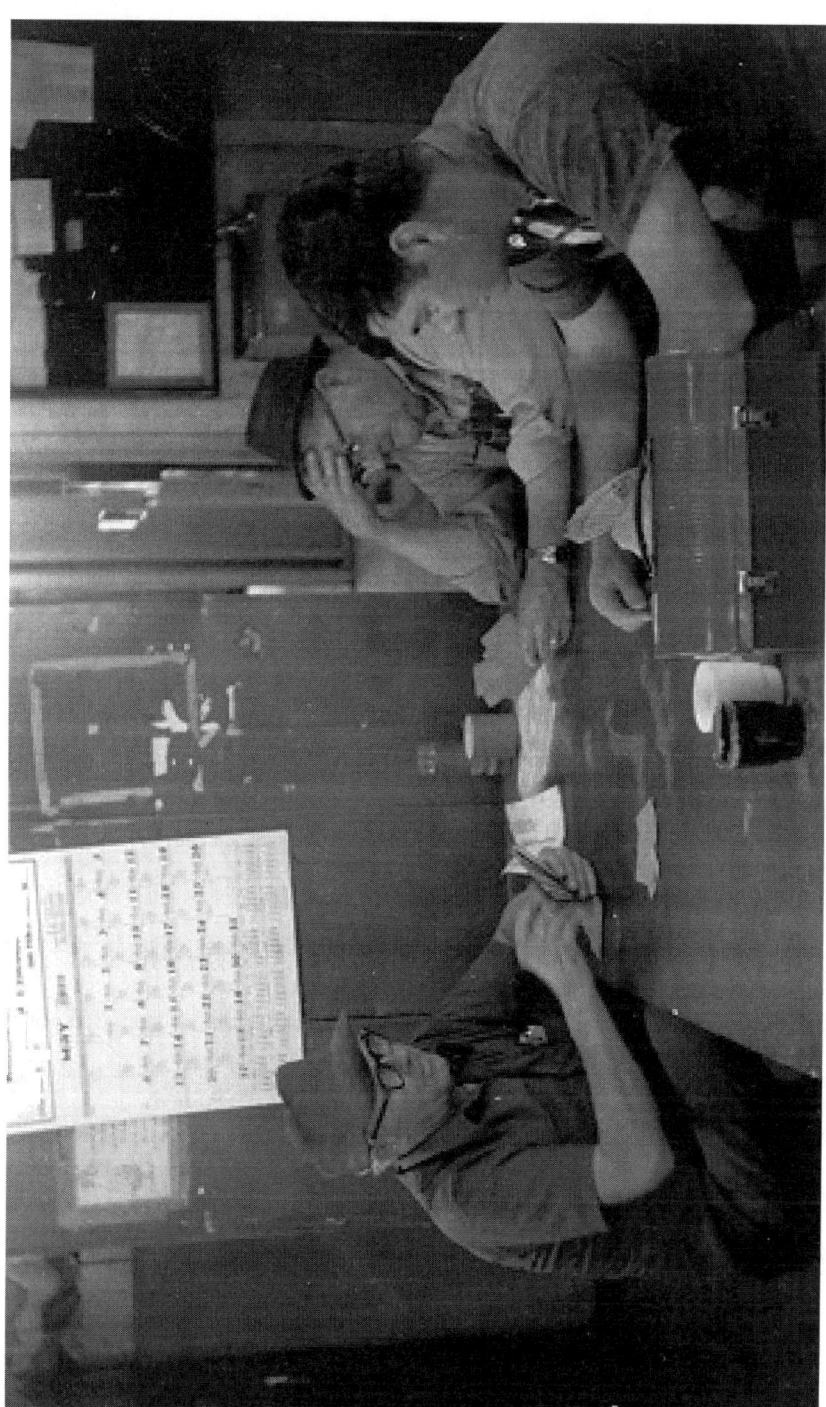

It was a short train.

They had a cabin built on a flatcar for living quarters. They cooked there, and lived, and slept, and everything — I don't remember for sure, but I think it was Chicago Northwestern. Maybe it wasn't even a railroad then, just a branch line goin' up there.

They would go up with the merchandise, and get a load back. They would do what ever they had to, if they had to sack wheat, they would.

The big thing up there was barrel staves.

In Wisconsin, they would cut barrel staves to get a load back south, where ever they were headed.

My grandfather cut barrel staves, time and time again ... there, from the time he was fourteen.

This uncle hired him, and paid him as he worked.

It wasn't a company deal at all.

It was kind of a contract with his uncle, my grandfather, and the other men this uncle had gotten for a crew. That's what I gathered, from what my grandfather told me.

The company they worked for had hired the conductor and the engineer to do the job; and the company paid the conductor and the engineer; and the conductor and the engineer paid the fireman, and from what I gathered, and the conductor paid the two brakemen.

My Grandfather's Boots

My grandfather told a story of buying a pair of boots, when he got enough money.

He didn't have any socks.

The boots hurt his feet.

He left them in the crummy or in the cab.

Somebody stole 'em.

He had to brake barefooted for quite a while.

He was about fourteen.

It was pathetic.

It gets real cold in Wisconsin.

1904-1917

My dad was workin' on the Shasta Division. He had established seniority on the Shasta Division. So he stayed there, I think it was 1904.

He stayed there until he retired, in 1944.

He was in the Fireman, when he went to work in Rockland. Shortly after that, he went into the Engineers. I think it was 1903.

He worked, and he was in an accident, a rear-end collision, in 1917 ... they shoved a train back into his engine; he was pretty-badly crippled.

Part of the settlement was when he went back to work, that he had a job for life.

But he didn't read the fine print.

It wasn't a job as an engineer; it was just a job with the company. He could've been a flagman, or a crew caller, or whatever.

But the union straightened them out — and he worked as an engineer.

He had one leg, two-and-a-half inches shorter than another. But he got around pretty good.

When that happened, I was six years old. I was aware of everything that was going on.

It caused him some pain and discomfort.

To get up to the cab on one of those engines, you had to climb a ladder, y'know, and get up, and it was six or eight feet from the ground.

I could remember my father, more when I worked with him, than when I didn't work with him, but he had a habit, rather than stepping up the ladder, of grabbing the grab-irons, and pulling himself up, see. And the same way coming down — he just grabbed the grab-irons, and slid down.

Once he got on the engine, he was just the same as anybody else — he didn't have that problem anymore.

He got a cash settlement too, it didn't amount to much today, but it was a whole lot then.

And in Dunsmuir, on account of the hills — it's all hills, it's on the side of a hill — he had problems getting back and forth to work walking; so he went to Weed, to work on the Weed helpers.

And that was flat country.

And he could walk good.

That's where we moved, in 1918.

And I stayed there in Weed, 'till 1930. I went all through grammar school and high school there.

During the depression, they had built the Natron Cutoff; that was the railroad extension from Black Butte to Eugene — that was the new railroad.

The old railroad, was what they called the Siskiyou main line, that went out through Ashland and Rouge River Valley and Grant's Pass and Roseburg and came in to Eugene.

They had helpers at Weed.

That had all kinds of engines at the roundhouse at Weed.

The had little Moguls, that they called Battleships; they were 2-6-2 engines, and they weighted possibly, 75 ton. Then they had the Consolidation, or the Hog.

Do you know why they called them a Hog?

Well if you ever had to fire one with a number 2 scoop on a grade, you'd know why they called 'em a Hog.

A lot of people'd tell you they called 'em a Hog because they waddled; but I know why they called them a Hog — 'cause I passed a lot of coal in those when I worked down on the Rio Grande in 1939.

The small engines were hand-fired.

I didn't have any seniority work on the main line; I worked switch engines, locals, and all of them were hand-fired.

It wasn't a bad job.

Bright Spots

What stoker-fired was, on each side of the tender, to the firebox, they had a screw gear conveyor; and it would pull this coal up, to what they called, the plate. And the plate was, oh, probably thirty-six inches square.

Then they had bats.

The bats would flip the coal different ways into the fire.

Every once in a while, you had to check your fire to see if she didn't have any bright spots — a bright spot would burn the grate.

And on those coal burners, the engineer always handled the

water; he took care of the water, not the fireman.

But on the oil burners, the fireman took care of the water. And the engineer, of course, he had his own water glass and the gauge cocks and so forth to watch so that it didn't get away from you. And the fireman, on the oil burners, he just sat, and adjusted his fire, to the work of the engine. And the engineer could, or couldn't, help him out if he wanted to. Same way with coal. It would all depend on how he worked the engine.

If he worked the engine too hard, then sometimes he would turn your fire over — if the engine wheels slipped, on a coal burner. And boy, you'd have a heck of a time gettin' your fire back regulated; when the engine would slip, the exhaust would lift the fire, and drop the coal back down, and sometimes when it'd do that you' get a half dozen bright spots.

On an oil burner, you didn't have to worry about that — because you just re-regulate your fire, and you're all right.

To keep the flues of a steam engine clean, when the engine was working hard, you had sand; and you'd sand them out. You'd sand your engines out just as soon as you got out of town, where it wouldn't disturb somebody's laundry.

And you'd sand it out, until you got the stack clean.

Sanding Them Out

They had a sand box on the steam engine, on all of them. And on the tender-in-back engines, the sand box was usually right back of the tender, coming into the cab.

We stood there with a scoop; we had a peep hole; you'd open the peep hole, and you'd just throw sand in the peep hole, and the fire'd suck it through, and you'd watch the stack, and when the smoke cleared up, that was enough sand, and you could close the damper down.

But on the Malleys, on the cab-head, the sand box on the 4000, was on the front end. But on the 4100's and 4200's, the sand box was right in front of the peep hole — 'cause it was too much of a walk back and forth to get your sand and so forth. And you sanded them out there, and of course, you'd make four or five passes with the sand scoop, and then you'd look at your stack, to see if the smoke was cleared up, and when it cleared up, you'd just quit sanding.

Because it wasn't going to do much good to sand anymore, if you had the flues clean.

And there at Weed, we had the Moguls, and the Hogs, and the Mikes, and the Decs, and the Malleys.

At Mt. Hebron, just before the war started, they had to have helpers again. And they brought a bunch of 1600's, 1700's, and 2900's up there for helpers. But they weren't quite enough. So they finally had to go back to hogs. And the hogs, we had three engines, and five crews. And they used to fleet those engines out of Klamath Falls about twenty minutes apart. And then you'd have a hog helper either on the point, or just ahead of the caboose.

The first engine to Grass Lake, they'd cut it off, would go up and turn on the Wye, and sit on the passing track, in the clear. The next two helpers would come up, and they would cut off, and they'd go on the passing track, and the engine that was headed down the hill would couple on, and tow them, backing down the hill to Mt. Hebron. That job, I caught those helpers out there any number of times when I was workin'. And it was supposed to be a pretty good job.

But my father lived out there. My mother used to work in Sears. And we used to go out there and go fishin', when I was a kid. I was out there for three years.

My dad couldn't work in Weed, and he couldn't work in Dunsmuir, 'cause he had trouble walkin', so he stayed at Mt. Hebron.

Then, when the war started, just before the war started, they put the helper back on at Reed. That's where he was when he retired, in '34. But I fired my dad a lot on the switcher there, and on the helper.

My dad was so easy to fire for, because he'd run those Malley's so much, he just knew exactly what to do with 'em. It was never a job to fire 'em.

You'd get some of these guys that'd try to make him do all the work on a Malley; he used to have a heck of a time keepin' 'em hot. To keep the steam right. I never had any problem with that, 'cause my dad had learned so much about them. That's all he'd ever done; he'd never had another job in his life.

A Story About a 4100

I'll tell you a story about a 4100.

The first time I ever saw a 4100 engine, my dad was on a helper at Mt. Hebron, in 1929. And that engine was pretty new. I don't know how old it was. It wasn't too old. My dad was on the Mt. Hebron helper. And a 4100 came in with a freight train, took water, and you could see the engine from where my dad had his place, his living quarters. And there was a fireman there, with my dad, talkin' with my dad.

"George, that's the end of the Mt. Hebron helper," the fireman said.

"Well, I'm afraid so," my dad said.

When they got engines that big, why, they didn't need the helper at Mt. Hebron any more.

I Wanted To Tell You About These Engines.

The small engine was that Mogul or Battleship; and then we had that Hog Consolidation — that was a little 2-4-0 engine ... and it was a very serviceable engine for the Southern Pacific company. The consolidations were a consolidated engine. They were all a simple engine. Some of the Hogs, years ago, were compounds.

Southern Pacific had more Hogs the places I worked than they had of any other type.

The S.P. built the biggest part of them in Sacramento. They'd get one or two engines from Baldwin, or where-ever, and then they'd build it. And that Hog was the 2500's, 2600's, the 2700's and the 2800's, they were all consolidations. Some of them were coal burners, and most of them were oil, that were built in Sacramento.

As far as I can figure from talkin' to my father and other older engineers, they converted from coal to oil, in 1911 — that was the last of the coal burners on the Southern Pacific system.

Then, the next size engine, was the MIKE, the Mikado. It was built and designed for Japan. The U.S. tried to change the name of it during the War, to the MacArthur, but it didn't go over. They were called MIKES.

They had the hot Mike, the cold Mike, and the screw Mike. I'll tell you the difference. The cold Mike was a saturated engine; it wasn't superheated. The hot Mike, was super-heated; the screw Mike, was super-heated — but it had a screw reverse-lever on it, instead of the quadrant type.

About the only place that the screw Mikes were used, were on passenger, that I ever worked on them.

Now the reverse lever on a locomotive was on your valve cut-off, when it was in the position of down in the corner, you had a full stroke on the valve — and the engine would only work in full stroke, up to a certain miles-per-hour, or up to a certain pulling power; and after that, it choked itself — it had too much back-pressure. So you had to hook it up, shorten the stroke; and to get speed out of it, like on passenger, you'd have the lever pretty much up on center — where there was just a little bit of steam goin' in, and a little bit of exhaust comin' out.

On the screw Mike, you'd have a wind-up, and screw the reverse lever in both directions to move it ... but it gave you pretty positive cut-off.

See, on the old reverse lever, on air reverse, when you pull it back, you had a notch; and sometimes, it would work better between the two notches; but on the screw Mike, you could keep the lever right where you wanted it.

And the Mike, the Mike was a very popular engine.

And a very good engine.

It did a wonderful job.

They used those Mikes on passenger over the hill from Hornbrook over to Ashland, and Ashland to Hornbrook.

"When you described the three locomotives, in terms of how they were heated, what did you mean?" I said.

The super-heated steam, is heated beyond boiler pressure. Super-heaters were actually dry; but when they had steam in them, they heated them up, dried out the steam, and built up the pressure a little more on the steam, to make the engine a little more snappy — exhaust wise.

On the old coal Mikes, and on the consolidateds that weren't super-heated, they kind of had a Swwwissh sound to the exhaust, a wet exhaust.

The super-heateds, they had a real CRACK! — a real positive CRACK!

Then, at Weed, we had the old 4000-class Malley.

Built for the S.P. company, about 1908 or 1909. And they came to the S.P. as coal burners. And when they made oil-burners out of them, they made cab-head engines out of them. They couldn't do that with coal. They made cab-head engines, which made them a little bit nicer engines to work on, a little cleaner engine to work in — kept the sand out of your eyes, and the cinders. 'Cause they had the cab ahead. And we had a lot of those up there at Weed, all the time. They used those for helpers.

We had at Weed when I was a kid there, at the roundhouse what we call 'storage tracks'.

The roundhouse would always have an engine in it, and there'd be a bunch of Hogs and Consolidations and Malleys and so forth on the two storage tracks; and they'd pull them out as they needed them.

The Sand-House

They had a stationary plant there, that made steam, to put pressure on the oil, to oil the engines. They also had a sand-house there, where they dried sand. See, they had a sand-dome on the top of the engines; and the sand came down to the wheels, to keep them from slippin' on the track — they had sander valves on all the engines. And before they slipped, or when you figured they were going to slip, you'd open the sander valve, and let the sand fall onto the track, to keep the engine from slipping.

But the engine's would slip anyway, sometimes.

And sometimes the sanders wouldn't be 100%.

But they dried that sand at Weed, at the sand-house. And pretty near every terminal had a sand-house; had one at Hornbrook; had one at Ashland; where they dried their own sand.

Here at west Oakland, with diesels, they have to sand those engines for slipping; but I don't think they dry sand — they get the sand already dried. I don't see any facilities to dry sand there. Of course, I retired before the big diesel shop was in gear.

"They don't have sand domes on diesels?" I said.

They do have sand high, yes. But they're not domes, out like they were on the steam engines. Diesels need to put sand on the tracks too.

Course a diesel, when it slips, you can feel it, or hear it. It isn't like a steam engine.

A steam engine, when it slipped, the exhaust sound would get so rapid, 'CHOP! CHOP! CHOP! CHOP!' — 'till it settled down; and usually we'd have to throttle them down.

And that was another thing. The more you had an engine hooked up for expansion of steam, the better chance there was for slipping — 'cause it was SNAPPY! see; but if you had the throttle worked down a little, it would blow more, 'WHOOSH! WHOOSH! WHOOSH! WHOOSH!' — it didn't slip so bad.

There Was Nothin' At Kirk

One time, another couple of kids and I, we rode the passenger train from Weed to Kirk. We got to Kirk; and there wasn't a darn thing in the world there.

Nothin'.

There wasn't even a place to eat.

But see, the engine crew, and the train crew, they lived there; wasn't no problem for them.

So we slept in the coach, and waited 'till we got back to Klamath Falls, for something to eat ... which was all right.

I think we had a blanket apiece.

We'd figured on camping out up there.

Kirk was on the Williamson River.

They had a few loggers there.

They used to load logs there.

Down at Chiliqwin, just below Kirk, they had a big mill. And then they had another one at Pine Ridge.

There was quite a bit of revenue came off that line. It went down into Weed, and then shipped south to Roseville, and then from Roseville over the hill to where-ever it was going — or it'd go to Los Angeles. And some of it even went east out of Roseville.

The Big Issue Was Always Lumber Up There. The Big Revenue Was Always Lumber.

And the same with Weed. There was a big mill at Weed.

When I was as kid, on the branch, which had been Weed Company Railroad, and S.P. bought it out, they had fifty-two loads of logs on flatcars come in, two trains a day.

And that mill worked twenty-four hours around the clock. That's a lot of logs.

Fifty-two loads a train; sometimes they'd only have forty-eight, I don't know why.

But we used to count them, when we were kids, when they'd come in to Weed.

Then when they built the Natron Cutoff, they abandoned that piece of track, from Weed to Grass Lake.

Then they ran the Logger, on S.P., from Weed to Black Butte, Black Butte to a place called Leaf — where they picked up the logs; then back from Leaf, to Black Butte, back into Weed.

But they only ran one train a day.

I don't know what happened.

I guess maybe the trucks were haulin' a few logs.

That would be, after 1927.

Spuds From Tulley Lake On The Spud Digger

You came out of Klamath Falls on the new railroad, and you went out through Tulley Lake. There was a big spud grower there.

We used to get about a hundred cars a day of spuds out of there.

A day.

When potatoes were being dug.

He must have had miles and miles and miles of potatoes; I can't imagine.

Anyway, that's all gone.

And they would fire those potatoes. They'd come into Klamath Falls; they'd bust up the train, and then they would consolidate another train, to go to San Francisco and Sacramento.

And they'd have about seventy cars of potatoes, on The Spud

Digger, they called it.

The Spud Digger would leave Klamath Falls, and at Davis, thirty of those cars would go to Sacramento, and that area; and the others would go into San Francisco — whatever was left.

But always about thirty to Sacramento.

And then the rest of the potatoes would come into Oakland, and San Francisco, and that area.

But no potatoes went to L.A., for some reason or other, that I can remember of. I used to go through the way bills on 'em, and I never saw 'em go anyplace but to Oakland, San Francisco, and Sacramento.

Of course, Stockton grows a lot of potatoes now — now the potatoes are processed there; and they're either potato meal, potato flour, or freeze-dried — they did away with the water, and they'll get twenty-five or thirty cars of potatoes into one car.

These french fry places, they all buy potatoes already processed; they're split, and frozen.

So there's no more potatoes, or potato trains.

People don't realize how cold it was on that Modoc Line. This is starting in 1929. I never worked on that line in '29; but they built it in '29.

I worked over there in '37. Modoc's north in California.

Oh my, was it cold?!

I'll tell you, we used to go outta Alturus with a train, and there'd be two engines on the point, two Malleys; and there'd be two Malleys on the rear end. It was a heavy grade, from a place called Likely, to the top of the hill, at Sage Hen.

And at Sage Hen, they usually cut the helper off the point. And he'd go back to Alturus, or maybe help another train from Likely up the hill.

And the other two helpers would stay on the train.

By that time, it was usually time to eat.

That's no foolin'.

You'd be seven or eight hours gettin' where you were goin'.

And they'd eat at Madeline or Bernal.

I'll tell, when there was cold weather there, and you went to eat, you never left your engine too long. You'd eat, and get back there — 'cause something'd freeze on it if you didn't. Oh Jesus, it'd get cold.

You'd usually have to leave a little spot-fire in it, because if you put the fire completely out, you might not get oil back to it; 'cause that oil'd get that cold, and you couldn't get it.

Then you'd go on, and then they'd cut the other two helpers at Crescent; that was the top of the hill.

And if the train was a little heavy, they'd run one of the helpers through to Vuland. Then cut it off at Vuland, and it'd go back. Then the rest of the train, without the helpers, went into Wendel; and from Wendel, they went to Bernal. And then S.P. main line picked up the cars at Farley. And they were usually blocked at Alturus, and they'd pick up the ones that came west, that came into Roseville.

What blocked is, say, they had a hundred-car train out of Alturus. Well, it would have the cars that were going back to Roseville on the point. We had twenty-one or twenty-two cars on the point, blocked, in a block. And all we had to do was pull 'em out, and go.

The freight we were haulin' was mostly lumber.

We had an awfully lot of pilings.

We had triple loads of piling. And there's the ones you had to be awful careful with, because you couldn't cut 'em, because you had poles sticking out someplace. It was mostly piling, raw lumber, and they had potatoes, too. But not so much potatoes, because they had the Idaho potatoes out east.

I've seen it 50 degrees below zero, at Madeline — that's in California.

One Morning Out At Madeline

I'll tell you what I did one morning, out at Madeline.

I took water, and I run the tank over, not by much, but I run it over. I was firin'. And not a drop of that water hit the ground, it just rolled over the top of the tank and froze. Course that tank is insulated. That's why it froze there, because the heat was focused in on the water and oil. But not a drop of that water hit the ground. It would freeze right in front of you. Your nose would freeze solid, just while you were out there. I didn't care much for that.

'Pop! Pop! Pop! Pop! Pop!'

I worked Alturus, on the extra list there, both as a fireman, and an engineer, at different times. It was a big pay job, but it wasn't an ideal place to work. You had to walk about a mile from where you slept to where the roundhouse was, and in cold weather, why it was pretty cold. Once you got on the engine it wasn't too bad, you had the heaters.

There was never any snow out there. Just cold, and frost. Might've had a little snow now and then, but not much to speak of.

That ground would be frozen six inches deep ... you'd walk on it, and it would go Pop! Pop! Pop! Pop! Pop! — when you walked on it.

That was real cold.

Charlie McLaughlin

I remember one fellah was firin' on passenger; he went to Gerber, and when he was in Gerber, they told him what had happened. He listened to 'em.

"I'll just take a hosslin' job when I get back to Dunsmuir," he said.

He took the hosslin' job, when he got back to Dunsmuir — the fireman used to hossle the engines to the roundhouse — when he got back to Dunsmuir he took the hosslin' job, and before he got a chance to work it the next day, he was cut completely off. And he was right up at the top of the list, firin' a passenger job.

He went to the Coast. I used to see him quite often when I worked the Coast Division. He's dead now. Charlie McLaughlin.

What The Hossler Did

What hosslin' is, it comes from hosslin' in the livery stable, where they used to hitch up the teams and stretch out the wagons. The hossler, at the terminal, usually took the engine after the engineer and the fireman left it, and took the engine in for service — for oil, sand and water. He took it in, and put in on the waiting track, or whatever track, or in the roundhouse (when I was at Dunsmuir), and they did any minor running repairs that had to be done. Then the hossler, when that engine was called to go to work, he'd take the engine out of the roundhouse, turned it on the turntable the way they wanted it to go, and set it out on a getaway track. Then the engineer and fireman would take it where ever it was going, in either direction.

That's what the hossler did.

We'd Knock Down Picket Fences & Throw Them In The Firebox

I've had engines dead, and tried to get enough fire in 'em to get oil in 'em; sometimes I did, and sometimes they wouldn't ... no matter what you'd throw in the firebox.

Sometimes we'd take all the packing out of the journal boxes that we could get, and throw it in the firebox — and if there was a fence along there, you'd knock all the pickets off it, and put those in the firebox. Then, once you got about twenty pounds of steam, you could get the oil back in 'em.

Later I'd have to tell the car man when you got to where ever you were going, 'I've taken the packing out,' and you'd usually give him the car numbers," Bill said.

Using Pickets To Heat Up An Engine

I ripped the pickets out of a fence there at Algona one time,. I had a young fireman and he didn't know much. I was tryin' to get a fire going in the engine, and all he did was help me watch it. We finally got the engine with about twenty pounds of pressure; we finally got the engine hot, so we could get out of there. It took a long time, though.

That was a 4200.

When we had the steam engines, it's was a dog's life. I'm not kidding you. And it was worse here (Oakland — what we call the Western Division) than when I worked up on the Shasta Division. 'Cause on the Shasta Division, we had decent places to stay, pretty good places to eat. And here on the Western Division, it was horrible ... places we had to stay, 'specially in Tracy and San Jose, and Rosall wasn't any better. And the places we had to eat weren't any good. On the Shasta Division, it was a little bit better. I don't know how much better. But like my wife said, I was gone the biggest part of the time.

It used to bug me to no end ... I'd be gone for three days, eatin' in these slop buckets and sleeping in the gas house, and I'd get home, and my wife would want to go someplace to eat. Jesus, that used to get me.

I'd had enough of goin' places to eat.

Some places in Tracy weren't too bad to eat. And we had some in San Jose that weren't too bad to eat. But Roseville never had any decent places to eat. And those were the three terminals we worked into, on freight.

Now when I worked on Amtrak, over the hill, Jeeze you couldn't ask for a nicer place to live than Sparks, Nevada. 'Cause you had a lot of action, and good places to eat, and good accommodations.

The same way in Dunsmuir.

You had very good accommodations in Dunsmuir on Amtrak. Places to eat were good.

I was with Amtrak '72-'77.

San Luis Obispo was just an ideal place to work into. I played golf twice a day down there. They had fabulous places to eat. And we didn't have too bad a motel to stay in.

I got there every afternoon at two o'clock, when I worked to San Luis Obispo. I would go out and play golf till it got dark. Then I'd go eat. Then I'd go back to the bed. And get up in the morning at six-thirty or seven, and go out and play golf till noon; I left San Luis Obispo, to come home, at one-forty-five. So it was an ideal set-up there.

Course in Dunsmuir, I always took a car up there, and I could go around the places I used to be, that I used to go to. I usually had a fireman who liked to go with me. And I used to go over the hill to Soda Creek ... I'd walk over the hill and go fishin' — I never could get a fireman who could make it.

Dunsmuir, I liked that job. The only thing was, it was all-night work. You went to work here at eight-forty-five p.m., and you got in there at two-forty-five a.m. in the morning.

And when you were scheduled out you left there at one-forty-five a.m., and you got in here (Oakland) at eight o'clock in the morning. You can see, it wasn't the ideal set-up.

When we went to Sparks, we left here at noon, and we got in there six-thirty, seven o'clock at night. And we left there at six-forty-five in the morning, and got in here about noon. So that was all daylight work.

Goin' to San Luis Obispo, eight-forty-five to two o'clock; comin' back, one-forty-five to eight o'clock — all daylight work. And fast track.

Goin' over to Sparks, that was awfully slow track. It took time. There were grades and cut-offs.

Going to Dunsmuir, some of it was fast track, and some of it was slow. But it was all-night work. But it didn't bother me, I was just goin' up there, it was like being back at home again. It didn't worry me much about what was goin' on.

I can tell you a story.

Here She Comes!

One morning, we were in a siding, another time, at a place called Erickson. It's no longer there. We were goin' east. We'd been there for quite a while. We dozed off. You sit there, and you doze off. The engineer dozed off. I dozed off. We'd been there an hour or so. Finally I see the headlight comin' around the curb. That train headlight looked like it was comin' right at us.

"Here she comes!" I says.

Old Ed opens his eyes and sees that headlight then jumps out the cab onto the ground.

He breaks his ankle.

He thought we had a mainline meet, I guess, in his dream, and he woke up, saw the headlight, and jumped out the cab.

I wasn't trying to scare him or anything.

You see, you have to verify a meet. If you have a meet with somebody, the fireman will say, "Well here comes 23."

And the engineer will repeat, "23."

So I says, "Here she comes!"

He had a heck of a time covering up about how he broke his ankle, I'll tell you that.

"Did he hold any of that against you?" I said.

"Oh no. He was dozin' off, or dreamin'. See, in those old cab-ahead engines, everything was out there in the front ... ... let me show you my number 2 shovel," Bill said.

We went outside to a shed, and he took out about a 4-foot tall shovel with a squared-off front end.

"That's what we used to shovel coal with, and that's what we used to on the section gang to tap the gravel underneath the ties ... ... and I bought that scoop, I didn't steal it.

"What they did, was they put the ties down, and then they run a ballast car over them, and dumped the gravel on top, and then you'd take a bar, and lift the tie, and try to get gravel underneath it as much as you could," Bill said.

"Why didn't they just set the ties on the gravel, in the first place? It seems backwards," I said.

"Well that's the way they did it. They must have had a reason," Bill said.

"So you made a bed first? Then you put the ties on the bed? And then you come back and put gravel under the ties?" I said.

"We'd take the pinch-bar, as they called it, and get ahold underneath the tie, and raise the tie up as high as we could, and try to get gravel underneath it ... ... Now I want to show you this oil can of my grandfather's," Bill said.

We went into a little cellar underneath his house. There was an old-fashioned oil can, about the size of a quart can of oil, with a 2-foot oil spout coming up out of it.

"Can you read what's stamped on it?" Bill said.

"Yeah. William Millard, April, 1894. 1894?" I said.

"I was named after my grandfather," Bill said.

"What was one of your happiest times on the railroad?" I said.

"One of my happiest times on the railroad, it's hard to say, I guess one of my happiest times is when I could work the year around," Bill said.

The Happiest Time I Had On The Railroad

The happiest time I had on the railroad was when I got set up,

couldn't work out of Dunsmuir, had to work out of Klamath Falls.
My little girl was about three years old.
We went to Klamath Falls, and we were there for a year. I think that was the best time I ever had on the railroad. Because in Klamath Falls, it was usually a local freight — you never went any place. And I got to be with my family.

"What about in the cab itself? You have any happy times in the locomotive?" I said.
"Oh yeah. One time I remember, it isn't happy, but it was funny. And I enjoyed it. And it's nice to talk about."

The Feast

One time over on that Modock Line we got stuck in the snow. I was with this old Swedish engineer.
And we started up the hill. And we had an empty tank on this Malley backin' up. We were just shovin' the tank. We were a light engine.
And we backed right into a snowdrift.
And Jesus, that darn tank raised up, and dropped back down. It scared the heck out of me. It probably didn't go near as high as I thought it did. I must've looked pale, 'cause the engineer watched me.
"What's the matter kid," the engineer said.
"Jesus, Johnny; that tank darn near jumped off the track," I said.
"You're all right kid. It didn't have any water in it," he said.
He hit a curve of snow on his side, and he cleaned the clock.
"We can go no further," he said.
So we go back to this siding at Horse Lake, that we had just left a few minutes earlier, and for some reason or other, he headed into the darn pass. And it was full of little snowdrifts about three feet tall.
And he got in there, and he gets on the phone, and tries to call the dispatcher, to see if he could go on to Windel.
Well he couldn't get anybody on the phone. He fooled around on the phone for an hour.
This was about two o'clock in the afternoon.

And he couldn't get anybody.

By that time, we couldn't move the darn engine, we had so much snow in front and back.

So there we were.

In wintertime. Colder than heck. We didn't have enough water to last too long with the heat in the engine.

I went out and tried to shovel snow into the tank; and that didn't do much good.

Anyway, it got dark, and Johnny start talking to me.

"Kid, we'll have a feast," Johnny said.

Did you ever hear of Martha Washington coffee? It was a liquid, instant coffee. Johnny had a little jar, a bottle of that. He had two cans of Beany Weinies, you ever hear of Beany Weinies? Two cans of sardines. And two boxes of crackers.

"Kid, we will have a feast," Johnny said.

So we had a feast all right. We ate everything we had.

It got dark, and we kept warm in the cab.

The next day, we were out of water.

Couldn't build a fire in the engine anymore.

And darn-it, all day we didn't have anything to eat.

It was gettin' pretty hairy.

But I figured, I wasn't particularly worried about it. There wasn't anything out in that darn country. At night you could see a farm light over there miles away; you didn't know how far it was. I was afraid to take a chance going out there; it was awfully cold.

By golly, I was gettin' awfully hungry.

I went back to the tender for some reason, and I could smell coffee.

I come back, and told Johnny.

"I can smell coffee!" I said.

"It's a mirage, kid," Johnny said.

Well it was a mirage all right. What it was, was a relief tender came along trying to find us, 'cause we didn't show up, and they were looking for us, and they were going along, and they had an engine, and they were pushing a car, and they had a flatcar in front, and every snowdrift they'd come to, if it was big enough, they'd poke a pipe in it, to see if our engine was in there.

Well they finally got to us.

Of course we were hungrier than heck. It was dark by that time. We just left the engine where it was. And they took us on in to Windel.

We went to bed, came back the next day on a job. And that darn engine stood out there, I guess, three or four days. And it froze up tighter than heck.

Everything froze up. The feedwater pump, the air compressors, injector, everything.

But we'd had our feast, all right.

I've kinda thought about that, and laughed about that, a lot of times. But if we'd been out there another day, I don't know what the heck we would've done.

'Cause it got awful cold that night and if we'd been there, we were out of water, and we couldn't have a fire.

"You couldn't have started a little fire, even without water?" I said.

"We didn't want to take a chance," Bill said.

"I would've probably started one in the cab, on the floor," I said.

"Well, we had a wooden deck, you know. We were talkin' about building a fire in the sandbox, but we never did," Bill said.

One Of The Biggest Thrills I Ever Had

One of the biggest thrills I've ever had was on the Dumbarton Line between Redwood City and the Dumbarton Bridge. We were goin' along there; we had an empty rock train, with about forty cars. It was pretty good track. You'd go right along out there. I was makin' the time.

We had two diesels on the point.

And here come a salt truck.

Jeeze, the way he was comin', I knew he wasn't going to stop. I thought maybe he'd make it across the track crossing.

He had two trailers, and the truck — the tractor. I caught him right between the trailer and the tractor.

And here come the salt.

Into the cab. The salt was knee deep in the cab. And it knocked the toilet out of the front of the cab.

I was sitting in the cab.

I went to emergency. We went pretty near a train length before we got stopped. We finally got stopped.

Then the electrical wiring in the lead unit caught on fire.

I had to shut that unit down, since it wouldn't operate any more.

Then we shoved the train back to clear the crossing.

Then when we got everything squared away, and got enough salt off the tracks so we could go on, we went on to Newark, and set that engine out. And then went on to Pleasanton.

I never saw so much salt in my life.

It knocked the windows right out.

And that salt came right around me too.

It was kind've hard to figure out where it all came from.

Plop, Plop, Fizz, Fizz

The biggest thrill you have, is when you're going down the coast on S.P., say from Coyote, down to Gilroy, the highway parallels the track. And there's two or three big crossings. But most of the smaller crossings are not used.

You'll see a tank truck going down on the highway, and you know there's a crossing down there that he might use.

But you don't know what to do — to slow down, or try to go faster, or whatever. You're going faster than he is, but he's still ahead of you.

And what a relief it is, to find out that that's a milk truck, instead of a gasoline truck.

It's bad enough to hit a milk truck.

But it's horrible to hit a gasoline truck.

I never did that.

I've Hit A Beet Truck

That was up at Elmira, I hit the beet truck.

I hit that beet truck on passenger.

The engine just barely hit it and shoved it off the track.

Darn near got stopped.

I don't even think he knew we were around.

It was what we called an unguarded crossing.

We Hit A Spinach Truck

One time there were two engines coupled together, runnin' light, on the old Altamont Line, and we come down off the hill there, the diesel, 1300 switch engine diesel was on the point, and I had a 3200 behind.

Had a crew on both engines.
At Verona, we hit a spinach truck.
I was on the second engine.
Art Wellis was on the front, lead engine.
I never saw so darn much spinach.
It was just loose spinach.
That cab was just full of spinach.
And it was all over everything ... ... the running boards, and the whole works.

We climbed down, and the crossing was even blocked with spinach.

The truck was still there, part of it.

The highway patrolmen come up, and they were making out a report on what happened, and talked to us.

"Why in the heck can't you guys hit a beer truck, or something like that? But spinach?" he said.

"Well we're workin' on dinner here; you got salt, you got beets, and you got spinach," I said.

I remember the engineer that hit it, Marvin Hargess ... he hit a ketchup truck. Over there between Elmhurst and Jack London Square. And if you ever wanted to see a bloody mess, that was it.

Marvin Hargess

There used to be a restaurant. It was the only one that was open at night over at Tracy. It was a restaurant and coffee shop right across from the Tracy Inn, a Greek restaurant.

And everything that you got there, had gravy on it.
You get a steak, there's gravy.
Fried potatoes, gravy.

Whatever you got, had gravy on it.

Marvin Hodges and I were down there one night. He had a hamburger steak, and they poured the gravy on it, you couldn't hardly find the steak. And when he got through, it was on the special, the waiter comes over.

"What do you want for desert?" the waiter says.

"What do you have?" Marvin says.

"Ice cream, rice pudding, and jello," the waiter said.

"I'll have jello. But for Christ's sake, hold the gravy," Marvin said.

One time we were there, a guy takes off out of the restaurant, goes to his car, and he has two buckets, one in each hand. I was with Marvin that time too. And this guy carryin' these two buckets is being very careful; they had a lid on them so he wouldn't spill anything.

I looked at Marvin.

"What the heck has he got in those buckets? I said.

"That's gravy. He's going to the Greek restaurant," Marvin said.

That Tracy Inn had a dining room on it. It wasn't a bad place to eat. But it was rather expensive. Couldn't afford it.

That was another thing. We never got quite enough away-from-home expenses on the railroad.

We were allowed a dollar-and-a-half for a meal.

Y'know, you couldn't get much of a meal even then for a dollar-and-a-half; this is back in '56, and '58.

A-dollar-fifty wouldn't go very far. And even then, you had to be away from home twelve hours before you got that. That was just one meal.

Right up until I quit work, in '77, we were only gettin' a-dollar-and-a-half for a meal.

That would buy coffee and a donut then, but not much more than that.

I could get a good meal in San Luis Obispo on the luncheon special; I never did go in the evening. I'd get a good meal for $2.75.

In Dunsmuir, you could get a good breakfast for a-dollar-and-a-half.

But boy, in Sparks, if you knew where to go, when you got in there at night, you could get a prime rib for 99¢.

"Did you ever work with any characters? Or were you a character?" I said.

"Possibly I was a character, I don't know," Bill said. When I went to work, you didn't ever call an engineer by his first name. He was Mr. Creasner, Mr. Smith, Mr. Jones or whatever. And after you worked with him two or three years, and bummed around town with him in Gerber, or Klamath Falls or someplace, you might get close enough to call him 'Jim,' or whatever his name was. But when you started out, you didn't call him by his first name. I don't think I ever worked with an engineer, when I first went to work, that I called by his first name, right off. When I was working around Dunsmuir, in the grocery stores, and then I had a little body fender shop there for a while, and service station, I called 'em all by their first names in the service station. But when I worked on the railroad, I didn't. They were Mister. And I tell you. An engineer, when I was a kid, had a certain amount of prestige. He wasn't just a regular railroad man."

"What about some of the characters you worked with? Any of 'em come to mind?" I said.

"Oh gosh, yes."

Frank Tirral — Full-Blooded Italian

There was a fireman here by the name of Frank Tirral. He was a character. He was an Italian.

And he used to pull out these wooden nickels he had, about as big as a poker chip. And they had printed on them, Frank Tirral, F.B.I. — Full Blooded Italian.

Frank was about as out-of-place on a railroad as a fireman as I can ever remember anybody being.

One time, he was firin' for me, and they had a city ordinance up at Suisun, that you weren't supposed to smoke or sand out an engine through Suisun — you were supposed to have a clear stack, and no sandin' the engine in the city limits.

And we come into Suisun, I'm not kiddin' you, you could'a walked on that smoke.

It was sure smoky.

I hollered at him.

"Frank, I think your fire's out!" I said.

He looked up.

"You're kiddin' me," he said. Then he regulates his fire.

He was one of those guys, that if you stopped any place any length of time, he was on his way to do somethin' else — usually he'd get a drink someplace.

And one time, we were over there on a switch engine, over on Fruitvale, and we went in there to wait until we were ready to pull a train.

"Bill, I'm going to take off. I need a drink of water," he said.

"There's water right here on the engine Frank; you're not going anyplace," I told him.

"I want to go. I want to go," he kept up.

Well I know what he wanted to do. There was a waterhole right up there nearby. He kept it up, and finally he got mad about it. And I told him.

"Frank, if you go get off, don't come back," I said.

He thought it over, and he didn't go.

Anybody'd tell you about Frank.

"Who were some other characters?" I said.

"Well, these guys are all gone now. There was old Razor-Neck Flynn," Bill said.

Razor-Neck Flynn

Razor-Neck Flynn was a contemptible old codger. Course I never fired for him.

All the guys used to use him for a yard-stick about the good-guy or the bad-guy ... he was the bad guy.

And old Razor-Neck Flynn, he gave these guys a bad time.

One time they stopped for water, up at Elmira, in a Malley. The fireman tried to have a spot fire in there, but he had too heavy a fire.

Old Razor-Neck come over, and he grabbed that firin' valve, and he turned it wide open. Well, when he turned it wide open, it went by the mechanical stop and he couldn't pull it back.

That engine just sat there and burned up.

The oil got underneath and caught on fire, and that engine just burned up.

The guy who was firin' for him, Hugh Parker, told me what happened.

They had an investigation.

But that never did come out.

You had a firin' valve to regulate the fire into the firebox. But you also had a cut-off lever on top of the tank to cut the oil out. What happened, was that cable was broken, and nobody reported it; and he couldn't pull it out to shut it off.

And the fireman back there takin' the oil, he saw what was happenin'; he tripped the valve manually, instead of the cable, but it was too late.

Hugh told me all about it.

He's dead too.

So's Razor-Neck.

Barney Price

We had guys that did things. There's one fellow, Barney Price. He was a pretty good drinkin' man.

One time the hill was tied up, and I got back firin'.

I was firin' for Barney.

We catch up with a passenger train at Crockett.

Barney looks at me.

"Bill, I'm going to go into Durelle and get a pack of cigarettes," Barney said.

Durelle is a little waterin' hole that's there before you get to Crockett. He goes in there, and he's gone for about two or three minutes, and he comes right back. By that time, the passenger train leaves.

We go to Port Costa, and Barney hollers down to the yardmaster.

"How long we gonna be here?!" Barney said.

"About twenty minutes. Just pull ahead, and we'll fill you (put cars on you)," the yardmaster said.

"I think I'll go over to Dutchman's and get a pack of cigarettes," Barney told me.

He goes over to Dutchman's.

He comes back.

I have to pull the engine up. I come back, couple up, and we're ready to go, and he gets on and we take off.

We get up to Elmira, and I see him pattin' his chest.

We get to Davis, before we had this 470; we set our train out at Davis, and pick up another one; and we'd usually eat there. He goes to eat, and I never did see him.

Come back, and we get ready to go, and we start out, we had a 4300.

And Barney pats himself.

"Well, if we stop at Elmira, and take water, we can go to Oakland," Barney said.

So he stops to take water.

"I'm going to go get a pack of cigarettes," he says.

So he goes into that watering hole down there at Elmira. When I get through taking water, he comes out, and we get ready to take off again.

And this brakeman I had took a look at me.

"Y'know Bill, I think that engineer you got is a cigarette fiend," he says.

Barney Price, they called him.

That was one of the characters that I worked with.

Frank Shoemakker

Then we had a fellah, he's still alive. He's still around.

When I first came down here, I looked pretty young. I was about thirty-two. And we made a trip around the bay. That time it was all in one pool.

I came in on the extra list; and I was lookin' on the board where I hit the switch and where I fit in on the extra board.

And this guy comes in and pushes me out of the way.

"Let the engineer do the registerin' in and registerin' out!" he said.

He didn't know I was the engineer.

Well I didn't know who he was. I thought he was the fireman I had, who was always horsing around. I just gave him a shove. He fell right flat on his ass.

He's sittin' there lookin' up.

"For your information, I am the engineer," I said.
He gets up, and goes in the change room.
He finds out who I was.
The next time I see him, he goes, "Hi Bill."
Frank Shoemakker.
Everybody disliked that guy.
He wasn't a very popular engineer.
After that he was always very friendly to me.

But some of the firemen, were they ever scared to death of him.

He was an obnoxious guy.

He retired, and went up to Portland. He came back a couple times. Christ old Frank must be darn near ninety now.

But he was a whole lot better once he retired, than when he was working.

Real Characters

There was Jacob Wilde; Johnny Cooper; Red Gardner. Some of these guys couldn't get an eye on a water spout. Johnny Cooper was one of them.

He was in the pool around the bay.

One time I had a fireman, name of Jacob Wilde; and we were goin' through Russell.

"Y'know Bill, you can't take water at Russell here in a 4400," he says.

"I didn't know that," I said.

"No, you can't," he says.

"Well why not?" I says.

"The tank's too high; it won't go under the spout," he said.

The 4400 had a real high tank.

"Well how'd you find out?" I said.

"Well I'm Johnny Cooper on a 4400," he said.

See, Johnny Cooper had tried to get water in a 4400, and couldn't get it 'cause the water tank was too high.

But can you imagine takin' water, coming around the bay? — on a tank that held 32,000 gallons of water ... Christ, you could go from here to Roseville with the water already in the tank, you wouldn't ever have to stop to take water there anyway.

Johnny Cooper

Johnny Cooper, one time, he was comin' off the hill there, on the Pacific pool, and come around what they called, Grecian Bend. He come around the curve there, and he wasn't goin' too fast or anything.

But see, those AC's as they called them, the Malleys, are articulated consolidations. See, they had a hinge in the running gear, but the boiler stayed straight. Two different engines, they swiveled.

Well, this engine that Johnny was on, it didn't swivel back; it locked. It went around the curve, the running gear swiveled, then it locked. And when Johnny straightened out, the engine wouldn't follow, it just went off the track.

And it had to happen to Johnny, off all people.

Oh he'd explain what happened.

'It wasn't my fault,' ... that's the way he'd always start.

Well it wasn't his fault. Everybody knew that already.

Johnny Cooper.

If anything would happen, it'd happen to Johnny.

Red Gardner

We had a conductor.

And you know the character in L'l Abner, Joe Bifsteak — always has a cloud over his head.

Well we had a conductor here, like that.

If anything would happen on a trip, it would happen to Red.

Everything happened.

If he got over the road, without somethin' happenin', that was a very successful trip.

He made things happen.

I don't know how the heck he did it.

It used to live here in Albany.

I haven't seen him for a long time.

I don't know whether he's still alive or what. He was a little bit older than I.

We used to deadhead to San Francisco.

We'd go down and leave our car at the lot at the roundhouse. Then we'd ride a switch engine down to the pier, with a cut of cars, or light. Then we'd go on the ferry boat, over to San Francisco. Then we'd get on a streetcar in San Francisco, and either go to Mission Bay, or where ever we were supposed to go. And if we got to Mission Bay, and we were supposed to work at Bayshore, they'd take us by bus.

The only time I ever remember, that a ferry boat broke down, Red Gardner was on it.

Stalled out in the bay for an-hour-and-a-half.

And Red would always start in by explaining.

"It couldn't happen to anybody but me, Bill," he said.

Red Gardner.

I enjoyed working with him, because he was such a heck of a nice guy.

A perfect gentleman.

I haven't seen him for a year.

I meant to ask, up at The Old Rails Club, if he was still around.

At the Old Rails, we meet once a month.

But the sad part of it is, when I first joined that Old Rails, in '77, we had about two-hundred-and-twenty members.

The last meeting I was at only had thirty-eight there. The sad part of it is, these fellahs die out, move out, the younger fellah doesn't want to go in with a lot of us older fellahs; they just don't have anything in common with myself, or some of these other fellahs.

"Did you have any favorite curves, or memorable ones, or curves you liked, or curves you didn't?" I said.

"Oh boy," Bill said.

The Curve at Keg Pit

Keg was the worst one goin' East.

That was between Bray and Mount Heburn, on the Shasta Division.

And that curve there, was fast track.

Myself, when I was runnin', I didn't go as fast as I could go around that curve; but when I used to go around there with guys, when I was firin' ... what I didn't like about that curve, was you come around, and the west switch, was right in the center of that curve.

And there's always the possibility someone had been springing that switch, and you would be going the wrong way.

It had happened.

Not there.

But other places.

That switch at Keg always bothered me.

One time they had a train, and they had a big storm, and the mainline was blocked. And they put this train in the siding at Hotland, and they cut the engine off, and the engine went around and got the caboose, and I don't know if they went back to Dunsmuir I don't remember now.

But anyway, after the train had set there for a week I guess, they decided to take it out.

When Snow Melts & Freezes On A Train On A Siding

We went up there with a 4400.

I wasn't on the train when they docked it.

While we were there, they coupled up the 4100, and they were going to pull that train out.

Well what had happened, it kept snowin'.

The snow would fall on the cars, and melt, and the water would run down, get underneath the trucks, and freeze.

They coupled up, and they figured they could pull ten cars out of there at a time. Well they coupled up, and the curve was on the fireman's side and my side, and they started to pull and I started screamin' at 'em.

"Stop! Stop!" I said.

Well what had happened, they started to pull, and those 4400's had a lot of Uummpph! And they were pulling the darned tops of the cars right off of the trucks — and they were about ready to fall over on the main line.

fig. 43 – 4-8-4 *Northfork & Western*, the steam engine of the future

I don't remember what they did, but they decided we couldn't pull 'em. We'd have to wait to see what they could do about it underneath the cars. The whole darn train had froze up that way.

We went back to Weed.

Another time, over at Alturus, we had a cinder pit over there ... red cinders, they called it, 'Keg Pit'.

And we used to get the cinders out of there for ballast.

Red Cinder Ballast

You've probably seen them on the rightaway, those red cinders, red ballast. They don't use so much of it as they used to. Nothing would grow in it. Even grass won't grow in cinder. And it's a pretty good ballast.

But it isn't a high speed ballast. It's just a ballast.

And they had a bunch of those cars over at Alturus, that had been rained on, between the time they'd loaded 'em at Keg Pit and the time they got to Alturus.

Well, they sat around Alturus for twenty-four hours, at fifty below zero.

Those cinder froze solid.

And they tried everything in the world to shake those cinders out.

They couldn't do it.

Y'know what they finally had to do with those cinders?

Send 'em down to Tucson, to thaw out.

More Curves

We had curves down in the canyon between Dunsmuir and Delta, that were pretty severe curves. But most of the time 25 m.p.h. was the maximum speed both for freight and passenger down there.

You never got much of a thrill, because you were going 25 m.p.h.

But we had curves on that Klamath Falls line up there, some of them were pretty sharp.

There was a big curve comin' into Leaf, that always bothered me. It didn't bother me so much when I was runnin', as it did when I was firin'. I knew what I could do when I was runnin' ... I could slow down.

But some of the other guys I was firin' for, they may not slow down.

Comin' into Leaf, you come around a curve, and there was always the possibility of somebody being down there, pullin' out down there, 'cause that's where we got our transfer from the Long Belt Lumber Company — logs and stuff.

And they didn't pay much attention to operating rules of the S.P.

They had their own railroad.

That curve always bothered me.

I saw one pretty bad accident there.

That bothered me too.

The Bridge To Leaf

Well I'll tell you, handling a train down a hill on a light grade, where you didn't have to use retainers and were trying to make speed, we bridged the train with the air. Instead of making a service application of the air, and letting it blow down, just let the train handle itself with leakage — as it leaked off, it set the brakes a little bit.

You get it set at just about the right spot, and just leave it leak a little bit, and build up a little bit, and your train would handle as a unit; but it didn't have the run-in-run-out service application.

Well this engineer, I knew him well, he was a heck of a good engine man too, he come down the hill on the bridge to Leaf; he'd evidently gone too much on leakage, 'cause when he gets on that curve, he sees a caboose sittin' down there. Well he goes to give a service application, he didn't have enough air to make the service application.

He plows into the caboose, and darn near kills himself with a Malley. I think he did hurt somebody in the caboose.

After that, if I ever used the bridge comin' into Leaf, I didn't use it to the amount that I knew I didn't have something left to stop.

I Was Out Of Air

One time, comin' off the hill there from Ambrose into Perez — there was a big, long siding there; I think it held a-hundred-twenty-one-cars, and I came off the hill on the bridge, and I had a long train, maybe a hundred cars, and it handled beautifully down the hill, just like I had a light engine, and they had a water spout down there and I wanted to stop at the water spout, and I missed the train link ... ... I was out of air.

So I got down to the other end, got stopped, cut my engine off my train, and had to go up through the pass to take water, had to come back down, get on my train, and go.

That bridge, if a guy knew what he was doing, why he got by pretty good with it.

Dick Was Out Of Air

I remember one time, over at Tracy, one of the guys comin' off the hill, he's long dead now, he was usin' the bridge comin' down the hill into Tracy — that was a pretty good little hill. You never used retainers, you had to use air, but most guys used the bridge. I used the bridge occasionally, if I had any loads I didn't pay too much attention to the bridge, because I could use air with the load.

But this fellah, Dick, he come down off the hill there, and he didn't have enough air to stop at Tracy.

He went right through Tracy on the fly.

He was layin' on the whistle all the way comin' into town. They knew something was wrong. They just lined him right down the main line.

He went down as far as he could, and he stopped.

Then he backed up.

"How long does it take to get the air back up if you're out like that?" I said.

Pops When Feelin' The Seat Box

"Well, the sad part of it, is that you go back over to release position, and you have to build up your air, then you charge the train up, and it runs faster than it ever did ... ... the air would release all the brakes then, see. When you had it on the bridge, some of the brakes were draggin'; but you kick it over to release, then it release all the brakes, and built up your air all right, but you were going pretty fast by then.

That's what the retainers were for.

You set your pops at the top of the hill, you're usually stopped — sometimes you'd set 'em on the go, but not very often; and as you'd start down the hill, you give your train a shot, and you knew just about how much you could give it from what the conductor told you you had. You'd give 'em a shot, and stay at ten or twelve pounds. Then you'd go back to running position — not necessarily to release position; then set your pops.

Now the pops retained seven to fifteen pounds on the brake cylinder after you released the train; it held the brake. And those pops would leak down in from 30 seconds to 90 seconds, it gave you that much time to charge the train up again.

Lots of times, you set your pops, then the train would hold back real good, and if you started to pick up speed, all you do is just fan them again.

The next time, you had to hit them a little harder, because the train had loosened up, and was rollin' better.

Then, when you released them, you went back to release position; and that charged the train up; but the retainers still held the air in the train, and held the brakes a bit.

Usually on the hill up there, on Siskiyou Grade, I used to leave the brake over in release position, 'till I got ready to use it again.

Then, when I had to use it again, I had maybe an overcharge, which would help brake, then I could fan them again — maybe it wouldn't take that much more air. Sometimes, it might only take six or eight pounds, the second time, when you had it over there in release position.

Now does that explain a retainer to you?

Now this retainer was a valve. On the newer cars, all A-B equipment, they had a two-position pop, a two-position valve.

Now that valve in release position, was hanging down, like a faucet, with the handle hanging down. You had two positions. The first position was seven pounds; and the second position was full pop, or full retainer — fifteen pounds.

But they never all had the same time momentum. I don't know why. Sometimes a pop would hold for seven or eight minutes. Sometimes it would only hold for a minimum of 30 seconds.

You could feel it, right where you were sittin' — how the train felt on the hill ... when you were using retainers, you had your train popped pretty well solid on the head end, and the rear end never run out or run in. What you were feelin' on your rear end, we used to call it, feelin' the seat box; just the feeling of what was happening — just like a flier, that flies by the seat of his pants.

And that's the way we felt, using retainers.

Now, does that explain retainers?

"You said you could feel how the train was runnin', in the seat of your pants. Is there any thing you could tell me that you could feel? I mean, if you're going by the seat of your pants, were there some things that you could tell?" I said.

You Hadn't Given It Quite Enough

If you were using retainers, and were coming down the hill, and you gave them a shot, let's say, eight pounds, and released them, and that train picked up speed — you could feel it right in the seat of your pants.

You hadn't given it quite enough.

You'd come back after them a little bit more then, or the next time. And you'd hold her over there in release position, to charge her up for the next time. That's the way I felt about it.

Speed is what you felt in the seat of your pants.

See, steam engines, very few of them had speedometers, until the last few years.

We had speed limits, and you'd take your watch, and watch the mileposts on the side of the track. My best way to feel speed, the quickest way, would be, all your whistle posts were a quarter of a mile from a crossing. All right, you come to a crossing in 15 seconds from the time that you went by a milepost, multiply it by

four, and that gives you 60 m.p.h.
  If it took you 30 seconds to go that far, you were only going 30 m.p.h.
  That's the way I always used to figure it.
  That would be the ideal way to do it.
  But you could go milepost to milepost, but the train could go different speeds if you went a whole mile.
  Do you ever notice on the highway, speedometer checks?
  It's the same deal.

"What was your responsibility like? What does it feel like to have that kind of responsibility? I respect someone with that kind of responsibility; you've got to be concentrated, you've got to pay attention, there's no goofin' off," I said.

You've Got To Be On The Ball

With a steam engine, there was a heck of a lot more going on than there was on a diesel. On a diesel, all you had to do, it's just like drivin' an automobile or a truck. You can regulate your diesel engine by your throttle or by your air.
  On a steam engine you were hookin' her up, or droppin' her down, or makin' her work harder, or make her work easier; and then you had the air just in case. And on your longer trains, you had to be awful careful how you used that air. 'Cause you might stretch that train out, and stretch it too fast, and pull it apart someplace ... break a knuckle.

"Well do you see part of the train gettin' smaller in the background when that happens?" I said.
  "Oh no. The train goes into emergency right now. You break an air hose, it goes into emergency."

How In The Heck Is A Woman Going To Handle A Hundred-Ten Pound Knuckle

If She Breaks A Train in Two?

The sad part of it is, they let these women run the engine, and they like to make you believe that they do just as good a job as a man. Like I tell you, what the heck if they had a break-in-two.

What I can't fathom, since I left, thirteen years ago, they've got these women runnin' the engine, with a conductor or a brakeman on the head end with them. Now these knuckles weigh a-hundred-and-ten pounds.

I never saw a woman yet that could do it.

I could handle it, nothin' to it.

They're heavy.

What I would usually do when I'd break a train in two, and a lot of guys, they'll say, 'I never broke a train in two;' well they have problems; they're dreamin'. Everybody's broke 'em in two sometime or another.

But you take the replacement knuckle, and there's always extra knuckles on the engine, on steam engines or diesel ... you know what a brake club is?

You don't use them very often. 'Cause all brakes now are power brakes. It's a club, it looks like a pick handle, only a little shorter, and they put it in the handbrake wheel, in the handbrake sprocket, and use it for leverage to screw down the handbrake tighter. By hand, you can tighten 'em up to a point; to make them really hold, you've got to use a brake club.

There's always a brake club on pretty near every engine. You take that brake club, and run it through the pin hole on the knuckle, and then get the brakeman with you, and one of you get on each side, and lift it — the problem you have then when you get the old knuckle out, or the old piece of the knuckle, is gettin' that off the brake club, and lift it up, and put it in and put the pin down back in.

Then when you take the old knuckle, and you throw it off the side of the rightaway 'cause you don't need it anymore, then I usually carry a piece of chalk, and I write, on it, 'Joe Cooper got me,' or write some other engineer's name on it.

Joe Cooper

I had one engineer, Joe Cooper; he's dead now, but he was a character.

Every time I had a broken knuckle, I'd take my chalk out, and write, 'Joe Cooper got me.'

"Even when you were an engineer, you'd help with the knuckles? You wouldn't have the two brakemen do it?" I said.

"Oh heck yes," Bill said.

The Broken Knuckle

Somebody had to stay on the engine. And if I had a fireman I could trust, I wanted to go see the broken knuckle. The whole thing is, you'd break a knuckle, and when you break it, you look at it, and see, it might've been a cracked knuckle to begin with. And if it was cracked to begin with, you have a rust stripe in there. And what you want to do, is find out how much it was cracked to see if it was a weak knuckle. I'm the only one who knows about that, or gives a darn about that. The conductor doesn't care. The brakeman doesn't care. The fireman doesn't care. I care.

And if I tell my road foreman if that had a 30% or 60% or 75% crack in it before it broke, it doesn't relieve me, but it takes the pressure off of me breakin' the train in two.

It can sometimes be clean as heck, and don't have a darn bit of rust in it. It was just a weak knuckle.

Joe Cooper Got A Drawbar Once

I had a road foreman here who was a heck of a nice guy; he's long gone now, Mr. Brae.

The road foreman is the fellow who instructs you.

And he's out in the office, and takes care of all that.

But he told me one time, that it took so many pounds to brake a knuckle on a jerk; and it took twice as many pounds to break the drawbar, or pull the pin on the drawbar.

So if you got a drawbar, you really had a surge someplace.

And that has happened.
I got one drawbar, all the time I was workin'.

Mr. Brae

That was up at Port Costa.

I had a big, long train, one-hundred-twenty-six cars.

I had a 3200. It took me a long time to get the train pumped up, or I thought it was pumped up.

I started to move the train, before it was completely pumped up.

Well, there was a car on the rear end that had been marked, 'switch to rear', and I jerked the whole guts, feathers and all out of that car.

What relieved me a bit, was that car was marked 'switch to the rear,' on account of a weak drawbar. And the conductor had it on his manifest, and it was also stenciled on the car.

I forgot now what was on that car; but it was some darn equipment, company equipment.

If you'd had that car next to the engine, you'd a pulled the drawbar right out of it right now. When you have it on the rear end like that, there's not much chance of doing any damage except to that one car.

It was right next to the caboose.

Evidently the air didn't release on that car like it did on the rest of the train, and it didn't take much to pull it out.

I got back to the yard, and I got a hold of the road foreman, Mr. Brae, and I told him what happened.

He went up there and looked. Then he come back.

"Yeah, that's what happened all right," he said.

"You ever run in the fog?" I said.
"Oh yes," Bill said.

410 In The Fog To Tracy Waitin' For The Owl, Old 53

One time, we were goin' from here to Tracy, on 410, that was the number of the train we used to have, and we set some of our train out at Pittsburg, and we picked up some empties at Pittsburg, and it was foggy, and we were foolin' around a lot longer than we normally would, trying to pass signals with a fuze-ie and all, and 'STOP' and 'GO' and all that stuff.

And I had a fireman there, and we got all together, and I had an hour-and-fifteen-minutes to go to Tracy, for the Owl — that was old Number 53.

You ever hear of the Owl?

That was a S.P. passenger train that used to run. They had three of them, went from Oakland to Bakersfield, or Fresno, all the way down to Los Angeles. They went over the hill too.

I had enough time to go, with just a little bit of leeway, not much.

Oh, it was foggy.

We took off, and I had this fireman, and you couldn't see anything. A signal, you had to practically know where the signal was gonna be, to see it.

I was going right along as fast as I could turn the wheels; I had probably sixty cars.

This fireman, he was gettin' pretty wormy.

Because he couldn't see anything on his side, see.

We had a diesel.

He was pacing around the floor, worried as heck.

I kept lookin' at my watch, and where I was and everything; and when I got to Tracy, I figured I had thirteen minutes to get in the clear; and that was up to them to get me in the clear after I got to Tracy.

Well I got to Tracy, and set there a while; I was pretty close on 53's time, and they start pullin' me in; and it was all over, as far as I was concerned.

They put me in the clear.

The passenger train was sittin' at the depot, by that time. He takes off, and goes, and that's all there was to it.

That fireman was promoted shortly after that, but y'know he never went back on the mainline after that.

He stayed right on the switch engine until he retired.

He's still here.

I see him every time at the Old Rails.

He didn't want to get in trouble.

He's a heck of a nice guy. But he's kind of a Milquetoast.

"Brakemen are giving you signals, right? You got to keep your eyes on the brakemen. Tell me a little bit about what that's like," I said.

"You know when you work with brakemen, you get to know a brakeman; you get to know their signals, that's their language — and you can depend, or not depend on them," Bill said.

A Brakeman Can't Signal Any Better Than He Can Talk, Some of Those Signs They Give Mumble

Some signals given by a brakeman, or switchman, are very, very definite, and easy to understand. Others are just like they're talkin' with their mouths closed, and they're mumbling; they don't signal any better than they talk. They're sloppy with their signals.

The signals of switchmen are different signals than signals of brakemen; it's a different class of service. (The switchman's inside the yard, and the brakeman's on the road; otherwise it's the same job — except the switchman's usually handling a heck of a lot more cuts of cars.)

Switchmen's signals are more decisive; more to the point. They're just signaled, and that's it. A brakeman, he'll be givin' you signals to slow down a long, long time before you get there. Whereas a switchman will give you a 'SLOW-DOWN', and then he just waits 'till you slow down; and then he'll bring you to a joint. But a brakeman will take you all the way up there.

But we have a lot of brakemen here who were switchman, and they use switchmen's signals.

I got a story on that.

That's The Time I Stopped

I had a young fellow a few years back, maybe twenty-five years back.

He'd just come to work.

His name was Dail; D, A, I, L.

We were switchin' here in west Oakland yard.

For switchin' we had ahold of maybe thirty cars.

When we stopped, the switchman went over to line the switch, and come back, and he gave me a signal to back up. Then he walks over on the other side, and when he gives me the last signal to back up, he gives me a 'COME BACK' sign on the fireman's side.

Well, I start backin'.

After a little ways, I start wonderin', 'Why doesn't the fireman say anything to me about the sign?' So I talked to him.

"Does that switchman say anything back there," I said.

"I'll tell you mister, he's so far back there, if he says anything, I don't believe I can hear him," Dail said.

That's the time I stopped.

Another Time I Was Shovin' Another Track

I had a young fireman.

The fireman was takin' signals on his side of the cab; and since I couldn't see on that side, I was kinda depending on him.

"What did that brakeman say back there?" I said.

"He didn't say a darn thing, he's just floppin' his arms, it looks like he's trying to fly. Yep, there he goes!" he said.

Well when you flap your arms like that, that's a 'STOP' signal.

Now this fireman wasn't jokin' me or anything.

No. He was serious.

About that time we hit.

See, this fireman, he didn't realize what that brakeman was doin' signalin' up there on the top of the car.

That was a very severe 'STOP' sign, that this fireman had never seen before.

You've got to be very cautious with a younger man.

I am.

Some of this young fellahs are just as good the day they go to work, as the day they retire.

And others, they never seem to give a darn.

"What's a pool?" I said.

The San Jose Pool

A pool is a group of engineers and firemen in one section. They have the San Jose pool, and we work between here in Oakland and San Jose, and here and Tracy. It's called 'San Jose pool'. Then they have 'Watsonville pool' — from Oakland to Watsonville. Then we had the 'Cal-P pool' — that went up to Roseville. When I was workin' we had six crews in the San Jose pool. That's the only pool I worked as a rule. 'Cause I had seniority enough so I could work it. I didn't like the Roseville pool, 'cause it had lousy places to stay, and there was no place for a decent meal. San Jose had better places to eat.

The Watsonville pool didn't appeal to me, because you had a long layover every time in Watsonville.

I didn't like Watsonville anyway.

So I never worked the Watsonville pool.

"I wanted to ask you if you wanted people to know about what it was like to be an engineer workin' the train, if you were going to tell people what the main impressions were, what would you want people to know?" I said.

"I'd want them to know, that you owed your life to the company store," Bill said.

You Owed Your Life To The Company Store

You were no longer an individual. You were an employee of the S.P. company. You did at their bidding, not at your own.

Now, does that answer that question?

A lot of things never bothered me, very few things ever bothered me.

I don't go for any of these things like at Niles, you know, the rail clubs down there. That guy who lives across the street, he belongs to that Niles railroad club; he's always around collecting crankcase drainings. See, they fire those engines with crankcase drainings. And I save all the crankcase drainings for him.

That club used to be out here for a long time. But you go out there, and you try to do something, and you're dealing with a bunch of bankers, and attorneys and school teachers; they don't have any railroad people.

Railroad people think too fast for them.

Well there's a lot of stuff that happened on the railroad that I could tell you; but a lot of the guys now are under ground; it wouldn't make any difference to them. What I'd like to do, is give you all the names of all the helper engineers and firemen in Weed when I was a kid, and things like that, and the helper engineers and firemen at Ashland – I worked all those places at different times.

I do what I can. When you get the age I am, you're not able to do the things that you'd like to do.

fig. 44 – *Ten-Wheeler*, narrow gauge engine in *SP* Ogden Division shop; Ogden Utah

fig. 45 – Niles Canyon, the *California Zephyr*, 1967

Jack Smith — (born 1947)

A Contemporary Diesel Engineer
Who Hopped Freight Trains As A Kid

Notices some management-heavy changes at Santa Fe, some shrinking crews & longer shifts. Likes to run down the main line watching the sun rise over the Sierras from the Central Valley. Wears a beeper, tries to keep his crew awake, & listens to the thoughts of the day goin' by, & the voice within.

"How old are you?" I said.
"Forty," Jack said.
"What's your job, anyway?" I said.

Well, I'm an engineer for Santa Fe. I've been working there for fifteen years as an engineer. Right now I'm workin' in the yard on a yard goat — that's the local term we use for switch engine. And sometimes I work on the road — which is the main line trains; it goes from Richmond out to Stockton down to Fresno. The choice is you can work main line, or you can work in the yard, on local trains — the yard's from Oakland to Pittsburg and back.

"Do you get a choice?" I asked.

It's all seniority. Whatever seniority will hold. But yeah, basically, it's a choice. Where ever you want to work, you have that option. You can work the road for a while. Now it's getting close to Christmas holidays, so it's nice to be back with my family.

The yard's a little bit nicer, because you have regular hours; you know when you're going to work, and you know pretty much when you're going to get off.

When you're working the road, you're always livin' out of a bag. In motel rooms. You take the train from Richmond down to Fresno; then you get off the train at Fresno and they put you up in a hotel. You're usually in the hotel an average of from eight to twenty hours. You get off the train, you shower, you get some food, get some sleep. Then you catch another train coming back the other way, from Fresno back to Richmond. So it's a rotating pool.

"How'd you get to be an engineer. I mean, a lot of people'd love to be an engineer. How did you even get there? How did you get into railroadin'?" I said.

Well, I've always liked trains, ever since I was a kid. I used to hop freights in college. I worked for AMTRAK out of college, got a job with AMTRAK. I just always knew I wanted to go work on the train.

I was in grad school, and I was workin' for the railroad part time, to pay my way through school. And it turned out that I liked the railroad; and it paid better than the job I would have had when I graduated.

It was definitely better working conditions.

So I just quit grad school. I was taking urban planning, city planning. I was gonna do that," Jack said.

I was goin' to Sacramento State College, going to graduate school there, working for AMTRAK," Jack said.

When I Hired Out

When I hired out into engine service, they have a training program; that lasted about nine months. Basically you worked with other engineers. You worked on the yard goats on the mainline trains and the locals, watching them and you run the train every once in a while, with them watching you and being responsible for you.

At that the engineering school was back in Topeka, Kansas.

They sent you back there. And that was more of the paperwork end of it. You went over the rules, the mechanical, and all that.

And they have a simulator back there. It's kind of interesting. It's a train engine set up.

With the simulator, it taught you the ways of running. That was kind of fun on that thing. Same idea as a flight simulator. They had film shot from a real engine going down the track, and they show the film in front of you, and then the cab was all set up like

fig. 46 – railroad excursion to Tracy CA, 1960

a regular train cab; and it was on springs. And it had these little things — a computer made it bounce up and down, to give you the feeling.

It's called shake and bake engineer school.

That's what it is.

In those films, they show you accidents and stuff; they'd just show what happened if you messed up. If you don't handle the brakes right. Not slowing down for curves, things like that.

In the old days, those old timers, it took them about fifteen years — they kept them as a student or a fireman for a long time; but I was promoted in nine months.

Not that I was better than those guys, but they just changed the program.

This last class, I think they were out in six months.

They're just rushin' them through a lot faster.

After you graduate, you go out by yourself, yeah.

"Do you have any kind of things that happen on the job that are in your mind?" I said.

"There's one story I thought of, as soon as you first got a hold of me," Jack said.

Cartoon In Fresno

Okay. This is right downtown Fresno.

We have the main line going on, we have a passing track coming off — so there's a switch, and the passing track goes off the side. And it's what we call centralized traffic control — it's all controlled from a central spot; switches are thrown automatically back in the operator's office.

And there was this one automobile that got stopped, it got stuck on the track. It was stuck on the mainline, but beyond the switch.

And we were coming down the main line, but we were lined through the passing track, which wouldn't bother him at all — but he didn't know this.

But we did.

We were in kind of an evil mood.

We were just runnin' down the track.

It kind of reminded me of the cartoons my son watches Saturday mornings.

That guy was running down the track waving his arms back and forth, trying to stop us.

And we were honking our horn, and waving him out of the way — 'cause we knew what was going to happen, that we'd pass him on the side track.

But he didn't know that, and he was really freakin' out.

His automobile was sitting out on the tracks, and the train came right down to it, then at the last minute, the train took the passing lane right around the automobile, and missed it.

And the guy just stood there with his mouth open, in awe.

It really blew him out, y'know.

We were making the train make as much noise as it could.

Then we just went around him.

"What's it like for you as an engineer in terms of responsibility," I asked.

On The Mainline

Uh, on the mainline, yeah you've got to be really awake; and be really aware of what's going on.

Because you get a train, it's a hundred cars long; each car can weigh one hundred tons apiece — we have like ten thousand ton trains. And some of the trains can go as fast as seventy m.p.h., the freight trains. So you multiply the weight of a ten thousand ton train by seventy m.p.h., and you're handling an enormous amount of weight.

So you really have to plan way ahead, on your stops, what you're gonna do. You have to really kind of project, 'What's two miles out in front of me? Uphill? Downhill? Are we going to have to stop at the station? Or what?' You really plan for it.

You have to know just everything; I'm not sayin' this because of an ego trip or anything, but I know every curve between here and Bakersfield — 'cause you have to, you have to know what's up there. Because it takes so long to stop one of those trains.

In the movies it shows, like when you put a train in emergency, everything goes slammin' against the front bulkhead; and it's not like that. Oh no. Emergency stop in a train, is like lightly putting your foot on the brake pedal of an automobile; it slows it down real slowly, like real easy braking on an automobile — it takes a long time to stop, oh yeah. You can't really just stop a train.

So if you see somebody hung up on a crossing when you come around a curve, or even if you see him a half mile away, you can't stop; you just can't.

Depending on the train, on how much weight's behind you, whether you're going uphill, downhill, what types of brakes are on there — but for a controlled stop, you'd want a mile, at least. Sometimes you go longer, 'cause there's different types of braking methods.

You can use what's called dynamics; basically the diesel engine turns a generator, which turns traction motors, which are electric motors mounted on each axle of the engine. And there's a way of braking where you convert the motors to generators, which slows you down because of increased resistance, and it actually slows the train down, and you create electricity.

"Do you have any curves that you like, or any one's you're suspicious of, or do you have names for any of them," I said.

Curves

There's old names for them; a lot of the curves have names, some of the bigger ones.

There's an old siding in Fresno, it's pulled up now, but the curve is still there; it's called Margarite Siding.

Usually they're names for, just the towns by 'em. Like there's Planada, a small little town outside of Merced, where there's a curve.

Running In The Fog

Freight trains can run up to 70 m.p.h. and passenger trains run 79 m.p.h.

In the fog.

You can't see.

It's real tough.
It can be a dangerous situation.
Even at 20 m.p.h. you can't see.
It's bad on the nerves.
That's when the job is not a lot of fun.

You're just real tired after making a trip in the fog ... from looking out the window looking for every block signal; every crossing — we have signs up a quarter mile before each road crossing, for where the road crosses the tracks.

You Count To 8, or 9

The trains going like 70 m.p.h. you see this sign; then you count off usually eight, nine seconds, and start blowing the whistle — and it usually works out right.

So there must be a hundred different crossings between here and Fresno; so you count from one to whatever — if you're going slower, you obviously count more, one to ten, so many times, you find yourself doin' it in your sleep.

Blowin' the whistle; you can't see the crossings, you just see the little sign, and you have a quarter mile, or ten seconds at that speed.

And just 'cause you blow the whistle, doesn't mean you know someone's not there; a gas truck, or something like that.

You sort of sweat out each intersection.

That's part of the reason why I'm in the yard right now.

'Cause I like being around the family — and it's dangerous out there, in the fog. I've worked it quite a bit, and it is dangerous. 'Cause you can't see what's going on.

It not everyday bad; sometimes you get fog that's not too bad. But sometimes you get it where you really can't see; and it's just really no fun in being out there.

You're just staring for every signal.

'Cause you're goin' fast. You only see it for a couple seconds.

You know it's out there. A green signal. It's by you.

Cab Signals

Some of the other railroads have something, it's called cab signals. It's not radar. But in the cabs, are reproductions of the signals alongside the track, about every mile or two, and some railroads have them — Union Pacific has 'em in some engines.

But I don't think Santa Fe does.

It's like little lights in the cab, that lights up green, yellow, red — whatever the signal is that's coming up, yeah.

Fog is bad.

It's not fun.

I don't know anybody that says that they like it.

Rain's No Big Thing

Rain's no big thing.

Rain's okay.

We have what's called mileposts. They have 'em every mile. There's a sign there. They have 'em in numbers. In our case, it's the distance from Albuquerque. And Albuquerque'd be milepost 0; then it goes 1, 2, 3, 4 ... Richmond, where I work out of, is milepost 1189. And it counts down to Fresno. Fresno is 1095.

So you know where you are.

You just know where it is.

If you go by 1156, that happens to be Pittsburg.

So you know where you are. That's really important when you're out in the country, where there's no landmarks.

Fog generally lifts a little bit in the cities, and sometimes you can see buildings, and where you are, but out in the country, it gets really tough.

So you know the milepost where you're at.

You should know what type of crossings are coming up — if there's a siding; whatever; if there's a reduced speed area.

Divided Responsibility

It's kind of a divided responsibility who's in charge of the train. There's usually three people on the crew; engineer, conductor, and a brakeman.

The brakeman assists the conductor. The engineer's in charge of the engine. The conductor's in charge of the train — he takes care of the paperwork, where to pick cars up at; where to set cars out at — from here to Fresno, it's not a straight shot. You stop in Stockton to pick up cars, Merced to set out cars, things like that. The conductor takes care of that, the paperwork of where to pick 'em up and where to set 'em out. The actual physical picking up and setting out.

The engineer's in charge of the engine, the speed of the engine, the condition of the engine, thing's like that; so it's kind of a divided responsibility.

It's not one person in charge.

"Have you ever been scared on the job," I said.
"Fog's scary.
"I've hit things before, and they've been pretty scary.

The First Person I Hit, or The Train Hit

He was about a twenty-four year old guy.

He was putting a dime on the track.

And the bad part of it was, not only that he got killed, but it was in front of his girlfriend — and she had two little kids there, and they saw the whole thing.

And the dime fell off.

And he went back.

She was tellin' him not to put it on — she told the cops that later; but he put it on anyway.

And for some reason, he just froze up there; and I hit him.

That isn't a good reason to give up your life.

Not for a dime.

I was pretty upset about it. Everybody was really upset. The whole crew was. The whole crew was really depressed about that. It was right at the end of the day.

When we knew we were going to hit him, we put it into emergency; but it takes so long to stop. We were ringing the bell, blowing the whistle. We saw him walk up. When we first saw him, he was in the clear. He walked up and put the dime on. Then he started to back off, which would have been okay. The dime fell off and he went back.

It looked like he froze. I've heard of that happening before. Sometime's guys will be playing chicken with trains; I haven't experienced that, that's just what I've heard. They'll wait 'till the last minute; somehow, they just kind of freeze up.

They'll see the train coming; the thing's so massive close up. It gets big, fast. And they'll look up. It would be a terrifying thing, such a big wall coming down on you. And even though you could jump in time, maybe you just freak out so much.

I think where a lot of people goof up, because a lot of people do play chicken ... some freight train's just draggin' along at 30 m.p.h.; then you have some faster trains — like AMTRAK goes along at 80 m.p.h.

And you can't tell at night. All you can see is one headlight. You can't tell if it's comin' slow, or fast. It's pretty hard to tell.

That's my own personal theory. A lot of cars, they want to go around the gates, and if the train was goin' 20 m.p.h. or 30 m.p.h., they'd be okay. If it was a 70 or 80 mile train, they have problems.

See, you really can't tell, at night.

I could see it all comin' down.

I didn't actually see him get hit, because of the angle, you're up so high.

We stopped the train, called the police; the conductor went back to see if there was anything we could do for the person — there obviously wasn't. He hit his head on the train — it was pretty gruesome.

So there was really nothing we could do.

The police got there real fast. I was surprised how fast they got there, almost before we got stopped. They talked to the woman and her kids.

I've been pretty lucky. Because most people have been in a lot more accidents than me. That was the first one. I've been there fifteen years. I'd never before hurt anybody bad. I've been in accidents, but it was like with a truck — where nobody got hurt; and some really low-speed accidents, but where nobody really gets hurt.

I was pretty lucky, in a sense, that that was only the first.

A lot of people have quite a few more.

Afterwards you just review things, like, 'What could I have done? — to avoid it? — and you really couldn't do anything.

The cops were pretty good too. Apparently they had some training; and they were saying, 'Hey, you couldn't have done anything. The guy was an idiot.' Which seems kind of cold to say; but it was a really stupid thing to do. It's unfortunate someone twenty, twenty-four, had to lose his life over that.

What Happened One Time

We hit a big truck and trailer at a crossing; it was going around the gates.

It was in Richmond.

Nobody got hurt.

The gates were down, and he went around them.

I knew we were going to hit him.

We went right through the middle of the truck trailer.

It was kinda like in a cartoon, goin' right through the middle of the trailer.

That was scary, 'cause you didn't know what was in the truck trailer. I remember all of us diving on the floor.

I just hoped it wasn't ... Standard Oil's right there; and they make all kinds of chemicals and stuff. It could have been something toxic. Or something explosive.

It turned out it was full of soap. Tide, I think.

But that was scary, 'cause in a few seconds you're gonna hit him, and there's nothing you can do — just hope he's not carrying something explosive.

We came around a curve, and he was going around the gates.

The gates were down.

The lights were working.

The bells were ringing.

And he came around. Some people just don't want to wait.

It was a short train too. It would only have delayed him a minute or so.

I put the train in emergency, then we went right through the middle of the van; cut it right in two, like going through butter.

The engine's are strong; they're made out of really hard steel. Usually when an engine hits a car, the car's all torn up in little pieces; and the engine might have a couple scratches on it.

They say the only two things that really hurt you, is a gasoline truck — if you hit one of those, you're dead; or maybe a big truck full of gravel or sand, something like that. Hit that and it would probably knock you off the track. But anything else you hit, you'll knock it clear of the tracks.

I haven't been in any bad train wrecks, where the wheels have come off the track.

That Part I Don't Like Too Well

The railroad is dangerous work. And people working there in the yard get hurt sometimes. Nobody I've been really close to has been seriously hurt. People get off and on while the trains moving — which is part of their job; and twist a leg, or get back problems, which is pretty common ... things like that.

But there's always that possibility. 'Specially those guys on the ground there brakemen, switchmen, there's always that possibility; that part of railroading, I don't like too well — to see people getting hurt.

The Part I Do Like

The part I do like, is I've always liked trains. I like runnin' up and down the main line, when it's not foggy; that's not bad, and it can be a nice, relaxing job, and there's some nice people there.

It's changing now, they're cutting back on crews.

When I hired out, there was one engineer, a conductor, and two brakemen. And now they're down to an engineer, a conductor, and a maximum of one brakeman; and on some trains, an engineer and a conductor only.

Some trains have just two people on board, the engineer and conductor — some of the express freight trains, that carry the mail; there's not a lot of work on that, so they cut the crew down, and so they've gotten down that low.

There's less people, and it's kind of lonely.

But basically, I just always liked trains. I still do.

"I think what impresses me the most, is the amount of concentration you'd have to have, to be an engineer, and the responsibility; but the responsibility's kind of meaningless without the concentration to support it. It seems to me you'd always have to be really concentrated," I said.

"Yeah, you kind of have to shift yourself into a higher gear, at least I do; especially like on the main line, where you do operate with high speeds, and quite a bit of weight. 'Cause I notice when I get done on a road trip, I just go kinda, 'WHEW!' — and just kind of let it out. And just relax."

"Is the road trip different from the mainline?" I said.

"No. The divisions are road and yard. Road is the mainline, it's another word for it", Jack said.

"So when you get back to the yard, you relax, you mean?" I said.

"No. Suppose I take a train from here to Fresno; when I get off the train in Fresno, I just kind of let go of my breath, and go 'WHEW!' — especially after being in the fog, Jack said.

"Is that typical of engineers," I said.

"I think it depends on what kind of trip you're having. You can have good trips, that just take a few hours; and you can have real bad ones. A lot depends on the crew; if they're in a good mood, or if they're not. Just the people you're with, can really make a difference. You get some people that complain the whole way; and that can really make it a negative thing. If people are in a good mood, that's a little more fun," Jack said.

You Wear A Beeper

Since last Thanksgiving, I went back in the yard. Pay's a little less money than the road. But on the road, you have to put up with a lot; you're also on call all the time; you wear a beeper all the time. You don't have a normal time of going to work, like Tuesday, at eight o'clock a.m. — it's whenever a train gets ready to leave. And freight trains are different than passengers. One day,

fig. 47 —*F-7 diesel* in the shop, Roseville, CA

they might only run four or five trains; the next day, they might run a dozen trains. It depends upon the freight load.

A lot of the trains go in the middle of the night. The business, say like the mail, UPS, we ship a lot of UPS — they finish their work in the afternoon, they get them all trucked up and shipped over to Santa Fe about 10 o'clock at night. Then they're loaded on trailers, and ready to go — these are piggybacks — it's probably about midnight. So, consequently, we get a lot of trains leaving between midnight and 4 o'clock a.m.; we get a bunch of trains then. So it's not the most ideal hours.

You are on the beeper.

That's pretty much how they get hold of you. Like if I was on the mainline, I'd be wearing a beeper.

That gets old.

But they do pay quite a bit more. So it's a trade-off," Jack said.

"It's nice you get to switch between road and yard a little bit," I said.

"That's a nice option," Jack said

"I guess you've seen plenty of nice sunrises and sunsets, because you work all different hours," I said.

The Tops of The Sierras

One of the prettiest things you see at night, rather the mornings, about four-thirty or five o'clock a.m. before sunrise, is the tops of the Sierras.

You can see the peaks up there, backlit by the sun coming up. So it's really beautiful. You go along, and the sky's just real dark, indigo; and then you see the very tops of the Sierras, Mount Whitney and all that, silhouetted in black — you see this in the valley, coming up from Bakersfield to Fresno; that's one of the prettier things ... . Goin' through the Delta, between roughly Antioch and Stockton, you cross the San Juaquin delta.

The only paved highway there's Highway 4, up in than area. But anyway, the train gets across quite a few bridges, and trestles; and it's really pretty there. There's islands in the delta. But by and large, it's pretty much all farmland we go through — and that gets a little old.

It's easy running, and it's fast, straight track, but it get's old.

"So what was it like today? What was a typical day like?" I said

A Typical Day The Way The Railroad is Going

Well, it was kind of interesting. One of the things that's happening, that's going on today ... it kind of gives you the trend of where the railroad is going ...

In Richmond Yard, right next to us, is a huge Standard Oil plant; that's real busy in there. They get in quite a few carloads of oil and what-not a day; gasoline, they ship all that stuff out. It's pretty railroad-intensive.

Now the railroad is moving to mainline only. They want to move things from point A, to point B — San Francisco to Chicago, for instance; and they don't want to do a lot of switching; because that's pretty labor intensive — and they want to move away from that.

Now there was this small railroad, called The Belt Railroad of Richmond.

Which is jointed owned by Southern Pacific and Santa Fe; they each own 50%.

And it switches at Standard Oil refinery.

And it goes in there.

For five years, Santa Fe crews work it; then the next five years, S.P. crews work it. And they switch this plant. It's like there's an engine on around-the-clock. Because they're pretty busy.

Anyway, they're selling this railroad off.

'Cause they just don't want to deal with it; and a private, non-union company is taking it over.

It's a small, five-mile railroad.

And I worked with some people today, who were on that railroad. They have like ten new-hires, that were going to be there, and I was talking to them today.

I was out there. They officially give it up on the first of the year.

Probably one of the last times I'll be out there.

It was kind of different, seeing all new people, and all that.

It's just some of the changes, some of the railroads are going through — in order to save money.

I'm not quibbling with the railroad, 'cause I can see that. Taking a boxcar into a certain place, or tankcars, is very labor intensive.

"How are you not going to deliver cars?! — are they supposed to come pick 'em or somethin'?" I said.

"Pretty much. They're really gettin' into piggyback, a lot," Jack said.

"Ohhh. So it would be a truck-trailer," I said.

"Yeah. The freight comes from Chicago to Richmond, and there's a big raft in Richmond, where they unload all this. It used to be there was all kinds of warehouses through the San Francisco Bay Area, and the train came in, loaded with primarily boxcars; switch engine would switch out the train to different tracks in the yard; and another train would take it around to these warehouses. It would pull the empty cars out, and put the loads in. Which is one way of doing it. They've been doing it that way for a hundred years, one-hundred-thirty years or so.

"But now they're going more to piggyback, which is a lot less labor-intensive. What happens there, is when the train comes in to Richmond, these big cranes unload the trailers. Non-union truck drivers, who are paid substantially less than the train crew — 'cause the train crew has three people on it — this way, one truck driver will deliver the trailer right to the door of the customer who wants it.

"And in some ways that's good; it makes the customer happy," Jack said

"Why doesn't the railroad just raise their prices. Charge more money. 'Cause there's no alternative is there, to trains?" I said.

"There's trucks... . So there's some changes going on railroads," Jack said.

"Yeah. I guess so," I said.

"The was a time, where you had a lot more independence. Conductor and engineer was the boss of the train. And you did pretty much what you wanted.

"Now, through radio, and centralized traffic control, they know where you are exactly, the whole time. They can contact you.

And keep their finger on you a little more — which in some ways is good. Because there was a lot of stuff going on. A lot of partying," Jack said.

"I was told that most of the derails are in the yard, 'cause there's lighter tracks," I said.

"Lighter tracks, right. But they're minor derailments. A set of wheels goin' off on the ground, something like that. Most people think of derailments as big crashes and injuries and all that — most of them aren't; a rail turns over, a car almost always stands upright ..."

"A rail turns over?"

"A rail? Will turn over?! I never heard of that.

"How can it do that?!" I said.

A Rail Turns Over

A rail turns over.

Especially after storms. The ground gets soft ...

Yeah. It'll lay on its side.

If the track's not kept up real good. It washes out underneath the track; it gets weak; undermines the ties. A lot of times, the rails spread. They just kind of move out a little bit.

There's only a little bit of wheel on the track. If the track moves out a little bit, about an inch or so, the car will fall down, or go between the rails; it'll still be upright; it'll just be off the rail.

The cars and the engines.

After a rain, the rails can just turn over sideways.

That's the way that most derailments in the yard happen; because the underlying ground is weakened so much. That's the way most derailments happen.

These are minor derailments, not big, major things.

Rail maintenance is such an expensive thing.

I guess they figure, in yards, they just keep it up to a certain standard; they know they're going to have a few derailments; they try to watch it pretty close — but there's always a few bad sections of track.

Like today, we were goin' out to Standard Oil. I was only goin' 1 or 2 m.p.h., 'cause there was real bad water, a lot of water around the tracks, it gets into the tracks, and weakens them.

So we were only going 1 or 2 m.p.h. — because the tracks were in such bad shape."

Sometimes the tracks get covered with water too.
That can happen too, yeah.
It's basically just muddy.
Just muddy.
It rained two days ago.
The main line, they keep up pretty well. That's in good shape. There's 80 m.p.h. passenger trains on there.
But the yard, see, it's 10 m.p.h.
They do maintenance on the yard, but it's obviously not as much as main line."

"So where did you go today, where you had to watch the rails?" I said.

"Went out to a couple of places. Went out to Ferry Point, where the train ferry boats used to leave from — Ford has a warehouse out there; brought some cars out there. Went out and worked in the Standard Oil plant for a while. And went to various industries around Richmond. A couple warehouses, things like that. Went around to switch various industries, brought a couple boxcars back. A general merchandise warehouse; Ortho has a place where they make bug spray — brought them a couple tankers in. Then went out through Standard Oil, out to this bulk terminal, out in Point Melody — it's a pretty place out there; it's over by the Richmond-San Rafael Bridge."

Fog and Sleep

It can be a boring job, in some ways. Like when the engineer is running the train from here to Fresno; the other people — and this has to stay in the background too ... this will get me thrown off, they'll tie me on the railroad tracks — the conductor and the brakeman, don't have a lot to do; it's kind of a kickback job.

But stations, where I stop, they pick up cars, and they're busy then, but riding from point A to point B, is pretty much all on the engineer.

That puts a lot of stress on the engineer, if the conductor and the engineer really aren't busy; it's totally on you. It's totally on the engineer. It can be stressful that way, especially in the fog.

'Bout a year ago, outside Stockton, there was a really bad

AMTRAK wreck. AMTRAK hit a truck at the crossing, and the engine turned over and killed the engineer, the fireman, and the truck driver. Three people died in that. That was one of those fog-related accidents, where apparently what happened, it was so foggy, the truck driver didn't see the gates 'till it was too late, and he went through it. The train hit him. Quite a few people were hurt in that one. All the passenger cars came off the rail.

He couldn't see the gates — when they were right in front of his truck; it must have been pretty thick fog.

I've seen it so bad, you can't see the ground from the engine cab. Once in a while it's been that bad. That's part of the reason why I'm working the yard, this time of year. September 'till March.

That can make driving the train real misery. You really earn your money. I don't mean to sound like I'm complaining.

The attitude of the guys who do take 'em in the fog — is it's just part of the job. They do it. The valley's has fog. It's always had fog.

It pays quite a bit more than the yard. I took about a 50% pay cut when I went in the yard.

Road trips pay pretty well.

Yeah, it's about 50%. Almost that. Yard pays about one-hundred-thirty-six dollars a day. For an eight-hour day. Road, a round-trip to Fresno, which can take from twenty-four to forty-eight hours to make around trip, pays about four-hundred-fifty-dollars.

I think it averages about two-and-a-half round trips a week.

It pays pretty good. But you have to consider, you don't have regular days off; you don't have scheduled starting times; you're on the beeper; you're liable to work weekends — you will work weekends; a lot of midnight stuff — in the summer's it's okay. It can be quite an easy job, if you're just cruising along.

Some People Get Sleepy

Sometime's in the middle of the night, you're just going along there, the train's all set up, you're just kind of sitting back with nothing to do.

Some people get sleepy.

Me personally, I kind of think in the back of my mind, 'If I go to sleep, there's going to be some really major problem' — and that just kind of shoots some adrenaline through me.

I have gotten sleepy.

Where I have to get up, turn off the heater, and put some water on my face, and hang my head out the window; something like that, just to wake me up. Sometimes we've had some phenomenally long trips. Four or five in the morning, the body wants to go to sleep, anyway. It's usually the deepest sleep during those hours.

In Your Blood

Yeah, railroads have always been real fascinating to me; I've always liked trains a lot. It kind of gets in your blood. Most people seem, once they've been there a while, they seem to stay.

It can be hard work. 'Specially being on the ground. Engineer's not hard work, it's not physical at all.

But being a switchman in the yard can be real tough physically. That's where you get on and off moving equipment, and in order to couple cars together you have to work with the couplers and the drawbars.

"I don't understand how you can hook up the air without getting in between the tracks," I said.

"You do have to climb in between," Jack said.

"You're not allowed to; you're not supposed to," I said.

"They do. That's the only way to do it," Jack said.

"But you gotta keep one foot out, to couple the air hoses, don't you?"

"Yeah. You have to go in between the rails, sittin' under there."

"But you're not allowed to. If anything happens, it's your fault. They fire you if you get hit by a train, with both feet inside the rails," I said.

"Well that's the only way you can make the air; I mean; you do that. It's okay then. That's the only way you can make them up, is to go in there. You have to have a lot of trust in your engineer, that he knows what he's doing, and he's not going to move. That could be real tough," Jack said.

"What do you mean?"

That Sixteen-Hour Day

Back when they had that sixteen-hour day, your whole social life was the railroad. Your whole life, period. You didn't know your kids. Your kids grew up without you. I personally wouldn't think that was a good way of growing up.

I like to do a lot of stuff outside the railroad. I like the railroad. And I like the job.

But there's a lot of other things.

Some guys, like I say, their whole life is the railroad.

Quite a few guys, right after they retire, it's surprising how many die so quickly.

I was a brakeman for a short time, for nine months; and I couldn't do that stuff for twenty years. That's some tough work. We have a lot of guys, out with back problems. They develop them over twenty or thirty years; gettin' on and off movin' equipment all the time; moving those heavy drawbars around — the couplers; it's tough on your body doing that.

"Do you have any favorite engines?" I said.

"Yeah. There are certain engines I like. They've got a new style of engines; they're going back to the old Santa Fe passenger engines, the red and silver one — it's kind of a famous design; most all the Lionel trains you see around Christmas trees are designed that way. A little bit of yellow-gold color. They're going back to that paint scheme. Those are kinda nice engines.

"There's characteristics of individual engines," Jack said.

"Do they have different names for different engines," I said.

"Well, this is going way back, to the '20s; but apparently they assigned an engine to an engineer, and you had that all the time. And you were the only one who used that engine. Cute, but enormously inefficient. I've seen pictures of engineers where they fix them up — this is basically the switch engine in the yard — they'd fix them up; they'd have names on them, and polish 'em up, and have names on them, and kind of paint them up their own way. Make 'em real nice. Same with cabooses too, back in the old days."

"Trains and the railroads aren't everything. It pays me more than enough to make the mortgage payments and all that," Jack said. "I don't think the last generation had to figure out life; I don't think they had that luxury. I can't say that they didn't notice that there was life. But a lot of them take it for granted. I don't think we get to take it for granted. I think it remains mysterious to us," I said. I'm feeling personally lucky; my wife does too — she's a registered nurse. And it gives me enough time that I can kind of get away from the job; being in a place where I'm surviving, where I can experience other things, take classes, look into the bible, things like that. We just have so many years to, maybe not figure it out; but to attempt to come to terms with it. And for me, meditation is just really important. Just being still. And listening to the voice within. Calming down, and listening to the thoughts of the day going by. Just having communication with your higher self. Not pushing any religion, or any isms or anything like that; just being quiet. The one thing I miss most about the railroad, is that it's not a creative job; it's a repetitive job ... take the freight from point A to point B — the freight doesn't care, one way or another; it doesn't thank you. The brakemen and conductor kick back and go to sleep on the job. They do. Between stations. And I'm running the train by myself.

No Cabooses

They used to have cabooses on every train. The conductor and one brakeman would ride back in the caboose, and the other brakeman would ride up in front in the engine with the engineer.

What they did, was they have this electronic black box. And it goes on the last car of the train. It does a number of things.

It will flash a light on. So an approaching train going the same direction can see that there's another train in front of it. It hooks up to the air pipe, so it tells you what the air pressure is one the last car. And it will tell you if the last car is moving. So it takes the place of the caboose — so there's no more caboose down there. Everybody rides in the head end. This box, which I guess is maybe three feet by two feet by six inches deep, sits on the knuckle, the coupler of the last car on the train; a big heavy thing, it weighs about forty pounds. It sends these messages through a radio, to the front of the train, what's happening in the last car.

And it does all the functions they did in the caboose.

So the caboose and a brakeman has been replaced by a little black box.

There Was A Whole Lot Of Sleeping Back In The Caboose

There was a whole lot of sleeping back in the caboose.

In fact, one of the older conductors, one of the nice guys, an honest guy, came up, right when I graduated from engineer school — 'cause I was pretty naive. "Hey, a lot of times, about in the middle of the night, 3 o'clock a.m. — you're gonna be on your own. A lot of people, they fall asleep in the caboose. I'm not sayin' it's right; but they do. They sleep in the caboose. And the brakeman up there in the head end with you, he'll be sleeping too — so it's all on you," he said.

And he was right.

Now it's happened up in the engine cab, right next to me, they'll be sleeping.

It happens, not a lot, but it happens.

Now that there's no caboose, they sleep up in the engine sometimes. And there's nothing really between stations; there's nothing for a brakeman, or for a conductor, to do, when they're not working between stations. It's tough stayin' awake.

Just the hum of the engine, the hum of the engine, and it kind of vibrates you, and it gets warm in the cab; it's tough to stay awake.

It's real tough.

Losin' the caboose is sort of like the undoing of the railroad.

The last generations of rails, their stories are, "Ahhhh! This is great! Isn't that wonderful! ... and I was standin' in the rain; the snow was cold, and I'd go back in the caboose and get warm! — and we used to play pinochle in the caboose. — Now there isn't even a caboose.

No caboose.

fig. 48 – caboose

fig. 49 – a train wreck on the *Western Pacific*

John Brown — (born 1951)

Started As A Santa Fe Switchman
& Ended Up An AMTRAK Conductor

The story starts in August 1965. I graduated from high school in Bakersfield, and decided to come up to San Francisco, and got lost trying to find the San Francisco Bay Bridge.

So I'm lost, and the bridge is in the rear view mirror. And so I'm looking in the rear view mirror, and all of a sudden this locomotive, pulling up this string of boxcars, came out of the ocean. That's what it looked like to me. Up this ramp, and on to the street.

It scared me.

Little did I know that ten years later I would be doing the same thing ... scaring motorists driving down China Basin way, seeing a locomotive coming up out of the water.

Years later it took me a little while to figure out that the place I was then working, was the one that had scared me badly years ago.

Neil Cassidy, whom Jack Kerouac made famous, worked for the railroad, as a brakeman, for Southern Pacific. Kerouac was a brakeman for a while too.

Kerouac's book, On The Road, how does that open? — "It was five o'clock on a ripe, sunny Saturday afternoon, I was layin' on my back on a rattling old flatcar that had rumbled its way out of Los Angeles heading north." Something like that. I thought, 'That sounds like a neat job.'

That's how I ended up working on the railroad.

We've Hit A Lot Of Automobiles

When I saw that train come up out of the water, I did not stop, I kept going. What a lot of people do, when they see a train coming, they stop on the tracks, and try to figure out the process of what's happening here.

I've seen that happen quite a bit on the head ends of locomotives. On locomotives, you're riding down the railroad 70 m.p.h.

Somebody will be wool gathering and they'll hit a crossing gate and break it. They'll stop on the tracks trying to figure out what did I hit?

Meanwhile, there's a ninety-car freight train barreling down on them at 70 m.p.h. which takes three-quarters of a mile to stop. And they're trying to figure out what exactly happened.

What happens then is you hit them. Scary. Real scary. Fascinating, but scary. It's like a movie. Your windshield's there, and it's kind of like a movie. It takes on a two-dimensional quality because of the adrenaline. You know, My God! They're not going to move! Then something drops in the old system, you know, they're really not going to move.

And everybody gets down on the floor because automobiles usually explode, and stuff comes through the windshield.

Get Down

The impulse is to stand up, to watch, to say, "I see it! Now I see it."

The last one we hit, the engineer was able to pull me down, and I was able to see a part of the hood go flying over the top of the locomotive.

You should get down, that's right.

We've hit a lot of cars.

My First Railroad Job

My first railroad job was in Bakersfield, with Santa Fe. That's where I hired on. I had moved from Long Beach, where I was going to college. I used up all the G.I. bill. I hit Bakersfield with twenty dollars, my bicycle, my guitar, and my typewriter. Then the car broke down.

A lot of them, at Santa Fe in Bakersfield, drank; there was a lot of denial.

They said, "Wait a moment, you're acting like John Dillinger."

I said, "Yeah, I got a drinkin' problem."

"No you don't," they said. "You drink with us, you don't have a problem."

"Oh okay," I said. "You guys are the authorities."

So I got lucky. I got a job on the railroad.

The World's Largest Whiskey & Water Salty Dog

It was in the Chronicle when we had the big storms back in about '83. A friend of mine, not a railroader, carried that clipping around, saying, "I know this guy."

I was loading tank cars on the barge, and I had two men who were not familiar with the procedure, who were brakemen, and were helping me that day.

We only had one radio. And I thought this one guy knew how to do it, because he had more seniority than me.

These cars were very heavy. We had nine cars. We could only load two at a time. That means you'd shove two down the center track, shove two down the outside track away from the barge, and shove two down the port track, next to the boat, then you'd have three cars left. And you'd go one, one and one. Because, you will capsize the son of a gun, if you try to go three, three and three. The hoosiers, the ropes, the lines will break.

It was raining like crazy.

I didn't have a radio.

I was on the opposite side, so I couldn't give a signal to the engineer. And it was raining, it was pouring like the proverbial cow irrigating a flat rock. The engineer start shoving them on, and he didn't stop.

I couldn't believe he was doing it.

I was flabbergasted. I thought, 'What!?' He was supposed to stop. I looked over, and the ropes that hold the barge to the tugboat, got skinny. It was gonna break!

And the captain was screaming out the window, but I couldn't hear what he was saying because it was raining so hard. And I figured, 'Ohhh. Enough of this.'

They shoved three on. They cut them off. And backed her up.

And shoved three more on, like they knew what they were doing. But the rope had gotten skinny. You could actually see it getting thin. A friend in a shipyard said that's what happens when they break.

And I had nowhere to run. Right before they break, they get real thin, and BOOM!, it's like a scythe cuts it. So I was scared. When it would go, it would happen fast.

So we loaded it, and the barge bounced. Part of the trick is knowing how to get the barge to balance out correctly, having the same tonnage on one side as you have on the other, which isn't always easy. Cause you have different weights.

But the barge balanced out. It was awful low in the water cause of all that weight.

The captain never did whistle off. That's the only weird thing about that. When everything is okay, he'll whistle off. We'd raise up the slip, and away they'd go. I guess he was painin' because he thought I was going to sink his barge.

So anyhow, that's what was the weak link. They got out here in the bay, and a terrible storm hit, and the rope broke out there. And the captain never did turn me in. I didn't think he was going to take the load, because I know he saw those hoosiers.

He saved my butt a couple of times. He was a good old guy. Effridge.

The barge was tied down to the tugboat with rope. And the barge has tracks on it. And you tie handbrakes on that, then you got little boards you put across so they won't roll off.

But he got out there, and the bow line broke, I think the barge was banging back and forth, and you get the oscillation of all this weight, they all fell in the drink. We had nine tankcars of whiskey in the drink.

It was in the newspaper. Everybody knew I was the one who did it. Nobody told anybody. They were mad. That was expensive. To lose a load like that. They lost the barge. Had the EPA out there. They finally recovered it.

At the Christmas dinner, the first and last one we had, we finally started getting militant, 'We're gonna change things around here.' We all had a big Christmas dinner, rented a bar, they gave me 'The Over-The-Edge-And-Into-The-Drink Award', which was a private joke. And what it was a little fish bowl, with a bottle of Kestler whiskey in it.

AMTRAK

In '85 I took a leave of absence from Santa Fe to go to work with AMTRAK. It worked out better than I ever thought it would.

You Get To Eat, Too?

Being on AMTRAK passenger trains as a conductor, people were glad to see me. You help get everybody a seat. You've got the smokers where they want to be, you've put the non-smokers where they won't smell the smoke. You answer graciously, what appear to be silly questions.

Like someone asking in a dubious, timid voice, "I'm going to take a train in January or July of '89, and I want to go to Boston, and I want to go to Canada, how long of a layover will I have?" Stuff like that. To answer those, sometimes I just smile, and nod.

Sometimes I take it as a rhetorical question.

Someone will ask me, "How many cars does AMTRAK have?"

I say, "A lot."

Let's say you're eating a sandwich on your lunch break, and they see you, and they say, "Oh, you get to eat too?"

Violence On The Reno Fun Train

Violence usually, almost always, comes as the result of alcohol. I saw violence on a Reno fun train, which was as private, chartered thing, where they take everybody up to Reno for the weekend.

It's chaotic. They start drinking at five o'clock in the afternoon. They're drunk when they show up to leave on the train. The train leaves at six o'clock. And I was real new on the job. I still didn't know how to deal with the public.

Some old man started throwing punches at this guy, the next thing I know, glasses are flying.

I make my voice low and gruff, and say, "Hey! You can't do that!"

These guys were both bigger than me. Their heads were brushing the ceiling. So I did a smart thing, I deputized one of them.

I said to the one who was winning, "Okay, good job. Don't hurt him. This will do it."

The quickest lip in the west.

Business As Usual

If you come into a yard, there'll be switch engines, switch crews, and there'll be the switchmen. A switch crew consists of an engine foreman, and two switchmen. And their job is to take the trains apart as they come into town, deliver the cars to the various industries, and to pick the cars from the industries, and put the trains back together.

Once the trains are put back together, they are given to an identical crew, except that's called the road crew — a conductor, and two brakemen. Pretty much interchangeable jobs, except those guys go out of town.

The people who run the engines are the engineers. The only difference between being on a switch engine, which they call a 'goat', and being on a road job, is on a road job, they have a fireman, who is an assistant engineer, a trainee engineer, sometimes maybe an engineer just working like a fireman.

The person who oversees the work, who kind of sorts everything out, is kind of like an air traffic controller, only not quite so dramatic. He's called a yardmaster. He sits up in a tower, and he gives you the lists of work orders for the various stuff.

Do they make mistakes? Oh, all the time. You see, when they make mistakes, you eat it, because you're out there on your feet, correcting their mistakes. So the idea is, if you know the job really well, that you don't do quite what they want you to do on the work order, because you know that they'll be wanting to make a correction later. And you kind of line the work up, without telling them, so that you save yourself some stuff later. You try to outthink them.

You've got to know your yardmaster, to do that though. The one that was over here, Billingsly, was very good. Most of the really old heads, were very experienced and knew the job well.

Some of them were not so together. Those are the ones, you would do the thinking for them.

A Major Mistake By A Yardmaster

A major screw-up by a yardmaster is having two crews working the same track, at the same time, at opposite ends of the yard. The tracks, some of them are over a mile long, a mile and a quarter. And it's impossible to see, when you've got a yard full of cars, that you've got somebody on the other end.

The danger is this, the switchmen are getting in between the cars, aligning the knuckles on the cars, and opening them up. Lining up the drawbars, and opening them up, so that you can couple the cars up.

Now when my engineer sees me give a 'STOP' sign, I step between the cars to do that, he's not going to move, until he sees me, personally step out, and give the signal. He won't take a signal from anybody else. Because my life is on the line.

However, the crew working on the other end of the yard won't see me because they'll be on the other side, virtually facing the other way. They'll be doing their own little thing.

I've had that happen, I've been between cars, and all of a sudden, they start moving.

The trick is, you keep one foot outside the rail, at all times. It makes it awkward, makes for a long stretch, but if you have one foot outside the rail, you have a chance of getting out. Where if you have both feet and you're crouched down between the cars, you don't have that same chance.

There's another craft, we call them 'carknockers', or 'car dogs'. They're the mechanical people who fix the brake shoes. They have the dirtiest, hardest job. They fix anything that's broken on the boxcar. They check the brakes.

I was off that night. I had a bad feeling. It was one of those nights where the moon was weird or something, and I did not want to go to work. I didn't have an excuse, so I just called in and told them I was sick.

What happened was one of these very hot trains, with high revenue, they wanted to get it out of town in a hurry. And so they had one guy standing one each side of the train, these car dogs, carknockers, inspecting it as it rolled by. That's called, rolling inspection.

Unbeknownst to them, a yard crew was shoving cars onto a

track where this man happened to be standing.

He could not stand any other place, but between the rails, to get the proper angle to see what's going on with the brake rig, the brake shoes, and these guys had no way of knowing the car dogs were down the track. The carknockers weren't where they normally did their rolling inspection.

The man was killed.

Protecting The Traffic

The biggest problem for us in San Francisco China Basin, and Potrero Hill, and up Indiana street to Jackson Square, is 'protecting the traffic'.

We used to have a lot of industrial work up 16th street. The problem there was that people would not slow down when they see the locomotive.

The switchmen are on the ground, walking around the cars, detaching them, tying on handbrakes, and that was the biggest problem, getting hit by cars, for us.

So you had to be very careful when you came around the edge of a locomotive, because of these people. I've had people run into me, apparently they didn't see us, we had bells ringing. They ran right into the locomotive. Yeah, I'm standing on the front, specifically for the reason of protecting the traffic, they call it. Waving your lantern at night time and yellin' "Hey! We're out here! Don't hit us!" And they still hit cha.

A Quick Way Home

It was a Willys Scout or something.

Fresno, we were leaving Fresno about three o'clock in the morning. That was the beginning of the run. My home terminal was Richmond. So we went down to Fresno, we took a train down there, we layed over sixteen, seventeen hours and they called us at midnight, took us something to eat. You get on the train at two-thirty A.M.

We'd just gotten out of town. We'd just gotten up to maximum speed, which was 70 m.p.h. We came around the bend 70 m.p.h.

It was mostly piggybacks, and it must have been fifty or sixty of 'em. UPS, United Parcel Service. They are the hottest thing on the railroad, or were, at that time. Because they paid a lot of money to get their stuff here from Chicago in forty-four hours. So everybody gets out of their way, and then, it's a big production, according to management.

It's a quick way home for us.

We came out of the bend for a long straightaway and we were going for it. And there was this white car on the track. The engineer is blowin' his whistle, and nothing's happening. I think, 'Oh, surely he'll move. They always do.'

It had been stolen, and the thieves got it high-centered on the rail, and they left it. We were doing approximately 65 m.p.h. when we hit it. It made a big Thunk!

The old guys say no, but I swear I could feel kind of a slack action, or a bumping. Because locomotives are very, very heavy. And they say you can't. But I always kind of thought you could. They say you don't, but I know you do, because I felt the impact.

You're awful vulnerable up there. There's not much protecting you from what you hit. From the windows up, there's just glass. And things do come through. And it tends to make an awful mess.

Wow! Man. Look At The Sparks

We were out there in Pinole, which is east of Richmond, and just coming out of the hills is curvy track, about five o'clock on a summer afternoon. Maybe it was early spring. There was still plenty of light, come around the curve and there's a kid standing on the rail with a lit match, waving at us. Striking a match, trying to flag us down. I didn't know what he was doing.

The engineer said, "What's going on?"

And I said, "Yeah, what's going on?"

So he was about eighteen years old, he was a kid, long hair. He was trying to flag us down. He figured, we'd see this match he was waving at us. So he jumps off the rail. We go into the S-curve, come out, and there's a '63 Chevy Impala dead smack center on the track, high-centered.

They'd got it hung up on the crossing. And about four or five kids standing there. We hit that. That was the first one I hit. And that car exploded.

It had a tape player in it, and the tape just blew out. It was quite impressive.

I was in the front, on the locomotive. I did kind of watch that one. I didn't get all the way on to the floor, cause I was watching. The 8-track tape cassette player, there was like tape, everywhere. I saw the aftermath. I decided at the last instant, that I better get down, cause the engineer looked like he knew what he was doin'. And I sure knew I didn't.

So he tells me, "My God, there was people in that car."

I went, "Oh no."

I was a medic in the army, so I have some experience, not much more than the average person on the street, but more. And I think, 'Oh no.' And I grab what I figured what I'd need for first aid, if you can give first aid, to someone who's been hit by a train. I don't know. I'd never seen one. I thought, 'Oh my God. What am I going to do to help people hit by a train. I don't know. Just play it by ear, when I get there.'

I go running back there, and there's nobody in the car. But there are these four long-haired kids, and they're four-sheets-to-the-wind.

And this one guy goes, "Wow man. Did you see it. Could you feel it in the sparks, man? Wow. Man, the sparks flew!"

I'm all pumped up, my heart's pounding, y'know, expecting to find hurt people, and here's this kid telling me about how cool the sparks are.

I said, "See what you did to the locomotive? How long do you think it's gonna take you to pay for that, kid? Your car was where it wasn't supposed to be. This is the railroad property here. You were trespassing." And that sobered him up real quick. Then I put him in the know, that they weren't gonna make him pay for fixing the locomotive.

To expect the worst, then to find these guys standing around, sayin' 'Wow.'

Accidents

But accidents do happen. Things break.

The scariest stuff is liquified petroleum gas, LPG.

I've seen pictures, these are the biggest tank cars they have, where from a distance, the tank car, which is ninety feet long, looks like it's about an eighth of an inch, with this huge giant flame coming out of it, hundreds of feet into the sky.

It's like a Bic lighter.

I've never seen one explode. It makes me uncomfortable handling them. Because there's so much potential destructive energy there, in this tank car.

When I saw that photo, of what happened when one did blow up in Texas. Wow! This car, I know it to be ninety feet long, but in the picture, it looks like an eighth of an inch, and the flame is like over six inches above it.

So putting all that into scale, man.

I guess they used a long distance telephoto camera. I think there was a derailment, and the cars were burning, and they evacuated the area, and they had people filming it. It was out in the desert.

Have You Ever Been Hit By A Train?

I was inbetween cars lacing them, and somebody shoved from the other end. To this day, I don't know how I got out. I sensed something.

I try to focus on that moment, when I sensed something. I couldn't hear anything. But I sensed it. I was halfway out, when the car hit me.

It'll be standing still, and when these cars move, all of a sudden they're moving, at ten miles an hour, right now. There's no gradual buildup. There are spring-loaded cushions, and BOOM!, they take off.

There was some higher power looking out for me. I thought about that a lot.

What was it?

I wanted to amplify that. And focus on it.

I thought suddenly, 'I've got to get out from between these cars!' I was coming out, and it hit me, and spun me around, and threw me out. The crew thought I had been killed.

I'd only been there about a year.

The Witch Of Davis

The witch of Davis looks like something out of Hansel and Gretel. She wears a black 'kerchief. She's in her sixty's.

I don't really know if she's crazy or not. I think she's been assaulted by the psychiatric establishment.

Some of her family put her on in Davis, and she goes on the night train up to Oregon.

But she started getting agitated one night. I think it was the second time I'd seen her. The second time, somebody cut me in, on what her story was.

As I walked by, she said, "You're not going to do it! I'm not going to let you stick those needles in me!"

And I flash right away, 'Oh, she's been treated by the wonderful psychiatric establishment.' So I'm not missing a beat. This is how this higher power thing works.

I whirl around, and knelt beside her, and looked her dead in the eyes, and I said with authority, "You know who I am. You know why I'm here. You know I won't let them do that to you, don't you."

She looked at me with vacant eyes, and whispered quietly, "Yes."

I didn't have a problem with her the rest of the night.

I don't know who I am. I don't know why I'm here. But I'm not going to let anybody stick needles in her.

I was really proud of that one.

If she wants to be crazy, that's okay. Just don't bother anybody. If you're scared, I don't want you to be scared and upset.

You see the costume I'm wearing, you think it's authority, you know who I am, you know why I'm here, you know I'm not going to let anybody do that to you, don't you.

If I was a social worker probably, I shouldn't be encouraging her craziness. But she went to sleep, and everything was fine.

The Lady With The Bag Full Of Ticket Stubs

This lady had this bag of ticket stubs that she'd fished out of the trash. Who tried to make such a nuisance, that you'd let her ride for nothing. This was on the Bakersfield to Oakland train.

She makes an art of it. On the Bakersfield to Oakland train, you are so rushed, and so hectic and so frantic, chances are, most crews will overlook it. But the guy I was working with, is such a ... he's a great guy, he's so compulsive.

But he's a workaholic, type A. And he's a perfectionist. And I like working with him, because you can count on him. When there's only two of you, it's got to be that way.

He's not going to let her by.

She's got old food spread all over the seat.

He says, "Lady, these are not the tickets. These are the receipts."

She tries to pretend like she's crazy, and doesn't know. He throws her off.

We see her the next day in Oakland. She made it up here, somehow. Going through the trash, getting tickets.

Suicide On The Tracks

There was one accident, there was a suicide, that was really kind of tragic, because my friend was the brakeman on the job, heading up a freight train.

We called him Raggity Andy. He was on the head of a freight train and this woman committed suicide. She sat down on the tracks. And it was almost like the Exorcist. She looked over her shoulder, dead into his eyes. And smiled at him. At the moment of impact.

Psychologically that damaged him. He was not ever the same after that.

He was out there helping the coroner get the bits and pieces together. He was in shock, and nobody knew it. But that really did him in.

He start getting into all kinds of negative psychic spaces.

He was finding black feathers people were leaving him. And he got involved with t.v. evangelists, and devil worshipers, so he was going to get thrown out of his Baptist church. And he wouldn't answer the phone.

It all dates from that time of that woman committing suicide, turning her head, looking him dead in the eyes, and smiling.

Love Story

I've had experiences on trains, where I've been knocked over by love.

One of the most beautiful love stories was on a train to Klamath Falls, there's a long night train. You go on duty eight-thirty at night, get there seven o'clock in the morning.

And you get in this kind of rolling along stupor, you don't want to be bothered. We came into Chico, and you try to have all these people in one car, who are getting off at one station, so you don't wake everybody up. It's about three o'clock in the morning.

Except for this one handicapped lady. She was three coaches back, and I had to go all the way back there, and help her down, and I'm thinking all the unkind thoughts I'm capable of. 'Why don't these darn people stay home!? Oh Jesus Christ, this lady's messing-up with my night!'

I walked into the lower level where the handicaps run, she had braces on. But there was something about the serenity, there was this clarity in her face.

That just made me ashamed of my thoughts.

I start thinkin' to myself, 'Boy can't I ever be an jerk? I just proved it.'

For some reason, I couldn't get the ramp down. So she's there, she can't bend her legs, and there's a three foot drop.

And I'm telling her, "Look, just fall forward on me. I'm a fat old brakeman. If you fall, you won't hurt yourself. I haven't lost one yet."

And I feel her afraid. And then she just surrendered to me. And I could feel that definite surrender and trust in me. And I started getting this tingling all over like I couldn't catch my breath. So I was standing there, trying to get her down on the ground, trying to get her crutches under her.

That woman, her son comes out of the darkness, cause we're three cars back, and there's no lights, the platform is 150 feet up. Out of the darkness, comes her son.

He said, "Mom!," with a catch in his voice, that, I thought I was going to cry.

"Oh, son. I thought you'd forgotten me,' she says.

So I'm holding her up, and they're hugging each other. And it was like an electrical charge. I was dizzy. I'd never felt anything like that love, in my life.

I go, "What the heck was that?! I'm losin' it."

My circuits are going. I'm startin' to really crack-up over the cripples.

Wow! What the heck happened?!

That was pure love.

Her resistance, and her surrender to me. Falling forward, never letting her fall off the train. That's when I started picking up, something was going on here. So I'm holding on to her, trying to get her crutches under her, and her son came up. It was like a circuit. Blippp.

Stuff like that happens, never often enough, but. It was pretty disorienting too. It was powerful.

It could have been my own hunger and need for my missing dead mother, who knows?

Something like that surprises the heck out of me. You confront yourself, and you're negative, in a safe way. I was thinking, 'Darn, I've go to go back three cars. Why can't she ride up here with the other people. Why doesn't she just stay home?'

It was like a Lily Tomlin routine. Boy, when I saw her face, I thought, 'Okay. I failed Humanity 101 today.'

It was like an electrical charge. Tangible. Like being plugged in. It was three-thirty in the morning. It was all makin' me a better person. Getting me in touch, in contact with people.

Basic elements. It's natural. As far as I understand that kind of stuff. It's not made by General Electric, that's for sure.

An American Indian Who Couldn't Stop Crying

One of the more interesting people I met, I remember him now, was an American Indian, who couldn't stop crying.

He was on the Klamath Falls train.

He was going down to the V.A. hospital, they sent him back to Oakland.

I met this self-styled, new wave composer, something of an arrogant prick. I wanted to learn about how to write songs, and I thought maybe I could get some ideas about how you get melodies and stuff.

He didn't want to come down to that level at all. He wasn't going to tell me. He had recorded a twenty-two minute tape of pretty much self-indulgent piano rolls. Semi-classical, it didn't have a beat, it was kinda like trance music I guess, I don't know. It put you to sleep.

So anyhow, I'm listening to it on the headphones, he insists, and it was so loud, that this Indian could hear it through the headphones, and I took it off halfway through, and went to run off, cause this guy had gone off to do something else.

The Indian leaned over and said to me in a quiet, broken voice, "That's the music they play, that's the music they play, before they do it to you."

I think, "Oh, a live one."

He's crying!

I say, "Who would do what to you? Who would do what to you?! On this train?"

He said quietly, "No.... I was in a Korean prisoner of war camp. Before they get ready to work on you, that's the music they play."

You talk about chills. By the look of this man, he had been some place terrible.

He said, "Stay away from that music. It's evil."

I looked at him, and he was not weeping, but his eyes were running. He was an American Indian, and his eyes were running tears all the time, and he'd been a prisoner of war in Korea, but the way he said, in a spooky, haunted voice, "That's the music they play, before they work on you."

Before he was brainwashed, or tortured, they played classical music.

That was like a Ken Kesey or something symbolism, of the weeping American Indian. Nobody would believe that if I wrote it. I think he was probably alcoholic. He was drinking, but he wasn't emotionally upset. He was going down to get some medical attention.

It looked like ripples of tears.

And this guy, the composer, he was weird. He kept wanting to know why people in Berkeley don't do this, or don't do that.

I told him, "Well why don't you go ask them?"

He wanted me to be a representative. He was a very strange, self-contained, prissy person, who was not real at all.

I said, "Hey look at this song writing book. Is it any good." But no, he didn't want to play. I think, 'You want me to sit and listen. Okay. I don't want to take any lessons from you, because I don't want my knuckles rapped.' It was strange. But the Indian was convinced, this guy was bad mojo.

The way he said it, I wish I could capture the cadence and the clarity. I almost knew instantly what he meant when he said that. I got this flash, he had been a P.O.W., and they had done terrible things to him.

But I didn't pry. I wished him good luck. God speed. And all that stuff. Take care.

Are We Almost There?

There's a 2,000 mile train trip from Oakland to Chicago, roughly. And to be thirty minutes out of Oakland, and to have somebody want to know if you're going to get into Chicago on time.

I said, "Well, Madam, there's 1900 miles between us and there, and we're only thirty minutes underway. Right now we're on time."

What a lot of it is, is that somebody will see, it's like kids with candy. The hungry bees. They'll see me talking to somebody and they'll think, 'That person's gettin' something I'm not getting.' All they want is some attention, some energy. It used to bother me. But now, I enjoy it.

Cause I want some too.

Life On The Job

If somebody's gettin' something I'm not, y'know. I try to be in a situation where they don't have to ask me, so that they don't have to ask me a question to get some energy.

I'll comment on a book they're reading. Or if they're getting ornery, I'll ask how they did gambling. Or if they're going to a destination that's unusual, and I haven't had one of those in a long time, Lincoln Nebraska, or something like that.

Usually when I'm takin' their tickets, they'll have the whole wad, and I'll comment, "Looks like you're doing a lot of traveling." And I'll tell them, if I'm writing the hat check myself, usually

I'm the assistant car gent, who writes the hat checks, a little tag, and I'll tell them "It's looks like you're doing a lot of traveling," y'know. "Is Lincoln a nice town?" I'll say, trying to establish a connection.

I'm not with those people the whole trip. I go as far as Sparks. The car attendant goes all the way to Chicago. So the passengers will have five or six more crews, five or six more personalities that get on.

Do the passengers come off the wall with different kinds of stuff? Sometimes hostility. Sometimes too much alcohol, cause we go from zero degrees sea level, to 7,200 feet. And they're drinking more than they normally do, because they're having fun. Got to have fun, quicker!

Before all the fun's gone, right?

Tough Street Guy On An Eleventh Hour Run

There was this lady who overdosed on the train.

A grandma, seventy years old, she's drinking gin. And taking heart pills.

She's a Black woman.

She had stopped breathing, apparently. Fortunately there was a woman Navy medic there, doin' CPR on her.

Her son was from a street gang out of L.A., a Blood, or a Crypt. He had it on his jacket.

So we were trying to find him. We get grandma back to consciousness, and she said, "Well, I'll be fine. I just won't drink any more gin."

I said, "Lady, you weren't breathin' when I got here. You owe your life to this lady."

Well, she wasn't going to get off the train. And we couldn't throw her off. So I got the grandson, and I layed it on him. I pointed my finger in his face, and I said, "Look, you're the man now. Your grandmother, you love her? She was dead when I got here. She was not breathing."

I layed it on too heavy. He starts coming to pieces, this tough street guy. He says, "Well take her gin bottle away! I'll take her gin bottle away!"

I say, "No. She's got to go to a doctor. I mean, she was ... . There was no pulse. No breathing. This lady saved your grandma's life. You got to make the decision. We can't throw her off, but you have to help. Just say 'Yes, Grandma, we're going over to the hospital.' And we'll send her to the hospital. I'm not lying to you."

He starts crying, "Oh Grandma."

It was too heavy, man. I used a sledge hammer, when I should have used a chisel. To sway this tough street kid out of L.A. A gang member.

This was the train from Klamath Falls to Oakland. That's a long night train, it's an eleven hour run. That was just out of Klamath Falls. The train goes all the way to Oakland, from Seattle.

Train 14 goes from L.A. to wherever it goes to.

The overnight train, when people are drinking heavily out of L.A., by the time they close the bar in Redding, they're all soused and loose and ready for just about anything.

There's Only Two Of You

I was on the Bakersfield run for quite a while, and that's a nightmare. It's not a reserved train. That means that you keep piling them on. Often times you have standees, more often than not.

Everybody's unhappy, because you're ruining their trip, cause you purposely put too many people on the train, so they can't have a seat, and it's all your fault!

I didn't like that job because I had to armor myself so I wouldn't make eye contact going through the car. Because if one person — you talk about hungry kids — if one person got me, ninety of them are going to get me. I don't have the time. Because a station stop comes up every eighteen minutes on that run. You have sixteen station stops in six hours. And you don't have any train attendants. There's two of you. Maybe 700 people. And it's overwhelming. So you can't make eye contact.

There was times when the old folks, the people who needed eye contact, were baffled or weird. There's only two of you, and there's four doors to open. And you got to get back to the old folks later. You go back to them, and you tell them, "Look, I haven't forgotten about you, this next stop, it will take me a while to get back to you." Cause you don't want them freaking out. Y'know, having a cardiac.

It's a taxing job. That's a taxing run. It just wears me out. From Oakland, to Bakersfield.

Old Folks

The old people all kind of run together, all old people, in a way. The old people seem to be a little more confused, sometimes.

They want to tell you the last time when they rode a train. That's the thing about old people.

They say in these quaking, broken voices, "I haven't been on a train since 1942."

It hasn't changed much. So I say, "Well don't wait another forty-two years until you come back to ride with us again."

Cops & Saturday Night At The Opera

That was up there by the Opera House by the Muni bus barn. And just a little bit north of there, they have the Opera House, on Tennessee street. About eight blocks from China Basin. I mean the Opera House storage facility.

That's when you go by, and you see all the great sets, and weird new stuff in there.

Well, it really scared the heck out of me. There was like this collision with a big Cadillac took place about three feet, or four feet, from the bottom of my feet. I'm saying I can't believe these people don't hear this thing. Well if they were drunk, they might not've. What was interesting was when the cops showed up, the sergeant was even drunker than they were.

fig. 50 – an excursion train from Oakland to Oroville in 1955; car was built mid-'20s 275

fig. 51 — engineers: Patricia Lollis & Herman, Christmas on the railroad

Pat Lollis — (born 1953)

1st Woman Engineer for Santa Fe in California

'Nothing Is Yours Until You Pass It On To Another.'

I was among the first group of women hired on the railroads in the U.S. — women didn't start getting hired until the early '70s. There were women working on other railroads, but there were so few of us, that I didn't know who they were.

I worked for the railroad as an engineer from 1974 until 1989 — for fifteen years; I'm proud of those years and I'm always glad to share my experiences.

I felt like I accomplished something. I was the first woman to run an Amtrak train out here for Santa Fe; and I was the first woman engineer in California for Santa Fe.

I'll never forget the day they called me, and I was the hoghead on an Amtrak train — my first one. I took it very seriously. There were passengers back there. I wanted to do well, to nail my stops, to do everything right.

So I went down to Fresno and when I'd stop in the larger cities like Stockton, the younger women were thrilled. This was back in the days of women's lib; so it was a big deal. Women would give me the power sign; they'd clap and cheer.

The reality of what I was doing, outside of just having a good time and an adventure came crashing in on me when a woman dispatcher told me her story. I was back in Topeka at engineer school. She had in her early years on the railroad held up the hoop with the written train orders on it, and the engineers going by would grab the orders off, then spit tobacco juice on her — because she was doing a man's job — she was able to do that because all the men were away at war. One of the reasons I felt this responsibility to pass it on, was not just because of that, but she wished so much, with all of her heart and soul, that times could have been different when she was my age; she really wished she could have been an engineer. The dispatcher's desk was as far as she could get. And here I was, twenty-two years old, doing her dream; and, 'I hadn't paid my dues'. I didn't have to do anything — I was a minority hire.' I really wanted to do well; and make sure I did well, so that any woman who followed would maybe have it better, or easier ... so no woman, none of us would ever have to go through what she went through, again.

And I realized that what I did, in the next however- many years I was going to be out there, was going to weigh heavily on the women that followed. I felt something that was bigger than myself.

One of the reasons I stayed for so long on the railroad, was that a part of me felt no matter how hard things got, no matter how bad things were, if I quit, then I would be failing, and not just myself.

It was a matter of consciousness, principle, and stubbornness.

One of my big regrets, frustrations, and a disappointment, is that as a woman, with all that experience behind me, I never got to pass it on, to another woman. There is a saying that has always stuck in my mind ... the whole thing of wanting to pass it on, and give what I got to another woman, 'Nothing is yours, until you pass it on to another.'

"What was it like for a woman to be working on the railroad?" I said.

It's especially hard to talk about it because being a railroad engineer is a mantle that has been handed down from man to man to man; even though I had been handed a mantle, my role models were men. I'm not a man. And how I work, and how I think, on one level, mechanically, I do what the men do — but how I integrate it, how I take it in and experience it is uniquely female.

The thing about railroading is, if they find where your soft spot is, then that's where they stay. They do this to men too, not just to women. They'll tease you, and they'll harass you, in a kidding way — and if you let it bother you, they'll never stop.

I wondered if it was just men, or just railroads.

"Could you give me some examples of what some of the difficulties were in talking to the guys?" I said.

One of my biggest frustrations working with railroad men, which is the only group of men I know, is that individually I could sit down with them, most of them, any of the ones I cared to do this with, and say, 'Hey, wait a minute.' — and they'd listen; and they'd understand. But when it came to the power of the pack, the power of the group, they could never go against the pack. And so it was extremely frustrating to have things that would go wrong, or points that I would want to make, and changes that I would want to try and bring, because there was an unspoken change in the men that was if they were thinking, 'Okay, we can't think or openly agree with the way she was talking to us privately anymore, because we're with the rest off the guys now, and there's a woman here.' It was always difficult to get it over on the group.

Those Old Guys Were My Favorites—They Were What Gave The Railroad All It's Color

"What were some of the positives?" I said.

The first five years were a lot of fun. There were a lot of things happening; a lot of fun and an adventure; hard work, but fun.

I really enjoyed myself. I was growing. I was learning. I was learning about men. I was learning about that kind of world. I was a woman in a situation where very few women had ever been before. Although there were some real jack-asses out there, the good ones far out-weigh the bad. I really want to stress that I have a lot of fond memories and feelings of affection for a lot of the people I worked with. And I was lucky I took to the work, I did a good job, I got along with most people; and I was young. It was all very exciting.

There was also a lot of drinking the first five years. I was right in there with the best of them, young, and crazy. We were just kinda kids cut loose in a candy store, in a way, but we had a tremendous amount of responsibility, involved in handling that kind of equipment and I didn't take it lightly.

There was a lot about what I did that was very, well, 'romantic' is not the world ... but it felt very 1930's. There was an aspect of it, it's like I felt that I was a part of something that was very old, and I was being let in to a secret club, that almost nobody really knew anything about ... an initiation. And I was very excited about that. It was very seductive. And I was the only woman doing it. At that time. So I felt like I had this special secret, and I was going to work doing this, I was running trains — I was doing something that little boys only dreamed about, and big boys dreamed about. So it was in that way it felt very special and unique.

Being With The Old Timers Was Wonderful

When I hired out, the men who were working on the railroad were all old timers, who came from the '30s, and the Depression, and W.W.II — so they had a completely different outlook on the world and the railroad than the pups did, the new guys. And those old guys were my favorite; they were what gave the railroad all its color.

There were so many characters. But most of the characters were the old timers.

A lot of those guys were wonderful — for me, the railroad dramatically changed when they all retired — because they took me in, and boy, they taught me. They were all the first ones to say, 'There shouldn't be women out here! — I'm not going to help her a bit!' But when I showed interest and also did my job, those old guys saw that, and they gave me all they knew.

I know it did help that I was a woman, because I didn't have to be macho, I didn't have to be a guy, I didn't have to prove myself in that way; I had to prove myself in many many other ways. But in that way I was able to get to these old men and say, 'Will you teach me? I want to learn — and they did.

The first nickname I got, was 'Sexy Hog'. Then they told me I couldn't be a hoghead, because I was a woman; I had to be a sowhead.

My Favorite Person

I'll tell you who my favorite person was. His name was

Herman. He's dead now. But he was an incredible man. He was a very gruff, very base, crusty old German. His parents and grandparents had come from Germany. His father worked at the Altamont shop in Pennsylvania on Penn Central, as a boiler maker. so he had railroading in the family. He was a character. I absolutely loved him. I found out after he died, that he had learned that there was going to be a woman on his job.

"That's it! I'm not going to help her! She shouldn't be here!" he said.

And within a week, he had taken me under his wing, and we were best buddies.

'Liebschen — Meaning 'Dear One'

There was a man named Herman. Herman was my favorite. His family came from Germany. His dad worked in the Altamont shops, he was a boiler maker for the Penn Central in Pennsylvania. All of Herman's stories, everything about Herman, had to do with anything German. He loved Saint Pauli's Girl; he loved German Shepherds; any kind of dog that was German; drove Volkswagens — that were classically fossilized ... he could fix them blindfolded; he loved Courvesier, bratwurst ... when he had a few belts in him he would yodel, German yodeling — and that was just who Herman was. He always wore the same clothes, old beat-up bib overalls. He always smelled like dogs and WD 40. When you thought of Herman, you thought of St. Pauli Girl beer, Napoleon Brandy, he always called me 'Liebschen,' which is German for 'dear one.' We were close. His favorite saying was 'Donder und blitzen schlagen das sheishaus — which means 'Thunder and lightning hit the outhouse'. When ever anything would go wrong, he would bellow this. You have to remember, to picture this guy, he was not very tall, kind of rotund, not fat, but rotund; he would laugh through — well I think George Washington may have used the same teeth that he used ... they were plates that a lot of the teeth were broken, and they didn't fit very well. And he smoked cigarettes with no filters. If he borrowed a cigarette and you gave him one with a filter, he'd say, 'Darn thing,' and he'd rip it off. This was just Herman.

One of the things that I remember about him is that when he

was working daylights and I'd be working midnights, and you're out there all night, and it was cold, and was raining, and you'd come in, and I'd look like something the cat dragged in. I'd walk in, and many many times, many mornings, he'd ask me if I wanted some coffee, because I looked so pitiful. He'd give me a cup with about one inch of coffee in it, and he'd look at me.

'Liebschen, you need some sugar in your coffee,' he'd say. He'd reach in and pull out this bottle of Courvesier and put two inches of Courvesier in my cup.

Herman's Gooseberry Pie & Papa Duck

Herman had very fond memories about his home in Pennsylvania, and his German Grosspapa and the farm — and he always talked about these gooseberry pies. He loved gooseberries.

There was a man out there, Papa Duck. Papa Duck had this very bizarre sense of humor. And he was always messin' with Herman, that would irritate Herman to no end. Herman, being a simple man, having a very simple outlook on life, 'Do onto others as you would have other do unto you,' he never understood why Papa Duck gave him such a hard time. He never got it. One day Papa Duck showed up to work and he had baked a pie — a real pie, with a bottom crust and a top crust, it looked beautiful.

"Herman, this is a gooseberry pie I baked for you," he said.

Herman was extremely touched.

Now you go back a little bit, and you have to realize, that one of the things that Herman hated most in life, was carrots. And everybody knew it. And so, we get on the engine, and Herman's talking about it.

"I don't understand it. This man, most of the time he's a son of a gun, and now he bakes me a pie. What am I supposed to think?" he said. He was very touched. He was a very simple man. There was no subterfuge in the way he thought. What you see is what you get.

So we got in the shanty, and he was drooling. We all sit down, and he cuts into this pie, and he cuts himself a big piece, and it's a carrot pie.

The whole shanty is hysterical. Herman, again, you had to know him, he would get these looks on his face. His face would screw up, and he'd look at you like, 'Can anybody make me understand? I don't get it.' He looked at me. We had lockers next to each other. I'm trying not to be hysterical; but the tears are coming out of my eyes. He looked at me.

"Liebschen, should I eat this? Do you think he was trying to be nice?" he said.

"Don't eat the pie," I said.

That pie sat there, I don't know for how many days it sat there as a monument.

When he cut that pie. Nobody knew but Papa Duck, that this was a carrot pie. And of course we all knew, Herman hated carrots.

Nobody ate it. It sat there until it got pitched several days later.

Papa Duck

Papa Duck had another nickname. 'Chef Boy-Oh-Boy'. He was into Sierra Club, camping, cooking out over an open fire. But he had this crack, when it came to Herman. He just wouldn't quit. Herman never understood.

He's retired now.

The one thing I want to say about Herman, another beautiful memory, I loved him very deeply, someways as a mentor, and how supportive he was of me out there. We used to get together every few months, and we'd go up to his house, and I'd visit his wife and his dogs. He had a wall full of cuckoo clocks. The man was very old-world. And he got cancer, sometime in the early 80's. He got extremely ill. He refused to quit smoking until he absolutely couldn't smoke any more. The last time he was hospitalized, he was very near death. So I was going up to visit him every chance that I got. And it just so happened, that on my off day, I heard that he was really failing. The last time I had seen him, he didn't look well at all. I went up to see him, and it was just one of those moments. His wife had been there a lot, and there was some business she had to attend to, so she left, and he was in the room by himself. I'll never forget. I went in, and he was out of it, he was not conscious. I remember I was trying to talk to him, trying to make some contact. He was very agitated, and I realized that I needed to just leave him alone.

And what we used to do, when we worked together, is when there was spot-time, which was when you had a coffee break or lunch break, we'd sit on the engine. He'd be in the engineer's seat, and I'd be in the fireman's seat. And we'd talk. It never failed, that my feet went up on the emergency brake valve, and my head went back, and I went to sleep in my seat. And his head would flop down against the window, and we'd sit there, and we'd sleep for ten or fifteen minutes, till it was time to go to work again. So what I decided, was that it needed to be like it always was. So I sat down in the chair by the bed, and I put my feet up, and I went to sleep. And I'll be darned, something woke me up, I'm not sure what it was. But when I woke up, he took his last breath. He was dead.

I was overwhelmed.

Being there with him at that time, it felt like a real privilege.

I knew that death was imminent. I'm sure that's what woke me up. But it was an honor and a privilege to be able to be there, just like always, on the engine.

He had someone being with him still, in a real quiet, easy way.

The 'Alerter'

They used to have these things called 'Alerters', that were attached to the wall, above-and-in-front-of an engineer. The 'Alerter' was a box about eight inches by ten inches. And it had a little red light on it. And how it was set up ... let's say you're sitting there, and you're going down the main line, and you haven't touched anything in maybe ten or fifteen seconds — the red light would start to flash, and it would start to 'BEEP!'. Gradually the beeping would get louder, and louder, and louder. And if you didn't either move the throttle, or touch something to ground the 'the Alerter', the emergency brake would apply.

When they passed a law in the 70's that there would be no more firemen — even though they had to bring them back — they came out with devices like this because they figured if there was only going to be one engineer in the cab; if he dropped dead on the floor, then the train would only go so far until it threw itself into emergency.

Well these 'Alerters' were old, and half of them didn't! work, and they would go, 'BEEP! BEEP! BEEP! BEEP! BEEP!' all the time.

It was enough to make you insane. It would be very distracting. None of us could stand them. But you had to live with them.

We had this trestle — it's a low trestle but it goes over the Orwood Bridge, which goes for maybe two or three miles, and you've got levee water on both sides. Well the 'Alerter' started to go off, and by the time this old head got to Orwood, he couldn't stand it; he couldn't take it any more. He was a big man, about six-foot-two, and he had his bib overalls on, and finally, he snapped. He took a hammer, and he started beating on the box. The more he hit it, the better he felt. And the more he hit it, the more he destroyed it, until the darn thing actually popped off the wall. He threw the windows open, took the box, pitched it out the window into the water, and then as the train was moving, and he yelled back at it.

"Now 'BEEP! BEEP!' at the fish for a while!"

The second five years, that's when I knew the job was changing and would never be the same. These five years were harder ... I was getting tired, the work was getting harder in that they were clamping down and making us work harder. We started losing ground contractually — we were just starting to make concessions. The old vanguard was retiring. And once the old vanguard started leaving, management started clamping down on us, 'cause we didn't know any better; we didn't have the clout or experience to really know what to do. And then, by the middle of that time, management started changing — around 1980 — railroad men didn't run the railroad anymore, college boys and corporate types did.

The railroad changed dramatically after 1980. But before then, one of the things about the job was they had enough manpower. The railroad was run by railroad men. In other words, trainmasters and yardmasters all usually came from the ranks of the trainmen, so they knew railroading, they knew it backwards and forwards; they knew the stresses of it. And you could, at any given point, lay off for up to fourteen days, without any questions. Most people never did that. Most people would take at the max, maybe five or six days off, or two or three. But you didn't get paid, but that was okay. Because you could work as much as you wanted, and make as much money as you wanted, then lay off. And take some rest. And they didn't say anything, because the job was, and is, so stressful, in terms of the hours.

It's changed dramatically. The bottom line is profit.

So that was a major turning point. The fun started to go out of it. Also around that time, I stopped drinking. You know, when you're in your twenties, you play and you party, and you either grow up, or you don't grow up. I grew up. And I didn't drink anymore. Then there was nothing to get between my feelings and the circumstances out there; there was nothing to buffer it. It just wasn't fun anymore. And it wasn't not fun because I didn't drink; but it wasn't fun, and I didn't drink. The toxic conditions on the job started getting to me, and the bad seats on the engines, everything started to catch up. My body started to tell a toll. I started getting headaches every day.

The third — and last — five years were excruciating.

I could no longer go to work on this job that dehumanized, brutalized, was very toxic; I could no longer do that, and feel the way I did in the world; and what I eventually did was I tried to marry the two, and I found an expression that fit my beliefs — which was the practice of acupuncture.

And then, the last five years, I was just hangin' in. It was a long time to hang in; but I was also going to school at the same time. It was excruciatingly difficult.

The experience of acupuncture school was for me, as exciting in its own way, as my first five years on the railroad.

I felt expansive again

(Pat Lollis currently is a licensed acupuncturist practicing in Berkeley, California. She is on the board of directors of the California Acupuncture Association.)

Wendy Weisman — (born 1949)

Switchman Promoted to Engineer

"What was your job capacity on the railroad?" I said.

I started out as a switchman in Stockton in 1977; and I worked in Morbin Yard in Stockton for three years; and then I went into engine service, spent a year in Richmond, then got transferred to Fresno. I trained as a fireman. I was a fireman for almost a year. What they do, is you work as a fireman — you're supposed to be there a certain amount of time. What it revolved around was when they could take you in the school. They could only take so many at a time in the school in Topeka Kansas. And so you just stayed in Richmond until you were ready to go to school.

I had heard about a lady engineer in Texas somewhere before I was working for the railroad. But there were not very many women.

"What was going through your mind at the time you decided to look for work on the railroad?"

Well I had a lady friend who got a job as a brakeman for Southern Pacific. She was telling me about it. And she'd just happened to get on a real cushy job — she rode from Tracy to Sacramento I think; brakemen, they spend most of their time on the road, so depending on what trip you're on, there's not a lot to do or whatever, and she was just telling me how much she got paid for the time that she worked.

"Hey, I could do that," I said.

She told me they were taking applications for Santa Fe. So I went and applied. I filled out some things, like 'previous jobs'; 'Why do you think you're qualified?' — I had worked in several male-dominated fields. I worked in construction. In a feed-lot working with cowboys and cattle. Things like that.

And it was funny, because when they called me in for the interview, the interviewer asked me three questions.

"You have to work midnight; is that okay?" he said.

"Oh sure; that's no problem," I said. And the whole time I'm thinking, 'There is no way. But I'll play along here.'

"There are hoboes; are you afraid of hoboes?" he said.

"Well I don't know, 'cause actually, I've never met one," I said. And I'm thinking, 'No possible way! I will not do this.'

"Well there's no women's bathroom," he said.

They were trying to discourage women, actually.

"Well there's a door on the bathroom, isn't there?" I said.

"Well yeah," he said gruffly.

And so I got the job.

It's real different to work with men, instead of women. Y'know, they have a whole different attitude. So I started out on that railroad job, and I thought, 'Well, I'm going to try this out for one week, and then, I'm outta here.' First of all, there was no way I was going to work at night. Second of all, I don't want anything at all to do with hoboes ... and who knows what's happening out there, in the dark.

Ten years later, I was still there.

Why did I stay? Really I stayed because there was a lot of freedom. You know they have an extra board. If you don't want to work, you just don't work. I mean there's a lot of freedom. In most jobs, they're eight-to-five five days a week, and you were there. Because if you're not there, there's no one there to do that job — that's the way most jobs are. But on the railroad, they have people just hanging out to take your place when you're sick. So if you have something really fun coming up, you just go do that. You don't have to make excuses; you just take the time off. Plus, for a woman, at that time, that was good pay, y'know.

They had several ways of running the extra board. If you get work depends on the officials who are at that particular location and how they run it. Like now, they have a guaranteed extra board. Nowadays you are guaranteed so-many miles per month; you're assured of that. There's a couple of reasons that they did that, but we don't have to get into that.

"What was it like, as a woman, workin' on the railroad? Is it even a relevant question?"

Oh yeah. It's a real relevant question. It sure is.

Now this is a generalization — but anyway, in general, the older generation of men were pretty nice — let's say maybe the over-forty's, forty-five, fifty at that time; somewhere around in there ... when I started there, I was about twenty-seven — they were polite. They still opened the doors kind of things; and they were very willing to help me learn. And most of them, if they had an attitude, I didn't know about it.

And then, the men that were in my age group, that were more like my peers, they were the worst ones. They treated me the rudest. There were hard on me. They kind of did underlying things to make me look stupid. They would withhold information and not tell me everything. They had an attitude. They didn't want me there. And I went home cryin' several nights. Because they harassed me. Just kind of pick, pick, pickin' at me all the time, and never quite ever accepting me. Now this was just in the first few years.

And then the younger ones, that were in their teens and real early twenties — they accepted me just fine, like, 'This is just the way it is.' They were used to women being in a more male-dominated field. So they just accepted me, like, 'Okay, there's another person.' And that was helpful. 'Cause that was really what I wanted all along.

But the ones that were closer to my age ... what happened, is I just had to learn to push back when they pushed. Or just refuse to be pushed. Or just give them a bad time. I just had to get mean for a little while. So that they'd stop pushing me around.

I Had One Guy Shove Me Into Some Cars That Were Moving

Well I had one guy shove me into some cars that were moving. I was real upset about that. But, after a while, everything got straightened out, and those guys just realized that they weren't going to push me around. And then there were rumors like, 'Don't mess with her, she's real ornery.' And I'm really not. But I just had to let them know that I couldn't be pushed around. Once it got established, which took probably three years ... when you work with six hundred people, you don't work with the same people every day. You keep changing on the crew; so you have to establish yourself, you have to get through most of the people. Then they start telling stories, like, 'Don't mess with her. She's grumpy,' or whatever. So then they start leaving you alone, you can get nice again.

I had lots of friends on the railroad; then there were the people that never never, after ten years, still never wanted me around. And then when I went to be an engineer, as far as some of them were concerned, 'She can't do anything right, and what is she doing out here anyway? It's like, after ten years you guys, 'Give it up!'

"How many other women were working at that time when there were about six hundred employees there, would you guess?"

I'm not sure how many in Richmond. I'd say I knew maybe three or four women switchmen in Richmond. And most of them didn't last very long.

These employees were kinda like from Fresno, Stockton, Richmond. I didn't know people from Bakersfield, 'cause I'd never worked in the yard and gotten to know those people. These were mainline people. Pat Lollis was one engineer; and there was another woman who had come from S.P. — two as a matter of fact, and I can't think of their names right now. Out of six hundred employees, there was about ten women.

"Can you tell me that story of that guy pushin' you around?"

A Fire in The Dark and The Cold

The shoving was over wood to keep warm. It was in the winter; it was real cold. I was probably working midnights, or something like that. We'd scrounged wood off of the cars when they went by. Y'know when they put tractors and things up on those flatcars they use wedges under the tires, and they chain them down. Well when they take the machinery off, they just leave that wood. So we'd get it off of there, and we'd start a fire down there to stand by while we're switchin' out there in the dark and the cold.

He would stand in one place where they had an electric box, and electric switchbox at the east end of the yard in Stockton there, and he'd stand there and push those buttons by the fire. And I'd get wood, and throw it on the fire, but I was maybe twenty paces down there. And I said to myself, 'Hey, wait a minute. I'm standin' in the cold, gettin' wood for him to stand by the fire. This is pretty dumb.'

So I built my own fire down there.

He'd come down and steal the wood off of it.

We kind of had a little argument.

"Wait a minute! Get your own wood!" I said.

He just wanted to get a little physical. I thought he was going to bop me in the nose for a while. He was a big guy, too. But it didn't happen. He just gave me a shove towards those cars.

And I just kinda left. I said to myself, 'I'm finished, I'm not going to work with you any more tonight.' I left.

I understood him. I just think he had a problem with women working there, really. I never really asked him about that. Several years passed and we didn't talk. I really liked him before that. He was a nice guy, basically. Then after a few years, I spoke to him.

"Do you want to bury the hatchet?' I said.

"Okay," he said.

"Were you ever scared, on the railroad, in terms of being a woman?"

One Thing That Happened One Night

One thing that happened, it was pretty scary at the time, I was working at night.

There's a transfer in Stockton, I was working in Stockton; and there's a transfer between the Western Pacific and the Santa Fe. The W.P. will leave cars there. And the Santa Fe, we'd go over and pick these cars up. Well we have a switch right in the middle of the street, called a 'submarine switch'. Somebody has to stay behind, and line that switch back after the train crosses — you know, there's ones you what to line back, and ones you don't; that's one you do.

So I stayed there, and caught the last car goin' through the yard. Well they always transfer them with air, so somebody has to go along and bleed off all those cars. Well I was walking up there, actually, while the cut of cars was being pulled by me, I noticed there was a pack of half-a-dozen to ten men that were on this car, and they were getting pretty drunk. They were getting pretty loud, and rowdy. I knew that I had to walk up by myself, past these guys — and it was two o'clock in the morning. So I was leaning up against these cars part way, and I knew that before I got there I was going to stop and figure out something else to do when I got close.

Well, the foreman was on the head end.

I got up, and I heard these guys, they were starting to yell and get pretty rowdy. In part of the yard there's gravel, and I heard these footsteps coming back — so I started walking back the other way. Then the footsteps started getting faster. So I started getting worried; so I went across the yard. In the yard there's maybe twelve tracks; I jumped across some other cars, about two tracks over, and was going to head up that way. All of a sudden I heard the feet that were following me jump over the cars. I was gettin' pretty scared. I was runnin' up to the other end.

"Wendy!" somebody yelled.

It was the foreman. He had noticed those guys were there. He was coming back to be with me.

But it was pretty heart-stopping at the time.

He was coming back to tell me not to come up that way, to go around.

There was definitely panic.

But that one turned out good.

Really I didn't have any other scary things, and I felt real confident that the people that I worked with were pretty willing, and they watched out for me too; I know that a lot of them did. They would take extra steps to keep an eye on me. I know they did. Because I had a good relationship with a lot of those people. It wasn't all turmoil you know, there were a lot of people who were really wonderful. And I know they watched out for me to a certain extent.

"What happened when you met your first hobo?"

The first? Nothing happened really. Basically he just stayed to himself. They just were real quiet. And they traveled together, two or three together. And they just asked which track was goin' west, or east or whatever. And I'd just answer. And that was it.

I know that there were dead ones found occasionally.

When we would see, when switchmen would see that a hobo was really drunk, we would usually call the gumshoe, and he would come and take him off; when it looked real dangerous like that, and a hobo could get hurt.

'Walk Like A Man If You Can'

I mostly avoided things that were about to happen. I had some guy yelling at me.

"Hey! C'mere you!" he yelled.

He was a big old guy, standing on the other side of the fence, which was only about three feet high; he could've jumped right over. He wasn't an employee; I don't know what he was, hobo, vagrant, or what. He wasn't in the road yard. He kept followin' me, and tryin' to talk to me. He seemed real shaky. Like that was a person I did not want to talk to. So I just kinda grumbled and walked away and tried to not look female. Walk like a man if you can. Luckily I had my coat on; so I put my collar up. 'Cause I had longer hair at the time.

I tried to look very unfeminine working nights. I put on the old baggy overalls.

"Were you married then?"

No. As a matter of fact, I met my husband Scott switching in the yard in Morbin. We were both switchman. He was from Richmond, and I was from Stockton.

Pink Cadillac

I remember kind of a funny situation on AMTRAK one time.
There was a big pink Cadillac.
You know those private crossings where they just have those

white crossbucks?

Well this guy was just sitting there in a pink Cadillac. He had his foot on the brake. But you know how on those automatics, you keep your foot on the brake, but the car will creep; but you don't notice?

He was talking to this guy who was beside him; and the car was creepin' on to the tracks.

It was on AMTRAK. And the engineer noticed this was happening, and he just blew on the whistle like crazy, and was ringin' the bell; he started slowing down, 'cause he saw what was happening. We were going at a pretty good clip, about 60 m.p.h.

The guy in the Cadillac, it was like he'd kind of look up like he was thinking to himself, Yeah, yeah, this train keeps blowin' it's whistle, blowin' his whistle more than usual ... being kind of obnoxious.' Well finally the guy looked up and realized where he was. The look on the guy's face, like his eyes almost popped out of his head. His mouth was open. You could see him push down on that brake with his whole body leanin' forward, trying to stop that car.

We hit him.

All it did was just hit his fender, and knocked his hood, he had just creeped out enough, that hood just flew up in the air. And I'll tell you, the look on people's face when something like that happens. It doesn't sound funny, but the look on their face sometimes is just hilarious afterwards.

It wasn't that scary, because we were almost stopped. And the engine just barely hit his pink Cadillac, like, 'Boink!' —like you hit it with your finger, and just flipped his car hood up into the air.

I bet that guy wet his pants.

I could tell you one sad thing; but I wasn't there. It happened to another one of the women engineers there.

I Hit a Car

Down the middle of the street in Fresno, it's 20 m.p.h. The railroad tracks run right down the middle of the street, so the cars have to move over when the train comes.

This woman came up to the stop sign, and she pulled right in front of me. The train was going the same direction as the car down the street. She had been over at the side of the road. What's normal is people just move over a little. And the stop sign was there. And she just pulled over right in front of the train. I was almost stopped. I was only going about 7 m.p.h.

And 'Boink!' Another one of those where the train dented the automobile. Well she got out, and she was so mad.

When the policeman came out he came over to talk to me. He shook his head.

"This lady has done this before. I think she's trying to get a new car."

'The Baby-Doll Train'

We were leaving Richmond Yard and coming to Fresno. The brakeman made the air on the train and he walked up. He got up on the engine.

"Hey, I found this doll here in the yard, I wondered if you dropped it?" he said.

He thought he was being real funny.

"No. It's not my doll. I don't play with dolls anymore," I said.

So he just put it down on the floor.

We leave the yard, and we're headin' towards Fresno. I don't know who got the idea to tie this baby doll out on the front of the engine.

"Let's give her the ride of her life," the brakeman said.

So here's this baby, maybe about eighteen inches tall, with all scraggly hair, and it's got these kind of rubber arms, loose rubber arms. So he put that up there. And we're going 60 m.p.h., and that little baby's flapping her little arms all over the place, and her hair's blowin' back in the breeze. And the people that were stopped at crossings, it was like, 'Ohhhhhh!' They'd point. They were hitting their spouses, pointing, and saying, 'Look at that! There's a baby up there!'

Well in Morbin Yard, there was a trainmaster, and his mission in life was to make sure that everyone wore their safety glasses. You had to wear safety glasses on the railroad. So before we got into the yard, I had gone out and with a pen drawn these safety glasses on the doll's face, so when we got into the yard, Van the

Man, as we called him ... so the doll wouldn't get into trouble with Van the Man for not wearing safety glasses.

It was a laugh.

We got off the train, but we left the baby on the train, and the next crew took the train down the line.

For years after, we'd see the guys.

"Hey, have you heard from the baby?" I'd say.

"Yeah, I heard she was in Davis, and she's goin' downhill," someone'd say.

There have been lots of baby stories from different people on the crew since we did that.

Van the Man

He was a trainmaster in Morbin. His big deal was to stand up in the tower with binoculars on, and watch, to make sure people had their safety glasses on.

He'd see somebody, and he'd come runnin' down, tip-toe across these tracks, and try to sneak up on people. They'd see him coming, and whip these safety glasses out of their pocket and put these safety glasses on. Well this one time this guy did that, and this guy's safety glasses didn't even have lenses in them. 'Cause these plastic glasses, the plastic lenses kept gettin' scratches in them, and they were just horrible to try to see through and horrible to wear.

Well Van the Man walked up to the guy wearing the safety glasses with no lenses in them, and didn't even notice there were no lenses in them. While they were talking, this guy would scratch his eye through the glasses, and Van the Man never noticed. I was on the side watching, and I was laughing away. Van the Man never did figure it out.

"Were there things that made you feel good?" I said.

"Let me see. I guess, camaraderie. There were several people that I really like. That I got to be friends with. And stayed friends with."

"What was business-as-usual like? What was a regular day like?"

"Well, it depended on the weather, of course."

"Are we talking about the central valley?" (Editor's note: in California.)
"Yes."
"So you were you running in the fog?"

Uuuuuuu. Running in the fog had to be the worst. You could get gray hairs running in the fog. Because, when your speed limit's 70 m.p.h., you go 70. It's not like in an automobile ... you don't slow down. You go the speed limit. And there are a lot of times you hope you recognize a twig, 'cause if you miss a milepost, and if you don't know where you are if you miss a whistleboard — you go by a crossing, you just thank your lucky star that there wasn't a car there. It's miserable.

A 'whistleboard' is a little sign that has a 'W' that is so-many feet before a street crossing, so you'll know there's a crossing coming up, so you whistle.

"I don't know how anyone can ride in the fog at 70 m.p.h. Because it's not a matter of skill or luck or training or anything ... at that point, it's just, is someone gonna be there or not? I said.

That's right ... ... and you also have to know where to stop. If you think about on a passenger train, doing that — I mean it's one thing to run a freight train in the fog. If you miss something — well you can't miss a red block — if you miss that, you could hit another train goin' 70 m.p.h.; on a freight train, if you miss it, you just call the tower and tell them you need to back up. And they'll tell you it's clear behind you, or whatever, and you back up. But on a passenger train, you have to stop at a particular place, and let the people on and off.
I was fireman on the passenger train.
I think the passenger train was almost worse.
Because you had to stop where you had to stop. It'd be more specific. And then you have all those lives in that train.

"It sounds like such a real thing — it sounds like it's such a dangerous, dangerous thing, to me."
"Well, it is."
"Have there been problems from that? From the fog, in terms of it being dangerous?"

"Not any more than from anything else. Most of the things that happened, would be automobiles would do dumb things, like go around gates. There have been train accidents; they're on the news all the time. Why they happen — a lot of times, you don't know."

No Matter What The Weather Is — You're Out There

The weather. If you're a switchman, and it's raining, you're out there. No matter what, you're out there. If it's 120 degrees between the boxcars, you're out there. There's no, 'It's too hot. I don't like it.' You just go do it; and it's miserable. The weather is miserable. You think about this rainy weather we're having right now, and you went in for coffee ten, fifteen minutes, you've had your break. Now the yardmaster walks in, and hands you a list, You just go out there. You put on all your rain gear. But you know what, when you're holding on to a boxcar in the rain, you're on this ladder — and you hold above your head to hold on, right? That's just kinda how you do it. You know where that rain goes? It goes in your sleeve, and down your arm, and into your armpit, it's like, 'Oyyyy!. I'm not going to ever do this again.' And that's the main reason I went into engine service. Because it was miserable being in the weather like that.

It's Good I Don't Get Colds Easily

But I get miserable easily... ... ... I knew there was a heater on the engine; you only get rained on when the rain was really blowin' in there.

Also, workin' as a switchman in the rain is very dangerous. Y'know, lots of people have been injured. I had a scary time, which was when cars were going by, and you're going to get on it, and you grab ahold of that ladder, you stick your foot on the bottom rung and your boots are slippery, and the ladder's slippery, and your foot slips through there — and you see those wheels turning, and you've heard all those stories. That's the first thing you hear is the stories, 'Oh, so-and-so got his leg cut off.' And that's what's on your mind, every time you get on, in the rain — and it's slippery, you think, 'Is this the time my leg goes?' It's always on your mind. That's another thing. Always, in the back of your mind, you know there can be death at any moment ... ... you step between some box cars to hook some hoses together, and somebody was not supposed to, but whatever miscommunication, whatever it might be, they couple into that, or throw a car into that track with those cars — you know all the time, your life is on the line; you don't daydream; you don't walk across tracks. Because you can't hear boxcars coming. They don't make noise. They are suddenly there, and 'BOOM!' So it's always on the back of your mind, that your life is on the line out there.

"What's it like working on the railroad when you're a mommy?"

Actually we had to take turns working. 'Cause we didn't have family who lived in town who would babysit. We took turns working mostly.

When we were first married, we used to have a password when he'd be heading for Bakersfield, and I'd be heading back from Bakersfield, we'd pick up the radio and say, 'Swordfish.' That means like, 'Hi. How you doin'? Too bad we're going the wrong directions again.' That's just the way it was. Then after having a daughter, we just had to take turns laying off and working. We tried to work yard jobs with different days off so that it would work out. It was difficult.

Because on the railroad there is so much out of town work, y'know.

One Of The Most Interesting Things About The Railroad

I think one of the most interesting things about the railroad is that it has a language all its own. The road is a different language. You can be sitting around with three or four rails, and there's somebody's wife sitting there, or a friend, and they just sit there with their mouth open, like, 'What are these people saying? I know they're English words, but I don't understand any of this.'

You say something like, "You stay here and line behind and then bleed up on that cut until you come to the cut, and then hang ten cars and kick 'em down the lead, shove six, hang the crummy."

Scott's sitting across the room, and he just told me a famous one.

"Pull your rear in the clear, drop your shorts and we'll fill your rear end."

I can tell you what that means. It means, When two tracks come together, there's like a 'V'. Well you've got to get your set of cars out of that 'V' so that if there are some other cars comin' down the track next to it they don't hit — that's 'Pull the rear of your train into the clear' so it won't get hit when other cars go down this adjoining track that comes to a 'V'. 'Drop your shorts' — say if you're going from Richmond to Fresno, cars that aren't going all the way, say you dropped them, left them, at Riverbank for example you're going only a short distance, are called 'shorts' — so drop those on another track, meaning 'Kick 'em!' in there. And then, 'Fill the rear of your train' — meaning that we'll take cars out of 6-track, put it on the end of your train, and then pick the shorts up and put them back on there, so that when you're going past stations, the cars closest to the engine are the ones you leave there first, then you go to Riverbank and you leave some more, then you go to Stockton and leave some more ... 'Blocking them' means putting the cars in order. So doing the above would block your trains properly for ease.

"What about old timers?"

"There are some real characters. Do you know that people on the railroad get nicknames more often than they're called their real names?"

'Flip-Flop'

He was the guy who had stock in the paper towel company. I guess he didn't want to get his clothes dirty. He'd tape paper towels all over his arms. He'd tape paper towels up on the windows. He had this roll of masking tape and these rolls of paper towels. He'd tape it up like for sun visors, so when he was switchin' the sun wouldn't get in his eyes. And he'd tape paper towels all down his arm, because when you lean your arms out the window, you'd get your sleeve dirty. I don't think he wanted to get his shirt dirty.

'Not-So-Bad'

'Not-So-Bad' is a switchman. He's one of those guys that y'know, dynamite could go off behind him, and he'd go, 'Oh, that's not so bad.'

He's a quiet, easy-going, nice guy — that's how he got his name, 'Not-So-Bad'.

'Tap-Dancin' Don'

He wore taps on his shoes. You always knew he was coming. He was a trainmaster. You always knew when he was trying to sneak up on you, 'cause of these metal taps on the bottoms of his shoes. He'd hang out outside, and be real nervous, walkin' back and forth. Nobody ever told him we could hear him coming — or we wouldn't be able to hear him sneakin' up on us.

'Giggles'

A lot of times they'd take people's initials, like S. D. Mott. Steve Mott, like they took parts of the engine, they called him 'Sliding Valve' — they also called him 'Giggles'.

'Chicken House'

C. H. Jones. Nobody knows how he got that nickname.

'Leaky Roof'

They called him 'Leaky Roof' because he had a bad memory.

'Shaky' Shayhan

He was nervous.

'Knuckles'

He broke a lot of knuckles. And that was his name, 'Knuckles'.

'Be-No'

'Be-No' was a yardmaster. He wouldn't let people go to beans.
"There will be no coffee. There will be no lunch. There will be no quit," he said.
So they called him 'Be-No'.
Be-no coffee. Be-no lunch. Be-no quit.

No Secrets on the Railroad

There are no secrets on the railroads. They write things on boxcars with chalk. You know the authors in every state. You know, that was another thing. There were certain people, I have no idea where they came from, but the same cartoon would be on the boxcars for years and years. It's like some switchman in a yard would have a certain cartoon for his trademark. They carried chalk with them. And they would draw pictures or write certain little quotes on boxcars with chalk.

"This one old timer I interviewed said he didn't think women would be good brakemen or engineers, because how could they change a knuckle?" I said.

They're not that heavy.
All women are not wimps. Good grief, I don't think they weighed that much. You know, there's more than one part to the knuckle. Usually it's that little part that moves, is the part that would break. Nobody can carry a drawbar. Then there's the big part of the knuckle, and the little part of the knuckle; and it just

kind of depends what's broken.

One point is that those guys often wouldn't go do that by themselves, so why would they go send a woman to go do it by herself.

Those Old Steam Engineers Didn't Even Talk To Their Firemen

One thing to remember about those old steam engineers, is they didn't even talk to their firemen. If they went to go eat somewhere, they sat at a different table, so did the brakemen. They didn't speak. They spoke to yell at each other in the cab. There was a time they went through that. Before the end of the steam days — but they went through that. There was a time when they didn't even speak. I've heard lots of stories about that. They'd go to lunch. They'd go to a little cafe place, and engineers and firemen would not sit at the same table. It used to be you spent many many many years as a firemen before you ever earned the right to be an engineer. Now, when you go to be a fireman, you're on for a little while, and after a year, you're an engineer.

"You told me when they interviewed you that they told you 'There was no woman's bathroom. And there's hoboes. And you have to work at midnight.' Well you told me about hoboes. You didn't tell me about the door on the bathroom. Did it work okay?" I said.

Yeah. Y'know — in the yard there was a restroom with four stalls in there; and right outside the door, was a private bathroom. It was like a restroom in a home, one sink, and one toilet. They just gave me a key to that. When they told me there wasn't a woman's bathroom, they were just trying to scare me off, to let me know what it would be like. So I had my own bathroom. Besides, the clerks, inside the yard office, there was a men's and a women's, two separate restrooms. I just went in there too.

"How did workin' midnights turn out?"

I just did it. I never really got used to it. It's hard to get used to not sleeping at night, for one thing. I'd just get called all hours of the day and night. In the yard there are certain times you go to work. Like the shifts always start at eleven, or twelve, or three or four in the afternoon, or seven or eight in the morning.

"Any other extreme weather stories?"

I remember the time that we were in Stockton, and I was switching, so I was having to get out of the engine, and it was in the middle of a lightning storm. And the electrical wires blew down, and they were whipping around sparking. And you know, the first thing you think of, is 'This wet engine is made of metal.'
That was a little trying to get past.

Favorite Curves

I liked them all. It gave me something to do. Y'know, if you're going along at 70 m.p.h., you just look out the window. When there's a curve and you have to slow down, you get to set the brakes, and you get to see how smooth you can make your transitions.

Back when there were cabooses, this is when I was an engineer, if you bumped them around, they told you about it. When they'd get off the train, they'd tell you.

"Well, I don't really mind wearing my coffee, but it was a little hot," they'd say.

There was other times they'd say, 'That was a real nice ride.' A lot of people would give you compliments.

And there was a pride in how smoothly you could run a train. Of course, without cabooses, it took some of the pride out of it, for one thing. I think it took some of the safety out of it too. Because when the conductor and brakeman would sit up in the caboose, they'd sit up in the cupola, and they could see the whole train forward. Trains derail in spots. Something'll happen, something will be on the track, like tires will be on the track. Sometimes it will bounce around, and knock things. Weird weird things happen. Trains derail. And the conductor and brakemen would see a problem before it could cause a lot of damage, and they call up, and say, 'Stop.'

fig. 52 – Sierra Nevada Mountains, *Nevada* at Colfax near Placer City

Wheel-Slip

When you have a train, let's say they give you two little diesel engines and sixty cars; you can only go 25 m.p.h. And the engines are whining and straining. You keep getting 'wheel-slip'. That's what you call a couple of 'bell ringers.' Meaning, when you get wheel-slip, the engine's not working properly, a bell will ring. And the engine will shut itself down, and you have to reset it. So they give you these two dog, bell-ringer engines, and too many cars that the engines can't even pull. You think about driving from Richmond to Fresno at 25 m.p.h. God, please, just let anything happen, just for a spark of life.

(Wendy Weisman is currently finishing a degree in Interior Design at Fresno State University.)

fig. 53 – Patricia's qualifying run on Amtrak

Linda Niemann — (born 1946)

Booming' Brakeman & Conductor

Author of 'Boomer', Winner of the 1990 Bay Area Book Seller's Award for Non-Fiction

I had a friend was doing this job, and he start describing it, and it sounded like something that I would be really suited for, and that I'd enjoy doing. That was before they were hiring any women as brakemen. So I called up the Southern Pacific.

'Are you calling for your husband?' they said. And told me flat-out they wouldn't hire a woman to do this job.

So I sort of put it away, and didn't think about it anymore. Lo-and-behold, about three or four years later, they were under some pressure from affirmative action, and did this campaign to get women to sign up. And I'd already had in my mind it was something I wanted to do, so when they opened it up, I went for it.

"What was it like working on the railroad?" I said.

It was hard. Because it wasn't just that the job itself was hard ... it's hard for anyone to learn it; you only get two weeks of training, and then you have to go out and do it — that was how you learned it, by doing it. And in order to do it, you have to get information from the people you work with. And there are just sort of initiation rites that go on. Basically, you need something from them; they don't need anything from you, and so they put you through this stuff — anybody, a man or a woman.

Being a woman, of course, it was additionally difficult because you had to deal with all their attitudes — and they were pretty boring attitudes. So learning the craft is in itself difficult, and oftentimes you're really tired; it might be two or three o'clock in the morning and you're working ... and when you're tired, as you know, things are a lot more difficult emotionally — and if somebody then starts harassing you at two or three in the morning it's a little harder to take than at nine or ten in the morning in some office. So that was the hard part, the additional harassment put on top of learning the job. Things like, in the middle of the night you'd be on some switch engine, in someplace like Texas, where you didn't know anybody, you're away from home, and you're isolated, and people just start in on you. You're just trying to stay awake, and not get run over by a boxcar. And all you need is to get the benefit of somebody's points of view of what you should be doing with your life who doesn't even know you. Like it's even their business, right? And they feel that you would just like to hear their opinions.

"You're takin' this job away from a man," they'd say.

"Well, what man?" I'd say.

"You should be married, home with kids," they'd say.

"Are you proposing?" I'd say.

There are these generic statements they would make that had absolutely no relation to your particular individual life. I'd try to make jokes about it, depending upon how tired I was.

Also, there's a generic problem which hasn't been fixed, and probably won't be fixed, which is simply because men have always done this job and they're really physically different from women — all the equipment is designed for them. So you take a difficult job to start with, and there you are as a woman, and your body is really different, and your size is different, and all the equipment is over-sized, and all the body mechanics used to operate this equipment is designed for men's anatomy — which is different from women's — and so that in itself is pretty difficult to get around. Just the height of the ladders, for example — getting on and off the cars, a woman has a really big step up, and when the cars are moving, they're sometimes moving ten m.p.h. when you're getting on and off.

The switches, throwing the switches, they're sort of levers, and the distance from your shoulders to your waist is really different for men, and men have a lot of strength in their shoulders, and woman have their strength in their hips ... and so when you're using your upper body to throw over a lever, how you do it, where your weight is, is really important — exerting force, with your weight on a lever. For a woman, your weight is in your hips, so you're gonna have to throw that switch differently. And the company had not studied this, and issued these orders on how you're supposed to do everything, based on how a man is supposed to do everything. And you can be fired for throwing a switch the way that it makes sense for you to throw it.

There are all these things that are built into a job where there's no provision. In the beginning we couldn't find gloves to fit; we couldn't find boots to fit; we couldn't find work clothes, it was pretty amazing.

"What was it like to be surrounded by all these groups of guys?" I said.

It was interesting for me. It was so different, it was such a different experience that it interested me — I felt like an anthropologist. I kind of liked that. That's sort of the part of the job that I liked the most; it's something most women don't get to experience much — the kind of a work environment where there's not a lot of politics ... there's just not a lot of personality attached; in a job like this, people want to organize most effectively to do the work. And so, they don't talk about politics, and they don't bring up things that are going to cause friction. So it was kind of a teamwork environment that actually was really interesting. And it felt liberating. I like to work on my own, and be left alone, and just to do things. I can't think of anything worse than to be in a work environment where people are making demands on my personality — that belongs to me alone, and if I want to share it, fine — if I don't, fine. But an environment where I would have to be nice to people that I hated, I don't think I could do that job. The railroad work environment with all these guys, it actually suits me. You're not expected to act like you like everyone; you're just expected to do your part of this job.

It turns out that I really do fit into that.

"You were saying that you feel like an anthropologist. Can you give me some anthropological observations?" I said.

Things like noticing that men don't talk about their personal lives much; and if they do, it's pretty formula-like — there are these formulas that's it's okay to use to talk about it. Like, you imply that you're getting one over on your wife or your girlfriend — forms of bragging, boasting, stuff like that ... never really sharing anything that's disturbing you personally.

It's interesting. Also the idea of the common denominator, that that's so important, even poetically — there had to be some common denominator of feelings about things that if people disagreed with that, they just wouldn't talk about it.

"Did any of the guys ever express their personal feelings?" I said.

No. See, being a woman, I would get men's confidential stories, if they got along with me, then they would sort of open up; but you could tell that they would never do this with each other.

It does go along with working in these groups, where things have to run smoothly, and the things that make things not run smoothly, are people getting into personal differences with each other.

"What are some of the nice things that come to your mind first, some of the most beautiful things, or some of the nicest things you recall?" I said.

I think what I like the most is the outdoor nature of the work. I really enjoy that. I enjoy physical work and this particular kind of work, where you're riding around on boxcars and switch engines, it's just sort of fun. It can be really fun work. And it's fun when the crew you're working with all works together well. It's like a team sport. It can be like a sport — I enjoy that a lot. I would be getting that experience somewhere else in my life if I didn't get it on the railroad. I like being outside a lot of the time; I would not like being inside all of the time.

"What are some of the worst things, or the ugliest things, or most unpleasant things? I said.

I guess some of the worst things are how tired you can get, and how physically uncomfortable you can get, and you really can't do much about it. Like having to stay up all night and work, and sometimes, being stuck out there for sixteen, seventeen, eighteen hours before you actually get back to a bed to where you can go to sleep; and being called back before you're fully rested. You can feel so bad physically, and that really affects your mental condition. Let's say you haven't had much sleep in the last three days, and I was in a place like Carrizozo, which is a turn-around place in Texas, actually, in New Mexico, but it's a turn-around for El Paso; and you get maybe three or four hours sleep, and you get called to go back to work, and it's something like eleven at night ... you're up all night on this train trying to get from point 'A' to point 'B', and various things can happen — you can have air trouble; and you can be really exhausted. And then you get almost into town; the sun comes out; it's 100 degrees suddenly; you've been up all night; and instead of expediting your train and letting it come in the yard and letting you go home; for reasons unknown — usually to save money — the company will then just park you on a siding until you run out of time on the hours-of-service. So you're sitting there baking in the sun in a siding; you're hot; you're hungry; you don't have anything to eat; you can't get a cup of coffee; you've been up all night; and you just've got to sit there until you die on the hours of service — which may be a couple of hours ... ... and then, you've got sit there until the company decides to sent a carry-all to pick you up — which they may or may not do for hours more. So you can end up feeling pretty physically terrible.

"In your book, some of your descriptions, like you were in a Texas oil field, with the black clouds coming up. That impressed me," I said.

Oh, those visual things. Well you're out in an environment that not everybody gets to see. It's sort of like the back door on the way the world works — the industrial landscape. Most highways, all you see is the front of companies; you don't get to go around the back. On the railroad, you go around the back in every walk of life. So it's really interesting.

For example, industrial colors — huge containers of things in junk yards, what colors things are painted; it's like a Cristo painting in a way, if you look at it that way. Like a gondola car filled with different-colored wires, huge spools and rolls of wires, orange, blue, pink — maybe ten feet tall, that's going to have some industrial application and needs to be transported; or parts that look like they've got some kind of high-tech, nuclear application — and they're huge ... just the over-sized nature of a lot of this stuff, is visually very exciting. In copper mines, there's huge slabs of shiny copper, they must weight tons each, and the gondola will be full of them, things like that. Or the colors of minerals. These things are beautiful, and they're unusual — if you saw a painting of them, you'd think it was really unusual. It's that kind of things that you get to see, that are really great.

"Can you describe that place in Texas with the smoke comin' up? Can I talk about that in terms of one of the worst places you ever worked?" I said.

Yeah, I suppose it was. There's this whole area around Houston, that's entirely petrochemical plants. I don't know if anyone who hasn't seen a landscape that's dominated by that can even imagine what it's like. First of all, the air itself is really hot and humid; the smell of those places dominates the whole situation — I mean, everything stinks like gas ... everything smells really bad; it smells like you might blow up any minute. And they're so lit up, that it's like being in a room with electric lights on at night — the whole landscape is lit up by lights. And they're firing off huge vats of steam, and burning off gas, so there's huge flares going up all the time. Everything is marked 'DANGEROUS', right? All these products, like they're going to kill you, and you're transporting them, right? So there are all these safety precautions involved with these plants, like showers all over the place, and people with gas masks following you around in case something gets loose. All the cars that you handle are full of dangerous material — often there's leaks; you can smell the stuff leaking out of the cars when you're walking the tracks — your eyes will start flushing. People get gassed all the time. So it's not like it isn't going to happen. When you handle these cars, you have to couple cars by impact, and you try to be as gentle as possible, but they won't couple up unless there's impact. So if the hatches aren't secured, on a lot of these cars, this dangerous stuff gets slooshed out.

These places the petrochemical crews are just like us; they're working around the clock; they're under pressure. So you've got people doing shift work and they're doing two shifts in twenty-four hours, and how careful are they gonna be? People want to make a lot of money, so they're working when they're tired, and they're working with dangerous stuff, and so they're going to make mistakes.

We're climbing on those cars; and we have to ride 'em; and to get on a car that's filled with sulfuric acid, hold on to the sides, ride it, couple it up ... ... it's like, 'hands-on'. So we're going to where they're being loaded, right into the plant, uncouple and couple and tie the brakes ... you're walking in this stuff. You're walking in and around a lot scary-looking stuff. If you've never seen it before, which I hadn't, and my railroad skills weren't very good at that point in my career — just regular old cars were kind of scary enough; and here were all these really dangerous cars. So that made it hard.

The tracks that this stuff was being moved over were in horrible condition. Houston is swampy anyway, and the ties would all disintegrate; and they really need to put in an entirely new track and ties — which they are in the process of doing. The track was so bad, that we would go on the ground every single day ... ... the tracks would just spread. You'd be coming along, and the tracks would just spread out in front of the train, and the train would go on the ground. Nobody said anything about it, because it was so common; it happened almost every day. When you go on the ground like that, the cars can tip over; that didn't happen, when I was working there ... ... as a matter of fact, it did — we tore up an entire track that they'd just put in; I guess they just didn't have it anchored down well enough. So we pulled in with our train, and we looked back. And there was a lot of dust, and we'd tore the whole track up, and the cars were all over the ground on the track.

"If they just put the track in, how can that happen?" I said.

I don't know. That was Englewood Yard.

The place with all the petrochemicals was Strang Yard. Both are in Texas.

"What about other places that were as awful as that?" I said.

That was about the most. That track really had to be fixed.

"How about things that were scary? Was anything scary?"

I think when you don't know a yard, when you don't know a place, that it's sort of scary 'till you get the picture on where everything is. And that happened to me so much — not knowing the layout, 'cause I had to move around so much, that, y'know, for the first week or two, you're pretty much scared most of the time you're working because you don't know what to expect in that yard, and yard's are dangerous places and you really have to know them well to work safely in them. For example, in El Paso, in that yard, there are two different railroads working in the yard, and the switchmen didn't really get along with each other. They would not cooperate with you; so they would leave switches wrongly lined for your movements; and if they made a movement, they wouldn't line them back for you — and so you could run through switches easily, and you could really get into trouble like that — you really had to check and double-check your line-ups all the time because of this weird situation of sharing the yard.

The railroads had different labor agreements, they had rivalries over who would get what traffic and who would get what jobs — which yardmaster belonged to which railroad at the time of the shift was controlling the yard — so it varied — there was rivalry. This was El Paso Yard.

"Does a funny incident stick in your mind, or something that amused you?" I said.

Well just the other day I was working around Salinas, and we switch out a sugar company out there, Spreckles. We were switching out some of their tank cars, and we made a joint. And this brakeman out there working the fields just got completely covered with sugar. That happened to me too, in Texas.

We've had water fights.

There's a fire extinguisher on the caboose, so we'd be passing another train on the siding, and we'd nail them with the water. You wanted to get the conductor, mainly. It would always be some old codger, with his feet up, and the caboose window open, and when we'd go by, we'd let him have it. Then later on, they'd retaliate on you. We'd be gone, but they'd have an opportunity to retaliate another day when they passed.

"What about sad events?" I said.

Luckily nobody I knew really got hurt; but things like that are sad — people do get hurt out there. No one I knew got killed, but various friends of mine had serious things happen to them. One of the women I know had to have a disc fused in her back because of throwing a defective switch; another one of my friends had her teeth knocked out 'cause of a defective brake; another one of my friends got chronic back problems from the railroad, and she got a settlement, and she's not working anymore. You know, things like that, things that are going to be permanent for people, are sad.

And other things are sad, that you'd see in any job — people who's lives are just not working. There's a lot of that because of the hardness of the lifestyle ... the fact that you really can't plan anything is really hard on marriages, it's hard on relationships — people being away a lot, and not being able to make commitments, and that kind of thing. There's a lot of divorce, with marriage problems.

"What's a regular day on the job like?' I said.

I just got back from a week on the Guadeloupe Local. That's way down in San Luis. Our board protects that board from up here. Instead of driving my car, I decided to take advantage of my contract, and I took AMTRAK down to San Luis, and then they had to get a cab for me in San Luis, and take me to the motel in Santa Maria. Then every morning a cab came and picked me up at the motel and took me to work. I went to work about 11:30. It was a local switcher out in Lompoc, and its main job is to switch out a Manville plant down there. Goes to work at 11:30, and what you do basically is go out on the main line and get over to Surf — Surf is the name of a siding — where an east-bound train has left cars for you, and do as much switching as you can do on the main line, as much as the dispatcher will let you do. Which can be fifteen minutes or it can be an hour or whatever. You sort of have to plan your work around how much main-line time you get. It's a regular crew, they work twelve hours a day, six days a week

Basically we get on the engine at Guadeloupe, a light engine, as head brakeman I line us out. We go along, we get to Surf, it takes forty minutes, an hour, something like that. We come on down the main line, let the conductor off, so he can line us to the crossovers to go into the yard on the opposite side of the track. Then we back up and the field man gets off and walks down the line of cars we're gonna pick up and makes sure they're laced together and makes the cut on whatever car we're gonna come out with — I'm the head brakeman, so I'll line us into the siding, and I'll work with the field man switching out our train on the siding, which we do. Let's say we take a couple cars with us and then we shove those cars — the field man will get on the rear car, I'll get on the engine, and we'll shove the cars through the crossovers, then I'll get off and line us behind so that mainline trains can now use the main track and then we release our block time on the main line. So now we're in this little yard and we're getting our cars together to go out to do our switching up the hill and in the little town of Lompoc.

So we'll switch out cars for maybe an hour, something like that, get them all switched out, get them lined up right, according to where they're gonna go. Then we'll get back on the engine and the conductor will give everybody cookies.

Okay, then we go into Lompoc and depending if we have any cars to pick up in town or not, we'll either get an hour lunch break or a three-hour lunch break — because we can't go up and switch out this other plant until 5 o'clock — it's just the way they work it. So in the meantime, if we have work to do, we'll do it. Otherwise, we go to this little shack called 'The Dog House', and sit around for two or three hours ... or I'll go shopping or something.

Then at 5 o'clock we'll get back on our engine, take whatever cars the plant wants, we'll go up the top of this hill where there's this plant. Then it gets a little bit tricky, because every track on the plant, they're going to want us to rearrange those cars; they want some of them where they are; they want some of them looped around; and the plant's on a really steep grade. We've got to haul everything down to a little switching yard to rearrange all these tracks. If you have old heads on the crew, you can do it in about two hours; if you have a crew that doesn't know what they're doing, it could take you all night long. With the regular crew, it usually takes us a couple hours; and that's where you're really throwing a lot of switches; you've got to watch out for running over these people who are zipping around the plant in their pick-up trucks — running right in front of your engine. Then after we're done with that, it's usually about eight-thirty or nine o'clock; we take all our cars and we go back down to 'The Dog House' ... ... and we sit there for another hour, and have a coffee break.

Then we start heading back to Surf, and we leave cars on the siding on the opposite direction for the next east-bound to pick up. See, they leave us cars there, and they also pick up cars. Then after we finish doing that, usually light-engine, go back to Guadeloupe; and we'll get in about eleven-thirty at night. And that's what they do every day.

It's really pretty. It's rural. There's the ocean. There's fields. It's a pleasant, long job. And this is what most locals are like. There's not very much pressure, but you're out there about twelve hours. When I got back, they had a cab ready for me, so as soon as I got off the switch engine, there's a cab sittin' there, and I hop in the cab and they take me to my motel; and then we do the same thing the next day.

Most people drive down, but I don't have to drive when I'm augmented someplace away from home, so I usually don't.

"What's workin' a humpyard like?' I said.

A humpyard is a hill; that's why they call it a hump. And what they use it for is classifying cars. So that means you take a train that comes in someplace and you break in up into cars that are going various other places — that's called classifying them. You may have blocks of one, two, three, four or five cars that are going certain places. So what happens is, you take a switch engine, and all those cars are down at the bottom of this hill in a bowl on all these sort of fan-like tracks. You grab a hold of one of those tracks and you pull it up the top of the hill, and you may have a couple hundred cars in your cut. The switch engine starts shoving towards the crest of the hill, and the pin-puller's job is to walk along and pull pins, and pull the cut levers on whatever number of cars you're going to let go sailing down the hill. While this is going on, somebody sits up in the tower, and throws the right switches for those cars to go into the right tracks — they're remote, power switches. That's somebody's job, to sit in the tower and throw those switches. The conductor's job is to sit in this little shack with a list, and figure out how many cars are going to go next, and communicate that to the pin-puller. And that's sort of the way it goes. It's pretty tedious. It's really hard. And all you're doing is pulling these pins and walking alongside of cars for hours. You pull the pins at the crest of the hill — there's a rhythm to it.

There are lots of humpyards that I've worked at. There's a humpyard at west Colton, there's one in L.A. — there was one — there's one in Roseville, there's one in Englewood yard in Texas and Houston.

"Did you have to move around a lot, and what were those places like?" I said.

Well you don't have to move around a lot — you're not forced to move anywhere. You move around a lot if you decide you don't want to be cut off, or you want to keep working — usually for financial reasons. But it's all your own initiative. There's no guarantee when you get cut off, you call up somewhere else and you find out your seniority will allow you to work there, there's no guarantee that by the time you get there you'll have a job.

That's happened to me more than I can imagine.

Booming is entirely up to you. If you want to move, you move, and you take your chances that there will be work when you get there.

"Where are some of the places you went to?" I said.

Well I've been lots of places on the whole Southern Pacific system, from El Paso, Texas to Klamath Falls, Oregon. I've been to Houston, Texas; Tucson, Arizona; Ogden, Utah; West Coleman , Los Angeles, San Francisco Bay Area, Dunsmuir, California; Roseville, California; I've been a lot of places.

"Would you make references to your book, 'Boomer', when you talk about some of the places you've worked? I said.

What I wrote about mostly in my book 'Boomer' were the stories of all the different places I had to go to, to work as a brakeman, because I hired out when a recession just hit ... ... and there were just way too many of us; and then, after getting trained and putting all this energy into figuring out how to do this job, then they just cut us off. So we sort of dispersed all over the country — if we wanted to keep working. You had the choice — you weren't forced to go anywhere. And there was no promise of when it would start up again where we lived. So it was sort of a shock to learn that, 'Yes, you could probably work' — but maybe you were going to have to chase it all over the country. Interestingly enough, a lot of the men didn't pursue it, 'cause they could get just as good jobs where they lived. But just about all of the women did pursue it, because this was a pretty big opportunity for us. The railroad often says that women don't want to do this kind of job; and I think the fact that all of us went all over the country, at a tremendous personal inconvenience, kinda disproves this — it's just bull — it's like when you call up and ask about a job, and they just tell you, 'Well, women just don't like doing this job,' and they really have no idea of whether women do or not.

I hired out in Watsonville, California in 1979; then I went down to L.A. and worked for a few months; then I went to Houston, Texas and worked for a few months; then I came back to Watsonville and worked; and I was cut off in Watsonville in the winter, and when spring came along I went over to Tucson, Arizona; and then I went back to L.A. and worked and then I came back to Watsonville and worked; and in the following year I went to Ogden, Utah; then I went down to Tucumari, New Mexico; then I worked in El Paso, Texas — during the time I worked in El Paso I worked on work trains all around that area, and in New Mexico too. And then I came back and worked in L.A. and Watsonville; and then I went up and worked in Dunsmuir near the Oregon border, we went into Klamath Falls. Then I went over to AMTRAK and did two years on AMTRAK, going wherever they go out of Oakland. And then I came back and worked on the commute line in the San Francisco Bay Area peninsula. And now

I'm working locals out of Watsonville — which is where I hired out ... and I finally have the seniority to work where I hired out after twelve years.

I have been over I would say, three-fourths of the track that Southern Pacific runs on, and into most of the major yards, and worked in most of those big yards. So I've probably seen more track than most road foremen or anybody else. I've been all through the system, except for into Oregon mostly — but I've been everywhere else.

In my book what I did a lot of was write about those places that I ended up working in. It was in a certain sense, an 'On-The-Road' book, and a travel-log about those places, and about what it was like being a brakeman booming in those places. So it's kind of a wild west book about the railroad and traveling.

"It's also a transformational book ... ... we've already talked a little bit about one of the chapters in your book, about the oil refinery job in Texas, with the plumes of smoke and flames rising up; would you highlight some of your other chapters a bit? Since your book was a wild West adventure, would you care to hint at a few of those places?" I said.

The thing about most of the places I went to is that when I went there, the reason I could go there in the first place was because there was a lot going on; there was a lot of work. That's why you're called a 'boomer', you turn up when there's a boom somewhere, 'cause that's when they need extra help. The situations I talk about are situations of pretty much extreme work conditions, where they literally don't want to give you any time to get any rest at all — they want to work as much as possible ... ... seven days a week.

Texas was pretty wild in those terms.

But also I was working in places like Tucson, Arizona, in the middle of the summer, where it's 110 degrees — and you're working twelve hours a day seven days a week; so it's a pretty extreme life style.

One of the places I ended up working was Ogden, Utah.

The reason they needed us there at the time was because they were trying to fix this causeway that the tracks run on that go all across the Salt Lake. And there were big-time floods. And so they were just desperate to keep this track open. They had work trains seven days a week, twelve hours a day, trying to dump rock in and fill this track in faster than the lake could eat it up. So that's what we were doing, seven days a week.

We were out in the middle of the Salt Lake on a work train dumping ballast into the lake, and there all these salt flies and a zillion spiders sharing this little piece of track with us; and it was really hot. It gets really hot out there in the summer. And we were losing the battle — the S.P. finally ended up making a breech so that the water on both sides of the track could equalize itself ... 'cause they just weren't keeping up with the lake. And then they finally created a new lake, draining some of the water off. But at the time I was working there they were losing.

I think AMTRAK at one point came over those tracks, and the waves were breaking against the engine. There was probably fifty feet deep of mud on either side of the tracks, and if an engine or some cars went into that, they'd never get the people out. The size of these waves were probably three or four foot waves, depending which way the wind was coming from and if there was a storm; that's what they were worried about Since the waves had to get up to the engine, and the track was five feet above the water, and the water would hit the engine, so they were pretty good-sized waves.

The salt water was pretty intense, it's very concentrated stuff. You can't go swimming in there. If you get it on you, it just cakes on you. We were sprayed with it all the time.

"When I was reading the book, it gets better and better. When you won the 1990 Bay Area Book Reviewers' Award, how did they describe the transformational aspects of the book?" I said.

A lot of people have talked about the book in terms of a spiritual journey; that's a term often used. The term spiritual journey is used to describe a journey in which something happens that makes a difference in your consciousness, a turning point in your consciousness; and then things are in some way different after that. That's what the term is about for me. That happened to me when I was right in the middle of this railroad adventure, and this spiritual journey changed what the railroad adventure was all about for me, what it was like, and how I could handle it.

"When I read the book, I identified really strongly with what you were writing about. The book was very meaningful and liberating for me. And I feel readers who enjoyed reading about the human side of the railroad in Old Rails' Tales, will certainly be caught up in and enjoy 'Boomer'... ... ... Can you tell me some more about what it's like for a woman working on the railroad in terms of it being a traditionally male vocation?" I said.

Certain aspects of the social situation I found on the railroad made me very uncomfortable, and made a lot of other women uncomfortable. It was just a fact that we all had to deal with that traditionally we, as women, weren't included in this workplace in any way. And there wasn't a lot of room made for us when we did show up. And there still isn't, really. It just wasn't built into the system that women got to do this kind of work. The work itself is hard, and the additional difficulties that didn't have to be there but were there because as women we weren't welcome, was just on top of it.

"As a woman, do you have to — in a way — every time you go to places as a worker, have to start all over in terms of dealing with men's attitudes about disliking women working on the railroad?" I asked.

Oh yeah, that's definitely true. It really takes time, anyplace, to get accepted — every single person there has to establish a relationship of trust with you and that takes a long time, because their initial response is distrust. So you start out on the negative with just about everybody, and then you have somehow got to get on the positive, and this is a long process.
Now that I have seniority and can work locally I'm not in the position where I have to go booming to all these places; if I did, it would be the same old story ... ... it wouldn't have changed at all. I know that.

"Any accidents or close calls?" I said.

I really haven't had any accidents or close calls since I was just learning the job; and that's probably pretty true for most people

— it's the first couple years of doing the job that it's really dangerous, because you just don't have the habits built in; you have to think about everything you're doing — and there's too much going on for you to be aware of every little thing at the same time. So you could have hair-raising experiences.

The two most common things that have happened to people that result in fatalities on the railroad are, falling off; and getting in the way of something. Because there's this whole jungle of tracks, they're pretty close together; and in a large yard, cars are being switched out on all these tracks by lots of different crews, so that other crews are working down there, besides your crew — and you don't know where they're going next, or what their game plan is, or what tracks they're working .... you may be working this one track, going and coupling up the cars, and hooking up your hoses and working on cars on that track, right next you, literally right next to you, suddenly that track might start moving.

Or they might kick a car into that track and the whole track will just bang together, and the slack will run in and if you're in the way, if you're not in the clear when a car comes rolling down on that track ... ... let's say you step into another track to look at your track, a car could come rolling down that track and hit you — and you don't hear it; and it's night, so you don't see it. And flatcars, particularly, you can't see their outlines. So they could be shoving a bunch of flatcars into a track, and it's nighttime, and you would not be aware of them shoving that car on top of you. So that's happened to a number of people, and it's almost happened to me ... but that's a real easy way to get killed.

After a while, you have these habits, even in a totally clear yard where there's nothing going on, a good brakeman will never be standing foul of any track, never.

You don't leave your lantern on the ground when you go between the cars, just little things like this could get you killed. Because if they saw the lantern they'd figure the brakeman was in the clear, and they'd give a 'BACK-UP' sign. Things like that, which if you're trying to figure out how to fix the cars up, you're not so worried about where your lantern is, right? In the beginning, you're trying to figure out how to get on and off, how to hook the cars up, how to hold your lantern while you're hanging on to the cars — it's all these little things. So you're not thinking of every thing at once.

I've turned my back on cars. I talk about this in 'Boomer' — adjusting the couplers; one time we came at the engine, we went against this car, and the two couplers didn't hook together. So I backed the engine up, and then I turned my back on the car, and start adjusting the couplers on the engine. Well, when we hit that car we started it rolling, and it rolled away from the engine; then it started to roll back to the engine — 'cause it was on a little grade. I could've been dead! Those two couplers could have met, and I'd be in the middle. But it didn't occur to me that there wasn't a brake on that car — I just assumed there was — but in fact, there wasn't. You really can't assume stuff like that — there are just little routine things that you do that as you get more experienced — until you get scared about paying attention, you really don't pay attention. And the only way you get scared is having close calls.

"What is most important about working on the railroad?" I said.

It's a job that I enjoy and that I'm pretty good at, and it satisfies me in certain ways. I've been able to work with it. It's not ideal, but it's been secure. I appreciate the flexibility and the security. Although the work hasn't always been there — it hasn't been a matter of losing the job; and I like the seniority system. I think it's a fair system. I think it's particularly good for women and for minorities once they're in. 'Cause once they get into a seniority system, then there's no politics about jobs.

It makes it harder at the beginning, because we're systematically excluded from getting in, but once we're in, and once we start to get some seniority there's no question about who gets a particular job — the person with the most seniority gets it and that's it.

Different racial minorities had trouble getting into the railroad; like women, they only have a certain amount of seniority and not more, because there was a certain time-frame when they were let in. I'm talking about Black people and Latino people primarily — they had been excluded just like women. It was a white man's job, period. It's hard for minorities, because there's all kinds of racism in the language and in the workplace, and it doesn't go away — it's just there ... and minorities just have to put up with it, or have to find some way to deal with it.

"Would you recommend for other women to work on the railroad?" I said.

Well yes! I know there are a lot of women who would like to do this job who could do this job and would find it financially very satisfying to do it, and in other ways. I know that the railroad is not in a big hurry to hire more women, because they're not under Federal pressure to do that these days. I would love to see more women in these jobs. There are certain women who really find this a pretty satisfying lifestyle. And those women should have the chance to do it. It really isn't for everybody, but for certain people, men and women, they just are really suited to do this kind of stuff, and live this kind of a life.

(Linda Nieman's award-winning book, 'Boomer', published by University of California Press, Berkeley 94720. Ms. Nieman is currently working locals as a brakeman out of Santa Cruz, California.)

fig. 54 – Pullman porter

Glossary of Rail & Railroad Slang & Terms

The lingo varies from locale to locale, and district to district, and line to line, and from one part of the country to another. However, these terms are basically the same everywhere, and specifically identified within the definition.

ballast — noun: an aggregate of gravel put beneath the ties to make a more secure foundation. Ballast is layed down after the ties are put down, and after the track is layed and fastened on the ties. The ties are lifted with crowbars, and the ballast is put underneath the ties, and in between them. Verb: to ballast, is to lay ballast.

ballin' the jack — is goin' fast.

beans — what you say when you go to breakfast, lunch or dinner, 'you go to beans'.

big hole — throwing the air-brake valve in an emergency, causing an immediate full application of the brakes

boomer — a railroad worker who goes from railroad job to railroad job, and consequently from place to place. Dates back to when railroads were built about boom towns. (Opposite of home guard.)

brakey — a brakeman's a shack. A brakeman is on a freight train, and he's with the conductor and the engineer. But a switchman stays right in the yard. A switchman, he works in the yard all the time. He may go a hundred miles, but he never leaves town. On a freight train, you have the head brakeman and the rear brakeman. Usually, it goes by seniority; the head brakeman has the least seniority, and the rear brakeman has the most. A lot of times, somebody'd say, "Well, I'm the head brakeman." And people'd say 'Ohhh!' — and people'd think he was the one in charge, but he wasn't; he just worked the head end, was all.

branch — a subsidiary line off a main line.

brains — conductor.

bullswitch — the lead switch into the yard. Usually the first switch off the lead that leads into a storage track.

bump — to get bumped; to lose one's job or position because a man with higher seniority bumped you off.

bumper — retaining post at the end of a spur track.

cabbage locals — what the lines are called down in Fresno, 'cause of the cabbage cutters.

caboose rocket — According to an S.P. safety poster, a caboose rocket is a rail who does not hold on while in the caboose.

crossover — A connecting set of tracks that bridges one set of tracks to another set.

captain — the conductor is sometimes called captain; as he was back in the early days of railroading when captain was the name of the job, not conductor.

car dogs, or car knockers — brakeman.

clearance points — clearance points are a point that cars or a locomotive on the other side of a clearance point will not come into contact with cars on an adjacent track. The clearance points are where two trains can't hit each other on adjacent tracks, where one track comes out of another or goes into another. What they do, is paint the tie orange that is the clearance point, so you can see when you're safe. Otherwise, you have to stand on the edge of the tie, and if you can raise out your arm length, and you can touch another car or engine, it won't clear. S.P. passenger trains on the mainline are twelve feet apart. It seems close. When you're standin' there, they make such a noise when they go by one another. Twelve feet, from rail to rail.

conductor — he's in charge of the train, passenger or freight. On a freight he has to ensure that if there's any work to be done, that all cars are going to the right places, and he's in charge of all the way bills, and all official documents, and he fills out the time slips.

corner — when you run into a car that is not clear and is sticking out from a siding.

crossover — two parallel tracks. You have two tracks paralleling, and you have tracks that go from one, and connect into the other one — the connecting track is the crossover.

crummy — caboose.

cut away from 'em — to uncouple cars from one another.

cut of cars — bunch of cars.

cut off — cut the engine off

deadhead — when an employee rides free to get back and forth to work, or when riding on a company pass; also, when an empty car is being taken back to its yard.

decorating — see 'riding high'

deep hole — see 'big hole'.

district — the length of track that is ordinarily the territory for a crew change. A division might have three or four districts in it, 'cause a division might be four hundred or five hundred miles, and it's broken up into districts.

drawbar — a piece of metal that holds the knuckle underneath the car. They have spring-cushion controls in there, and shock absorbers. It kind of pivots, so it can be moved, so if the cars aren't perfectly aligned, you can still make a joint. And it also means that there will be movement when the train goes around a curve. The drawbar is the device that holds the knuckle and it has lateral movement so that when the train goes around curves, it won't hop off the rail.

drop — when the engine's pulling a car, and let it go, there's an interval, when the draw bars are stretched out when you're pulling, and the engine has to hesitate, so the man can pull the pin, to release the knuckle, then the engine has to pull away, and he has to get out of the way; and between the time the engine gets over the switch, and before the car, or cars, arrive at the switch, a man has to line the switch, so the cars will go down a different track from the engine. It takes a little bit of coordination. It's usually the last car, or last string of cars, that gets dropped.

dropper — man who rides a car in a gravity yard.

field man — is another nickname for switchman.

fireman — not a current job. But what he used to do, on steam engines, in the East, he'd shovel coal into the firebox. In California and the western states, most of the engines burned oil, instead of coal; it was much cleaner. And he had to tend the firing valve, he had to keep the fire in the fire block. He had a big job. But when the diesels came along, all he had to do was sit there and he had a little lever, and he rang the bell, this little air bell, that went 'Ding Ding Ding Ding.' He'd turn it on at crossings, or approaching depots, and turn it off afterwards. And he was a lookout. They still have firemen on passenger trains. It's a federal law. There always has to be two men in the cab of an engine, at all times. So that's all the job he has now.

flying switch — that's where you give a car a kick, and it goes by itself — the engine gives it a push, so you don't have to shove it into each track, you just kick it in; a switching move when cars are cut off behind a moving engine and the switch is thrown after the engine has passed, so the car goes onto a siding or another track.

foreman — equivalent to a conductor.

goat — a yard switch-engine.

go high — get on top of a freight car to set brakes or signal.

going into deep hole — see 'deep hole'.

going into the hole — from a single track to go into a siding to clear a train coming the other way.

going on the ground — when the train goes off the track. It can be upright. Most of the derailments are in the yard, because for one thing, there's a lot more action. There's a chance for wood or debris to get on the rails because the rails are not as high as they are on the main line — they don't need heavy rail in the yard, it's only 110 lb. rail in the train yard, and 150 lb. on the main line. That's 110 lbs. per yard of rail in the train yard, and 150 lbs per yard on the main line.

gravity yard — when cars are pushed up a hill then cut loose to go by gravity down the hill onto a choice of sidings.

hand signals — you could almost carry a conversation on from 200 feet away with different hand and arm and signal light signals.

highball — One of the most common things one hears on the radio, is a highball. Highball means giddy up and go. That means, everything's okay. We say that a lot. And that dates back to the old days, when they actually had a staff, with a big ball on it, that they raised that up, so the train could see it, that was the highball.

highballing — to go fast.

highball 6 by the green flag — When you have speed restrictions, repairing track, or something was wrong with it, and you're by that restriction, you see, you have a little green flag out there, and you'll say, highball 6 by the green flag.

hog — a particular series of old steam engine.

hoghead — Hoghead for engineer. They call them hogs, or hogheads. The reason they call engineers hogheads, dates back to the steam days. It was a nickname that firemen gave to engineers, because an engineer could literally work a fireman to death, by the way he manipulated the steam. If the engineer wanted to use a lot of steam and keep the poor fireman shoveling to keep the steam level up, he could do that. And once you did that, they called them hogheads. He would hog the steam. Apparently you could get the train to do the same thing, without using all the steam, it'd be a little bit slower. That dates back. The fireman was the guy who stoked the engine.

homeguard — opposite of boomer; an employee who stays a long time at one railroad job in one location.

hoopla, hoop — old-fashioned method of handing up written orders to an engineer on the locomotive, by fastening the written orders in a wooden hoop on the end of a long stick.

hotbox — a journal bearing that's overheated and burning its packing.

humpyard — see 'gravity yard'.

in the ditch — derailed or wrecked cars.

janney — to couple.

joiner — a 'fish-plate' that holds the rails together.

kicking a car — to 'kick a car'; to drop off one or more cars.

knuckles — Knuckle is a hinge thing on the end of a drawbar, and they come together, and they open up, and there's a little pin on the inside, that's called an automatic coupling device. The knuckles hold the boxcars to each other, like two hands clasping. In the old days, they used to literally stand between the cars and drop the pin in by hand, to lock the joint together, so the cars wouldn't separate. The knuckles are on the cars themselves.

link and pin — old-fashioned coupling set up that usually cost a man a few fingers.

making the air, making the air hoses — Connect air brake hoses between cars.

making a joint — 'Making a joint' is when you couple two cars together.

Malley — same as Mallet. A cab-forward engine design.

meets and run-aheads — when two or more trains from opposite directions 'meet', one is obliged to pull onto a siding and wait for the other to clear ... the engineers are normally aware of all meets, because meets are described in the train orders they pick up from dispatchers, or receive on the radio. A 'run-ahead' is the train that is given the rightaway.

nose on — to couple on to the front end of an engine.

pin puller — nickname for a switchman, 'cause the switchman also pulls the pins.

pig, or piglengths, or piggybacks — a car that's ninety feet long, that has trailers on it.

Pocatello yardmaster — a guy who usually's hired out under a flag; that means, that's something's wrong with his record, and he claims he was a Pocatello yardmaster. Well, a long time ago, they had a fire in the yard in Pocatello, and all the record's were burnt up. And so anybody in the world can claim that they were a yardmaster in Pocatello. And there's no way of ever really tellin'.

pool job — a chain gang. Pooled freight is usually a through-freight, and it's called a 'chain gang' — 'cause you relay it, you go your district, then you turn the train over to another crew in another district.-

pops — retainers.

plug it — Make an emergency stop.

rails — What train people call one another.

reefer — refrigerator car.

riding high — 'going on top' or 'decorating' a car. Most enterprising people at night would tie their lanterns to a grab iron up on top of the car, and they'd get down in the boxcar.

rip rap — stone used to protect railroad beds from erosion by water.

road crew — the engineer, the conductor, and the brakemen. They're in charge of the train for their district.

rule G — railroad rule against drinking on the job.

run-aheads — see 'meets' and 'run-aheads'.

runaways — a train or car or locomotive out of control and racing down a hill or straightaway.

setting air — The engineer controlling the air pressure in the brake lines from the cab; also the brakeman setting retainers.

sign, or, giving a sign, or, hanging a sign on you — switchman's or brakeman's hand signals or light signals to the engineer.

slack — running in & running out — there's a little distance between each car, and when the train starts out, the engine pulls and it stretches out all that little distance till the last car starts to move; and then when the engine stops, the same thing happens in reverse — the slack shoves up against the engine.

spur — a side track, of no particular length. They're all different lengths.

spot, to — to put freight cars alongside their respective industry destination.

string — two or more cars couples together.

switch crew — as opposed to a road crew. Brakemen are on the road; switchmen stay in the yard — but they are essentially the same job. A switch crew stays in the yard. They go maybe a hundred miles a day, but they never leave the yard — an engineer, possibly a fireman, and two switchmen, and a foreman.

switch list — a list of what order to line cars up in.

switchman — he works in the yard all the time. He may go a hundred miles, but he never leaves town. (see brakeman)

tie cars together — to couple them together.

tie-down — to set hand brakes on a car, or on each car.

torpedo — a signaling device and it makes a loud noise, because it's gun powder placed in a little packet; and there's a little metal strip to hold it to the head of the rail. And a 'gun', as it's called, is placed approximately 150 feet apart. And when the train runs over them, they make a loud BANG that can be heard in the cab. And when you hear that, you're supposed to stop the train immediately. It's a warning device. Normally, there's two torpedoes placed as a stop signal. But if you just hear one, you're still supposed to stop. It signals danger up ahead. They still use them. They're in the rule book.

track gang — the employees at work keeping the track in maintenance.

trainmaster — he's an official. He's not on the train. He's in charge of the day-to-day operations in the yard.

turn 'em down, or, turning them down — to set handbrakes on individual cars.

wabash — to 'corner' a car.

wabashing — going fast.

washout — emergency stop signal signified by waving both arms in a downward circle in daylight, or swinging signal-lamp wide in a low semicircle across the track at night.

workin' under a flag — means you got not too good a record.

working limits — train orders that apply when they're working on a track. When you approach a yellow flag, you get two miles to reduce speed down to the indicated speed over that section of the track — which is included in the working limits. At the end of the working limits, you get a green flag, where you resume speed. But the entire train has to pass beyond the green flag. They're flags at day, and lights at night — or reflectorized disks.

wye — tracks in the shape of a letter "Y" that lead from a main track for the purpose of turning cars or engines around when there is no turntable.

yard — tracks for the storage of cars.

yard crew — engineer, conductor and brakemen who just stay in the yard.

yard goat — see 'goat'.

fig. 55 – Depot at Cisco, western summit, alt 5,900 ft

Figure Caption Narratives

(keyed to List of Illustrations, page xxi)

Cover illustration by Mike Kotowski. It was the Orchard Supply calendar pin-up for March '91. Mike has been illustrating the calendar for eighteen years. He is a train graphic artist, has an advertising company, and at the time was Mayor of the Silicon Valley city of Fremont, California. Illustration is of a 4-4-0 American-Type, built by Norris-Lancaster a year before the end of the Civil War. When it came around the Horn in 1865, it was named 'Mariposa' for the Western Pacific Railroad (not related to the later railroad of the same name). It was sold to the Central Pacific in 1870. In 1906 it was re-numbered the Southern Pacific 1488 and developed the reputation as being the fastest steamer in the west. It was sold to the S.T. & E. in 1909. By that time it was the oldest operating steam locomotive west of the Rockies. In 1953 the engine was retired from service and donated by the S.T. & E. to Travel Town at Griffith Park in Los Angeles. The Stockton Terminal & Eastern Railroad was privately owned and ran its first train on August 17, 1890, on its total run of thirteen miles from Stockton east to Linden. This was a railroad that owned one steam locomotive, one combination coach-baggage car, one boxcar, four flat cars and a Hall-Scott motor coach. Through bankruptcies, hard times, and equipment failures, the S.T.&E. somehow survived to this day with diesel locomotives and plenty of work to do in Stockton's east side industrial areas.

Unless noted figure caption narratives are by John Hogan.

(1) A would-be brakeman.　　　　　　　　　　　　　　　　　　ii
(2) Washing out impurities in boiler in roundhouse, West Oakland 1948.　v
(3) SD-9, early diesel locomotive online a year. I was a brakeman on this passenger train workin' at Northwestern Pacific Railroad, 1956, near Willits, Calif. Didn't wear uniforms – coveralls okay; conductor coveralls, or slacks and a hat that said 'conductor' on it. Engine front: side lights – marker lights; double light – regular headlight; top – oscillating Mars headlight. Marker lights display white if you're an extra train; green on first train if there's a second section following – so train on the

siding would know there's a train following and wait. Second train would run no marker lights, and that means that it's the last section. If the yardmaster has enough cars to call a train then he'll call an extra. They have scheduled freight trains that run on the timetable, but if he doesn't want to run it as a timetable train, then it's called an extra train. xi

(4) A steam engineer's throttle (top) steam guage, rectangular air brake gage, power-reverse that makes makes the engine go forward or backwards (hand-lever middle-right); steam & boiling water piping and valves for the gages xx

(5) This is a West-Side Lumber Company locomotive. This picture was taken in 1952. The engine is what was called a 'Climax Engine.' The cylinders are diagonally under the boiler, and they run a big steel shaft along the bottom of the engine, that has big gears on it, that actually turn these wheels. It's a high-powered engine, that goes very slow. He's basically a switch engine, who can move forty or fifty cars at once. It goes real slow, but it has a real rapid exhaust, and it sounds like a steam engine going 90 m.p.h. – but it's going real slow. That guy standing in the back there, I hope he's payin' attention, 'cause that was a very dangerous place to ride ... called the footboards. He could be up in the cab – but on the footboard, particularly a leading footboard; if they're going forward, it's not so dangerous. But if they're backin', that's a very dangerous place to stand. You always had to hang on, and he's got one hand in his pocket. You can tell 'cause there's exhaust, that they're moving. I remember taking that picture. I've got movies of it too. This is in Tuolomne, California. 4

(6) 1951. That was a wreck down near Mountain View, CA one time. The engine ran into a gravel truck. 10

(7) Sierra Railroad Overland Ltd.; open observation platform, quite the cat's meow, w/deckchairs & awning 17

(8) Switch engine in Berkeley, California, in 1957, at the University overpass. Switch crew riding on the back of engine; he's going out backwards to spot those six cars someplace. 23

(9) Roundhouse switch engine and roundhouse in west Oakland, 1947. When I took that picture I was in the Navy. I climbed up on the top of a tender to take the picture. This particular little engine was really a jewel. It was a switch engine, and they took the tender off of it, and instead of pulling the tender around,

they mounted some water and oil tanks around the boiler – so they didn't need a tender. That made it a short little engine, so it could get on the turntable with another engine – that was it's primary function, to move the big engines around. It was kind of a pet of the roundhouse crews. They kept all the gauges clean and kept it all washed off. It's got a silver front to reflect the light so it's most visible and easy to see. It was kind of a pet – then, all of a sudden, it was obsolete, and they junked it. 29
(10) Erecting hall in Sacramento; engines under repair; one of the biggest locomotive shops west of the Mississippi, 1946. 35
(11) Cleaning & washing-out the boiler; getting the scale out. west Oakland CA, 1943. 37
(12) Western Pacific 39
(13) This is a 'Back-Up' Mallet – a running model I made. 50
(14) This was a later series 4-6-2. The boiler was called a 'milk-bottle' boiler, because of the distinctive shape; also called 'wagon-top' boiler.' 50
(15) GS-4 on the turntable. On the garden tracks – to either side of the roundhouse –a diesel's on the far end of the left garden track. The roundhouse tracks are numbered from left to right. On #3 track is a 4-8-2. #4 track is a 2-8-2, Mikado. #7 is another GS-4. #8 is a Mallet; and the tender for it is in #9. And on the right garden track is a 4-6-2. 56
(16) This is part of my train board. I'll eventually have storage tracks where these cabooses and other cars are sitting – the prototype for those cabooses is one of those old Southern Pacific wooden cabooses. You can see the cupola sticking up out of the roofs of the cabooses. That's where you sit to watch over the train. They've got ladders going up inside of them to the cupolas. On the track is a model of a Pacific-Type 4-6-2. 58
(17) This was a wreck near Pasa Robles in 1942. One train ran into the back of another. You can see it just demolished that car. Luckily it was early in the morning and there was nobody occupying that part of the train – or they would have been severely mangled. As one old-timer pointed out to me, this short guy in the middle of the tracks was J.J. Jordan. He was a division superintendent. And he never fired anybody for Rule G – which was the rule against drinking on the job, 'cause he was the biggest violator himself. He was a two-fisted switchman once. He had a face like a bulldog. Anyway, a freight train was following too

close; he was supposed to be following at restricted speed – there was a yellow indication on the block signal; apparently he was not paying too much attention. Then all of a sudden, he ran into the back of a passenger train. What had happened was that a taxi cab got stuck on the track in front of the first train. In fact, he wasn't stuck, he just missed the crossing and ending up on the track, and his automobile fell onto the electric switches for the signals and completed an electric circuit on the signals, turning-on the signals that displayed the red indication for the engineer on the passenger train to stop; well the freight train that was following along behind it, he had a yellow block, so he shouldn't have been going so fast, and all of a sudden, he gets up

fig. 56 – Observation lounge car on the *California Zephyr*; Oakland CA, 1968

to the red block, and BAM!, he ran into the back of the passenger train. With really disastrous results.   64

(18) This is one of the greatest pictures. My friend took it. In 1968. We were going to Connecticut, and we took the California Zephyr, which was nicknamed The Silver Lady. There's a book out called *The Silver Lady,* devoted entirely to this train. It was probably one of the greatest trains in the world. It was just absolutely fantastic. The cars ... there was a big to-do about it when it was inaugurated in 1948, about how it had the latest of everything ... it had telephones in the lounge car, you could call anyplace. It was very successful. The train was always full because the service was always good. And the train went through some of the most beautiful areas in the world – but it failed. For a lot of reasons. Inflation probably; age; other forms of transportation. Evens the unions had a shot at it. It was the changing picture of America's lifestyle; I think people would rather take their cars, or fly ... and the train just seemed to come in third place. And it was such a shame, because it was such a beautiful train. They had a lounge car fixed up like the interior of a cable car, and scenes of old-time San Francisco in it. Luckily I rode on the train three times; this was the last time. It was such a great train. It left early in the morning, got to Stockton about 10 o'clock a.m., 10:30 maybe. Then in Sacramento an hour later. Then I went up through Oroville, Marysville, through the Feather River Canyon – boy, that was spectacular. And then the train dropped down into a desert of Nevada; then through Colorado – which was just so beautiful. The track still goes there, but it's not passenger; it's freight train only. It's hard to conceive that only freight train crews have the benefit of the scenery. I hope they bring that back. There's no highway through there. Train is the only way through Feather River Canyon; the only way you can see it is through an airplane at 30,000 feet. Western Pacific was bought up by the Union Pacific. It was such a shock when I heard they were going to pull the train off. The train used to have an average occupancy of 97%. And they said they could just not make it pay. Anyway, it went into oblivion. All the cars had names having to do with silver: Silver Plane; Silver Country; Silver House; Regal Silver ... see, the interesting thing was that these cars had names, instead of numbers. And we got the Silver Rifle over in

Hunter's Point, where we're restoring our steam engine. And there's another one, The Silver King, that is still in existence, and they're the only two that I know of. The Union Pacific, they had the Pacific series: Pacific Ocean; Pacific Beach; Pacific Gate. And the Santa Fe had the Regal series: Regal State; Regal on and on and on.   71

(19) Job of a *Redcap* is to load luggage on carts & train   75

(20) Oakland.   79

(21) I had a camera with me – I wasn't in the picture, because I was taking it. Some other guy took a picture of me, with all the crew there. And we were sitting in a siding waiting for this other train to go by. I remember that train, it was real slow. And we took in every siding there was, I think. Taking in sidings means 'going into the hole'. This guy on the bottom, his nickname was 'Blinky', and he said, "I'll take a picture of you." And the fireman, he said, "No. I'll take it of you and Blinky." Blinky was always blinking his eyes. I have that other picture put away somewhere out in the garage with a couple more boxes of train photos I haven't unpacked yet ... we just moved in here a year ago. Working the railroad is not the most glamorous job in the world. But I think it is. You're outdoors all the time. The railroads have always kind of gotten into my blood, you might say.   83

(22) Overland Limited; F-7, first-generation of diesels replacing steam power, built 1948, arriving in Berkeley from Chicago, 1956. A friend took this picture; we were passengers.   86

(23) Great Salt Lake, north end at Monument Point   87

(24) Bound for the mountains, 12-mile tangent – 4 miles from Sacramento   88

(25) Sierra Railroad, west of Jamestown, CA. Engine 24 was a little 2-8-0, built not too long after the turn of the century. The fireman is up on top filling the tender tank with water.   96

(26) *Sierra Railroad,* west of Jamestown, CA. I took this picture, one of my favorites. This train was moving, not stopped. It struck me as a back-woods railroad, where everything goes along at a leisurely pace, where you're in no hurry. You can see this man is riding on the front of the steam engine – of course it is a dangerous place to ride – any other railroad, would just have a fit if you did that.   107

(27) The Race Track Special, at Bay Meadows, waiting for horse races to finish. Southern Pacific had something worked out

with the track, a siding to let the whole train sit there. I was working the train when I took that picture. Everybody on the trip down was all jubilation and everybody was wearing suede shoes and bright ties and ladies with leotards on, and everybody's jovial. And coming back, there was quite a change, half of them were still celebrating, or drunk, and the other half were sitting there dejected. 113

(28) 4-4-0 American-Type engine, one of first engines built by Southern Pacific, in mid-1870's. 119

(29) 4-6-0 Ten Wheeler, probably built in 1880's. 119

(30) 4-8-2 Mountain-Type, built by the American Locomotive Company for Florida East Coast Railroad in 1934. The Western Pacific Railroad acquired them over an equipment trust default, from the Florida East Coast Railroad. It was used on through-passenger trains: The Scenic Limited; and later on, The Exposition Flyer. 125

(31) El Gobernador, 4-10-0. This engine lasted from about 1860 to 1903. The boiler actually lay around in west Oakland roundhouse serving as a stationary boiler till 1940, so it was very well made. On the front of the engine are two flag-poles in lieu of electric marker lights – they used to carry green or white flags. A scheduled train would display no flags. If he had another section behind him, he'd put up his green flag. If he's an extra train, he'd display white flags – an extra train is one that's not on the schedule. They would use a red flag if they were backing up and this was the rear end of the train. 125

(32) 4-6-6-4. These were faster than the 2-8-8-2. But they didn't have the same pulling power of the 2-8-8-2. These basically were used in Nevada flatlands. 131

(33) 2-8-8-2, Western Pacific. About as big as they got. They were very successful engines, used principally between Ketty and Salt Lake City, about 600 miles – built for that run. They were also used in Feather River Canyon. They were built for power up grades through hills and mountains. There was only one engine larger than this, called 'Big Boy', on Union Pacific Railroad. It's just enormous. In fact, the 'Big Boy' was a 4-8-8-4. 131

(34) (Grant Allen:) Here's a centralized traffic control board. The dispatcher can throw all those switches; those switches control the entire subdivision – from Portola to Oroville; 119 miles. The switches control the road signals that control the move-

ment of the train – red, yellow, green, see? He could line the track switch from there, by throwing the panel switch up, and that would tell the train crew that the mainline was red and the siding was green, which meant their train would go on the siding. I used to sit in front of one of those boards. He's handling the district between Stockton and Oroville. 147

(35) (Grant Allen:) There's the dispatcher for the Feather River Canyon, and two maintenance men. That was right after the second world war. I was the chief dispatcher there. I was the youngest dispatcher in the office; all the other dispatchers were older than me. 153

(36) (Grant Allen:) That's me on one of those track motorcars – in 1919. That's about seven miles east of Helper, Utah. On the N.P.R., Northern Pacific Railway. The lineman was with me; he was checking the lines. I got a kick out of riding it around. I used to run it for the lineman, and he'd keep his eye on the lines, and I would run the car. That was my recreation. I was working graveyard shift. To get it off the track, you just lift it off. Pull the front wheels off; it was all one man could handle. They still use motorcars like that. 159

(37) (Grant Allen:) Margarite – my first wife. This is when we were workin' at Montebello – it's the first subdivision out of Ogden on the S.P., going west; we used to have those cabins built out of ties. They were nice and warm. Sure. You betcha. That's Margarite and me. We were married in 1918, and that's the following winter. We were married in 1918, and we were in Idaho Falls. She was working the afternoon shift; and I was working the graveyard. And while we were there, I got acquainted with a Priest that gave me my Catholic instructions. So Margarite and me got on the train one morning, and went to Roberts, about fifteen miles north of Idaho Falls; we got married; and when we come back, we got back home about three o'clock – so we had one hour's honeymoon. I was married to Margarite for fifty-one years. 165

(38) (Grant Allen:) Here's a picture up in the Siskiyou Mountains. We got layed-off one winter, so there was a forest service fireman's shack near Big Bridge there, so we spent the winter in that shack. They had a fire ranger watchman up there watchin' for fires in the summer, and they didn't use the shack during the wintertime. So I got permission to use it all winter. 173

(39) (Grant Allen:) Ten Wheeler No. 77, train No. 11 at Sacramento,

August 1941. That's the only passenger engines that they had when they built the railroad – Ten Wheelers ... 4-6-0 (ooOOO), on the Western Pacific. That's the engineer, and that's my secretary. She was a little cutie. 173

(40) Southern Pacific coachyard, San Francisco, 1959. 177

(41) Sierra Nevada Mts., *Huntington* at Alta, Placer City 178

(42) Playing pinochle in the switchman's shanty, John Hogan (r), Harold Clark (l), Pappy Way (t); Richmond, CA., 1973. 181

(43) 4-8-4. Northfork and Western built this steam engine. It may look simplified, but what went into this engine was really something. There were a lot of new developments on this engine. If the diesel hadn't come along, this probably would've been the engine of the future. The springing, for one thing ... most railroads turned later on to a drive-wheel, box-pox driver – it wasn't spokes in there; most driving wheels have big spokes radiating from the hub. Well, box-pox were a new kind of driver, and instead of having spokes, they had kind of elongated holes. The reason for this was, the old spoke driver, every time the counterweight went around, it hit the track, and it would just pound the track. Well box-pox drivers were balanced to a greater degree, and rode with a greater degree of balance. And then Stoline, another company, came out with a driver that was similar to box-pox; almost identical – but they were still a radical departure from spoked drivers. Anyway, Northfork and Western developed this engine, and the springing was so good in it, that they didn't need box-pox drivers – they stayed with the old spoke drivers; because the springing was just absolutely superb. They had all these equalizer bars that were counter-balanced; spring-rigging; parts of the frame were all incorporated in the equalizing. It was just mind-boggling. And this engine would go at nearly 90 m.p.h. And it was so smooth, it didn't hurt the track, and it didn't bounce the crew around, or anything. This really was the high-water mark of steam development. They only built about twenty of these. Another interesting thing was that because of superior feedwater heaters, they raised the percentage of efficiency two percentage points; so instead of fifteen percent efficiency, they went up to seventeen percent efficiency. This was because of research and development on these engines. But it was too late, because the diesel was already running at thirty-five to thirty-eight percent efficiency. The efficiency equation is the possible

number of BTU in the fuel versus the work the engine does on the rail. For example, if you put a hundred BTU's in, and only get seventeen BTU's out on the rail – then there's a tremendous loss there. The diesel was almost twice as efficient as steam. That was the story right there. 213

(44) Ten-Wheeler. A Southern Pacific narrow gauge engine, that ran from Keeler to Laws. The tender's sitting behind it. This particular shop is at Ogden, Utah, because the Ogden Division had jurisdiction over the narrow gauge, even though there was more than 400 miles to Keeler and Laws; but for some reason they gave the Ogden Division jurisdiction over the narrow gauge, so every time they had to bring the power in for maintenance, or even the cars, they'd put the engine and cars up on a flatcar and ship them to Ogden – 'cause it was narrow gauge, and they couldn't run them there on standard gauge tracks. Even the freight cars, they'd just put them up on a flatcar and they'd haul them to Ogden. 227

(45) Niles Canyon, the *California Zephyr*, 1967 228

(46) Railroad excursion train trip to Tracy CA, 1960. 231

(47) Diesel shop at Roseville, California. These are the first generation of diesels – F-7. The first generation of diesels; they replaced the steam engines on Southern Pacific. Southern Pacific was one of the last major railroads to start buying diesels. It was principally because Southern Pacific had a reputation for letting other railroads try something out first, to see if it worked out. 242

(48) Caboose. 253

(49) I cut that out of a newspaper. It was a train wreck on the *Western Pacific*. Some kids put a cement manhole cover on the track, and the train ran over it and derailed, and it was really a mess; and luckily nobody got killed, or even hurt, but they did an awful lot of damage. How the crew ever survived that, I don't know. You can see the engine's facing the opposite way that the train was going. And the cab is off. That track's in a *figure 'S'* from being bent. You bet it is. Just 'cause kids can't keep their hands off somebody else's property – those kids probably didn't realize what it would do. All you have to do is raise the wheel a few inches off the ground, and the flange won't hold the wheel to the rail, and it's gonna derail, and at that speed, you don't know what's going to happen. 254

on the road & in the yard

(50) An excursion train from Oakland to Oroville in 1955. Car was built in mid-twenties. 275
(51) Two engineers at Christmas time. 276
(52) – Sierra Nevada's, *Nevada* at Colfax near Placer City 305
(53) Pat Lollis on her Amtrak qualifying run. 306
(54) Pullman porter 326
(55) Depot at Cisco, western summit, alt 5,900 ft. 336
(56) Observation lounge car on the *California Zephyr*, Oakland, 1968; nice inside too; had a form to them— so beautiful and so nice to ride in; note the observaton Vista Dome on top; this lounge car was always on the rear of the train — there was a fantastic view from the Vista Dome; below,there were real wide windows, car was so comfortable; but now it's all gone. 340
(57) Nevada, Truckee Meadows 349
(58) John Hogan when he was a conductor for the Southern Pacific commute trains. 350
(59) Dedication. 351
(60) Southern Pacific engine 2372. 352

photo credits – :permission to use granted by

John Hogan – figures: 1, 2, 3, 4, 5, 7, 8, 9, 11, 12, 13, 14, 15, 16, 18, 19, 20, 21, 22, 25, 26, 27, 40, 42, 45, 46, 48, 50, 54, 56, 58, 59. Grant Allen – figures: 34, 35, 36, 37, 38, 39. Patricia Lollis – figures: 51, 53. Alameda Newspaper Group – fig. 49.
Stanford University Archives – (*Central Pacific* mid-1800's before absorbed by *Southern Pacific*), figures: 23, 24, 41, 52, 55, 57. Norfolk Southern (Norfork & Western) – 43. Union Pacific (absorbed *Western Pacific*) – figures: 30, 32, 33, 34, 35. Southern Pacific Lines – figures: 6, 10, 17, 28, 29, 31, 44, 47, 60.

A 'Thank You' To The Men And Women Who Contributed Stories To This Book

I would like at this time to personally thank the men and women Rails for their heartfelt participation in this book series. It was a pleasure for me to meet and talk with them; and I'm sure it will be a positive and entertaining and enlightening experience for the readers of this book, as it was for me, to share their stories.

As Pat and Wendy and Linda already know, it was very challenging for me to locate women working or once working on the railroad to interview — in so far as the book was ready to go to print, I had reserved the final chapters as to contain a collection of stories by Lady Rails. I am so very pleased that Pat and Wendy and Linda shared their experiences with me, for me to share with you.

Women were not permitted to work in the operating department of the railroad until the early 1970s. At that time men did not want women to be working as engineers, firemen, switchmen, brakemen or conductors on the railroad — and to this day women would not be allowed in the operating department of the railroad in these jobs if it were not for the protection of Federal mandate.

I feel that these women are very special, very brave, very strong individuals, who in addition to being very competent in their work, also stand out as bright spirits. And I want to thank them again and say how fortunate I feel to have met them and to have their stories in this book.

A Note About the Photographs & Their Captions

Most of the photos in this book came out of two boxes of photos in John Hogan's garage he shot or traded-for throughout his career. Unless otherwise noted (in credits) photos were taken by John Hogan or crew members or other rails. Captions beneath photos except where otherwise noted are from Mr. Hogan. Photos provided by Grant Allen & in Grant Allen's chapter bear Mr. Allen's captions. Pat Lollis provided her photos.

fig. 57 – Nevada, Truckee Meadows

fig. 58 – John Hogan, when a conductor for Southern Pacific

How To Order Copies Of This Book

For Trade or Single Copy purchase information contact
www.Trafford.com

Go to the 'bookstore' to order one or more copies.
At the bookstore you can go to 'trade orders'.
Or in U.S. or Canada call toll free 1 888 232-4444
or from all other countries 1 250 383-6864
or email to emailorders@trafford.com

fig. 59 – Dedication: John Hogan: A Brakeman Tried & True

fig. 60 – Southern Pacific engine 2372

ISBN 1-41205113-4

Made in the USA